PREEMPTION

A KNIFE THAT CUTS BOTH WAYS

Issues of Our Time

Ours has been called an information age, but, though information has never been more plentiful, ideas are what shape and reshape our world. "Issues of Our Time" is a series of books in which some of today's leading thinkers explore ideas that matter in the new millennium. The authors—beginning with the philosopher Kwame Anthony Appiah, the lawyer and legal scholar Alan Dershowitz, and the Nobel Prize–winning economist Amartya Sen—honor clarity without shying away from complexity; these books are both genuinely engaged and genuinely engaging. Each recognizes the importance not just of our values but also of the way we resolve the conflicts among those values. Law, justice, identity, morality, and freedom: concepts such as these are at once abstract and utterly close to home. Our understanding of them helps define who we are and who we hope to be; we are made by what we make of them. These are books, accordingly, that invite the reader to reexamine hand-me-down assumptions and to grapple with powerful trends. Whether you are moved to reason together with these authors, or to argue with them, they are sure to leave your views tested, if not changed. The perspectives of the authors in this series are diverse, the voices are distinctive, the issues are vital.

HENRY LOUIS GATES JR., SERIES EDITOR
W. E. B. DU BOIS PROFESSOR OF THE HUMANITIES
HARVARD UNIVERSITY

Issues of Our Time

PREEMPTION

A KNIFE THAT CUTS BOTH WAYS

Alan M. Dershowitz

W. W. NORTON & COMPANY
NEW YORK • LONDON

For information about permission to reproduce selections from this book, write to
Permissions, W. W. Norton & Company, Inc., 500 Fifth Avenue, New York, NY 10110

Manufacturing by Courier Westford
Production manager: Julia Druskin

Library of Congress Cataloging-in-Publication Data

Dershowitz, Alan M.
Preemption : a knife that cuts both ways / Alan M. Dershowitz.— 1st ed.
p. cm. — (Issues of our time)
Includes bibliographical references and index.
ISBN 0-393-06012-8 (hardcover)
1. Violence—Prevention. 2. Preemptive attack (Military science) 3. Pre-emption.
I. Title. II. Series.
HM1116.D47 2006
363.32—dc22

2005027728

W. W. Norton & Company, Inc., 500 Fifth Avenue, New York, N.Y. 10110
www.wwnorton.com

W. W. Norton & Company Ltd., Castle House, 75/76 Wells Street, London W1T 3QT

1 2 3 4 5 6 7 8 9 0

This book is dedicated to my dear friend and colleague of forty years, the Honorable Irwin Cotler, Attorney General and Minister of Justice of Canada, who always carries out the biblical command to pursue justice, and who inspires me and so many others by his constant example and his unwavering commitment to principle.

CONTENTS

ACKNOWLEDGMENTS

I wish to thank the students from my spring 2004 "Preemption" seminar at Harvard Law School with whom I shared insights, testing my ideas and theirs. They are: Erin Abrams, Itzhak Bam, Avigael Cymrot, Michael Fluhr, Eric Heining, Marc Jacob, Amos Jones, Shiek Pal, Anna Santeramo, Daniel Tenenblatt, Lina Tilman, Michael Tivin, Jessica Tuchinsky, Dan Urman. I also wish to acknowledge the special efforts of two people: Joel Klein, who went on to become chancellor of the New York City public school system, for his research assistance on the *University of Cincinnati Law Review* articles of 1974, which served as the basis for one of the chapters of this book. And Alexander Blenkinsopp, a researcher in my office who spent endless hours checking every source and giving me interesting suggestions. Other student researchers also worked at various stages on this book, including Mitch Webber, Aaron Voloj Dessauer, Danielle Sassoon, C. Wallace DeWitt, Alexander Slater, Bill Gray, Daniela Saltzman, and Taly Dvorkis. Thanks.

My assistant, Jane Wagner, my agent, Helen Rees, my editor, Roby Harrington, and his assistant, Mik Awake, all made my life easier by doing their jobs so well.

My friends and colleagues Jeffrey Epstein, Gabriella Blum, Philip Heymann, Jack Goldsmith, and Richard Goldstone provided valuable insights. My family—as usual—gave me both encouragement and criticism, each in appropriate doses.

Many people in Israel, the United States, and elsewhere listened to my ideas and responded with useful information and critiques.

Finally, we all owe a debt to those on the front lines who seek to balance security and liberty, a never-ending task of great importance to all democracies.

PREEMPTION

A KNIFE THAT CUTS BOTH WAYS

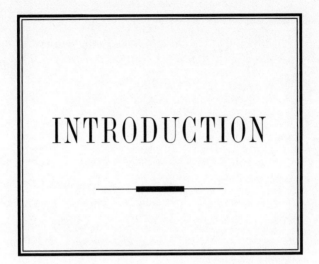

INTRODUCTION

*I*f reliable intelligence determined that a large-scale terrorist attack in your city were highly likely during the next few weeks, and it also pointed to a particular suspect, would you support the preventive detention of that suspect for a period of time—say, a month—until it could be determined whether he or she was, in fact, planning the attack?

What type and level of interrogation would you authorize to elicit the information necessary to prevent the attack?

If arrest were not feasible because the suspected terrorist was hiding in an enemy country, would you support his targeted assassination if that were the only way to stop the attack?

What if the attack could be prevented only by a military strike against a terrorist base in a foreign country?

What if a full-scale invasion were required?

If the feared attack involved a weaponized virus, such as small-
pox, whose deadly impact could be substantially reduced by massive
inoculation, which would, however, kill 150 to 200 of those inocu-
lated, would you support compulsory inoculation?

If an article demonstrating how to manufacture and weaponize
smallpox were about to be published, would you support the pre-
ventive censorship of that article?

These are the kinds of tragic choices that every democratic soci-
ety is now—or soon will be—facing. Yet we have not even begun to
develop an agreed-upon jurisprudence or morality governing such
drastic preventive and preemptive actions by our government.
Instead, we are simply taking such actions on an ad hoc basis as we
face the ongoing threats.

———————

The democratic world is experiencing a fundamental shift in its
approach to controlling harmful conduct. We are moving away
from our traditional reliance on deterrent and reactive approaches
and toward more preventive and proactive approaches. This shift
has enormous implications for civil liberties, human rights, criminal justice, national security, foreign policy, and international
law—implications that are not being sufficiently considered. It is
a conceptual shift in emphasis from a theory of deterrence to a
theory of prevention, a shift that carries enormous implications
for the actions a society may take to control dangerous human
behavior, ranging from targeted killings of terrorists, to preemptive
attacks against nuclear and other weapons of mass destruction, to
preventive warfare, to proactive crime prevention techniques
(stings, informers, wiretaps), to psychiatric or chemical methods
of preventing sexual predation, to racial, ethnic, or other forms of
profiling, to inoculation or quarantine for infectious diseases

(whether transmitted "naturally" or by "weaponization"), to prior restraints on dangerous or offensive speech, to the use of torture (or other extraordinary measures) as a means of gathering intelligence deemed necessary to prevent imminent acts of terrorism.

Although the seeds of this change were planted long ago and have blossomed gradually over the years, it was the terrorist attack against the United States on September 11, 2001, that expedited and, in the minds of many, legitimated this important development. Following that attack, the former attorney general John Ashcroft described the "number one priority" of the Justice Department as "prevention."[1] The prevention of future crimes, especially terrorism, is now regarded as even "more important than prosecution" for past crimes, according to the Justice Department.[2] In his confirmation hearings of January 5, 2005, Attorney General Alberto Gonzales reiterated that the administration's "top priority is to prevent terror attacks."[3] The tactics that have been employed as part of this preventive approach include tighter border controls, profiling, preventive detention, the gathering of preventive intelligence through rough interrogation and more expansive surveillance, targeting of potential terrorists for assassination, preemptive attacks on terrorist bases, and full-scale preventive war. We are doing all this and more without a firm basis in law, jurisprudence, or morality, though there certainly are historical precedents—many questionable—for preventive actions.

From the beginning of recorded history, prophets have attempted to foresee harmful occurrences, such as flood, famine, pestilence, earthquake, volcanic eruption, tsunami, and war. Attempting to predict crime—to determine who is likely to become a criminal—has also captured the imagination of humankind for centuries. From the Bible's "stubborn and rebellious son," identifiable by his gluttony and drunkenness,[4] to nineteenth-century criminologist Cesare Lombroso's "born criminal and criminaloid," identifiable by the shape of his cranium,[5] to Sheldon and Eleanor Glueck's three-year-old delinquent, identifiable by a composite score derived from familial relationships,[6] "experts" have claimed the ability to spot the mark of the potential criminal before he or she has committed serious crimes. Though the results have not generally met with scientific approval, it is still widely believed— by many police officers, judges, psychiatrists, lawyers, and members of the general public—that there are ways of distinguishing real criminals from the rest of us, even before they commit any crimes.

In the 1920s and 1930s eugenicists not only in Nazi Germany but in the United States, Great Britain, and other Western nations believed that they could prevent criminal behavior in specific, and the weakening of particular races or of humankind in general, through sterilization and other eugenic measures.[7] Even before the Holocaust, the German government forcibly sterilized four hundred thousand men and women, nearly 1 percent of Germans of childbearing age, believing that "[i]t is better to sterilize too many rather than too few."[8] The legislation authorizing sterilization was called the Law for the Prevention of Genetically Diseased Offspring.[9] Although this "science" became justly discredited following the Holocaust, as recently as the 1970s it was suggested that the presence of the XYY karyotype in a man might be associated with, and consequently predictive of, certain kinds of violent crime.[10] The mapping of the human genome has stimulated contemporary genetic research into the predictability of violence and other harms. Racial, ethnic, religious, and other "profiling" is now thought by some to hold promise in the effort to identify potential criminals, especially terrorists.

Historically, the widespread use of early intervention to preempt serious threats to the state and its rulers has been associated with tyrannical regimes. Hitler and Stalin excelled at killing their enemies before they could rise up against them. But preventive approaches have been championed by progressive forces as well.

Over the past several decades, especially in Europe, the so-called precautionary principle has become "a staple of regulatory policy."[11] It postulates that one should "[a]void steps that will create a risk of harm. Until safety is established, be cautious; do not require unambiguous evidence. In a catchphrase: Better safe than sorry."[12]

The *New York Times Magazine* listed the precautionary principle as among the most "important ideas" of 2001.[13] This principle, which originated in Germany and grew out of efforts to prevent environmental and other "natural" disasters, has now moved beyond these concerns, which have traditionally been raised by the left. According to Professor Cass Sunstein, the precautionary principle has now "entered into debates about how to handle terrorism, about 'preemptive war,' and about the relationship between liberty and security. In defending the 2003 war in Iraq, President George W. Bush invoked a kind of Precautionary Principle, arguing that action was justified in the face of uncertainty. 'If we wait for threats to fully materialize, we will have waited too long.' He also said, 'I believe it is essential that when we see a threat, we deal with those threats before they become imminent.'"[14]

Professor Sunstein points to an interesting paradox in the different attitudes in Europe and the United States: "[T]he United States appears comparatively unconcerned about the risks associated with global warming and genetic modification of foods; in those contexts, Europeans favor precautions, whereas Americans seem to require something akin to proof of danger. To be sure, the matter is quite different in the context of threats to national security. For the war in Iraq, the United States (and England) followed a kind of Precautionary Principle, whereas other nations (most notably France and Germany) wanted clearer proof of danger."[15]*

This observation can be generalized beyond Europe and the United States and beyond the contemporary scene: All people in all eras have favored *some* preventive or precautionary measures, while opposing others. The differences over which preventive measures are favored and which opposed depend on many social, political, religious, and cultural factors. As I shall argue through-out this book, it is meaningless to declare support for, or opposi-tion to, prevention or precaution as a general principle because so much properly depends on the values at stake—on the *content* of the costs and benefits and on the *substance* of what is being regulated.

One can of course sympathize with efforts to predict and pre-vent at least some harms before they occur, rather than wait until the victim lies dead. Indeed, Lewis Carroll put in the queen's mouth an argument for preventive confinement of predicted criminals that Alice found difficult to refute. The queen says:

> "[T]here's the King's Messenger. He's in prison now, being pun-ished; and the trial doesn't even begin till next Wednesday; and of course the crime comes last of all."
>
> "Suppose he never commits the crime?" said Alice.
>
> "That would be all the better, wouldn't it?" the Queen said. . . .
>
> Alice felt there was no denying *that*. "Of course that would be all the better," she said: "But it wouldn't be all the better his being punished."
>
> "You're wrong . . ." said the Queen. "Were *you* ever punished?"

---

* Following the London subway bombings, signs were posted in train stations reading, GUILTY UNTIL PROVEN INNOCENT — TREAT ABANDONED BAGS WITH SUSPICION.

"Only for faults," said Alice.

"And you were all the better for it, I know!" the Queen said triumphantly.

"Yes, but then I *had* done the things I was punished for," said Alice: "that makes all the difference."

"But if you *hadn't* done them," the Queen said, "that would have been even better still; better, and better, and better!" Her voice went higher with each "better," till it got quite to a squeak. . . .

Alice [thought], "There's a mistake here somewhere—"[16]

There are numerous mistakes and perils to liberty implicit in this kind of thinking, and they are not being sufficiently debated today.

Part of the reason for our neglect of the issues surrounding prevention is the mistaken assumption that any form of preventive detention would be alien to our traditions. Lord Justice Denning, one of the most prominent common law jurists of the twentieth century, purported to summarize the irreconcilability of preventive punishment with democratic principles: "It would be contrary to all principle for a man to be punished, not for what he has already done, but for what he may hereafter do."[17] It may be contrary to all *principle*, but as we shall see, it is certainly not contrary to all *practice*.

The shift from responding to past events to preventing future harms is part of one of the most significant but unnoticed trends in the world today. It challenges our traditional reliance on a model of human behavior that presupposes a rational person capable of being deterred by the threat of punishment. The classic theory of deterrence postulates a calculating evildoer who can evaluate the cost-benefits of proposed actions and will act—and forbear from acting—on the basis of these calculations. It also presupposes society's ability (and willingness) to withstand the blows we seek to deter and to use the visible punishment of those blows as threats capable of deterring future harms. These assumptions are now being widely questioned as the threat of weapons of mass destruction in the hands of suicide terrorists becomes more realistic and as our ability to deter such harms by classic rational cost-benefit threats and promises becomes less realistic.

Among the most frightening sources of danger today are religious zealots whose actions are motivated as much by "otherworldly" costs and benefits as by the sorts of punishments and rewards that we are capable of threatening or offering. The paradigm is the suicide terrorist, such as the ones who attacked us on September 11. We have no morally acceptable way of deterring those willing to die for their cause, who are promised rewards in the world to come.[18] Recall the serene looks on the faces of the suicide terrorists as they were videotaped passing through airport security in the final hours of their lives. It is not that they are incapable of making "rational" cost-benefit calculations, by their own lights. But these calculations involve benefits that we cannot confer (eternity in paradise) and costs (death) that to them are outweighed by the expected benefits. They are in some respects like "insane" criminals who believe that God or the devil told them to do it. Because they are not deterrable, the argument for taking preventive measures against them becomes more compelling. Blackstone made this point in the context of "madmen": "[A]s they are not answerable for their actions, they should not be permitted the liberty of acting. . . ."[19] Nations whose leaders genuinely—as opposed to tactically—believe that their mission has been ordained by God (such as some in today's Iran) may also be more difficult to deter than those who base their calculations on earthly costs and benefits (such as today's North Korea or Cuba).[20]

The *New York Times,* in its lead editorial on September 10, 2002, a year after the 9/11 attacks and six months before the invasion of Iraq, recognized the distinction between the theory of deterrence and the theory of prevention (or preemption or first strike) in the context of the war on terrorism: "The suddenness and ferocity of last September's terror attacks tore the United States free from the foreign-policy moorings that had served the nation well for more than five decades, including the central notion that American military power could by its very existence restrain the aggressive impulses of the nation's enemies. In its place, the Bush administration has substituted a more belligerent first-strike strategy that envisions Washington's attacking potential foes before they hit us. That may be appropriate in dealing with terror groups, but on the eve of the anniversary of Sept. 11 there is still an important place in American policy for the doctrine of deterrence."[21]

Deterrence, in the context of international relations, boils down to "a brutally simple idea": If America or its allies are attacked, we will retaliate massively. The *Times* continued: "Deterrence is diplomatic parlance for a brutally simple idea: that an attack on the United States or one of its close allies will lead to a devastating military retaliation against the country responsible. It emerged as the centerpiece of American foreign policy in the early years of the cold war."[22]

According to the *Times*, this approach has the advantage of inducing "responsible behavior by enemies as a matter of their own self-interest. . . . Aggression becomes unattractive if the price is devastation at home and possible removal from power."[23] The *Times* then argued that while preemption may be appropriate against terrorists, it was a far more questionable strategy in dealing with Iraq: "In the wake of Sept. 11, President George W. Bush has made a convincing case that international terrorist organizations, which have no permanent home territory and little to lose, cannot reliably be checked by the threat of retaliation and must be stopped before they strike. Whether Saddam Hussein falls into that category is a question that the country will be debating in the days ahead."[24]

The debate predicted by the *Times* did occur, but only in the relatively narrow context of the Iraq War. In this book, I shall broaden it beyond any specific war, and even beyond the issue of war itself, to the wide range of harms that may not be subject to (or may not be *thought* to be subject to) the strategy of deterrence.

The classic theory of deterrence contemplates the state's absorbing the first harm, apprehending its perpetrator, and then punishing him publicly and proportionally, so as to show potential future harmdoers that it does not pay to commit the harm. In the classic situation, the harm may be a single murder or robbery that, tragic as it may be to its victim and his family, the society is able to absorb. In the current situation the harm may be a terrorist attack with thousands of victims or even an attack with weapons of mass destruction capable of killing tens of thousands. National leaders capable of preventing such mass attacks will be tempted to take preemptive action, as some strategists apparently were during the early days of the Cold War. Again according to the *New York Times*, "During the Truman administration, some strategists suggested attacking the Soviet Union while it was still militarily weak to prevent the rise of a nuclear-armed Communist superpower. Wiser heads prevailed, and for the next 40 years America's reliance on a strategy of deterrence preserved an uneasy but durable peace."[25]

With the benefit of hindsight that decision was clearly correct, but if the Soviet Union had in fact subsequently used its nuclear arsenal against us, our failure to take preventive action when we more safely could have would have been criticized, just as Britain's failure to prevent the German arms buildup in the years prior to World War II has been criticized. One of the great difficulties of evaluating the comparative advantages and disadvantages of deterrence versus preemption is that once we have taken preemptive action, it is almost never possible to know whether deterrence would have worked as well or better. Moreover, at the time the decision has to be made—whether to wait and see if deterrence will work or to act preemptively now—the available information will likely be probabilistic and uncertain. It is also difficult to know with precision the nature and degree of the harm that may have been prevented. For example, if a preemptive attack on the German war machine had succeeded in preventing World War II, we would never know the enormity of the evil it prevented. All that history would remember would be an unprovoked aggression by Britain on a weak Germany.[26]

The conundrum, writ large, may involve war and peace. Writ small, it may involve the decision whether to incarcerate preventively an individual who is thought to pose a high degree of likelihood that he will kill, rape, assault, or engage in an act of terrorism. At an intermediate level, it may involve the decision to quarantine dozens, or hundreds, of people, some of whom may be carrying a transmittable virus like SARS or avian flu. At yet another level, it may raise the question of whether to impose prior restraint on a magazine, newspaper, television network, or Internet provider planning to publish information that may pose an imminent danger to the safety of our troops, our spies, or potential victims of aggression.[27] Since the introduction of the Internet, which, unlike responsible media outlets, has no "publisher" who can be held accountable after the fact, there has been more consideration of before-the-fact censorship.[28]

At every level, preventive decisions must be based on uncertain predictions, which will rarely be anywhere close to 100 percent accurate. We must be prepared to accept some false positives (predictions of harms that would not have occurred) in order to prevent some predicted harms from causing irreparable damage. The policy decisions that must be made involve the acceptable ratios of false to true positives in differing contexts.

Over the millennia we have constructed a carefully balanced

jurisprudence or moral philosophy of after-the-fact reaction to harms, especially crimes. We have even come to accept a widely agreed upon calculus: Better ten guilty go free than even one innocent be wrongly convicted.[29] Should a similar calculus govern preventive decisions? If so, how should it be articulated? Is it better for ten possibly preventable terrorist attacks to occur than for one possibly innocent suspect to be preventively detained? Should the answer depend on the nature of the predicted harm? The conditions and duration of detention? The past record of the detainee? The substantive criteria employed in the preventive decision? The ratio of true positives to false positives and false negatives? These are the sorts of questions we shall have to confront as we shift toward more preventive approaches—whether it be to terrorism, crime in general, the spread of contagious diseases, or preventive warfare.

Decisions to act preemptively generally require a complex and dynamic assessment of multiple factors.[30] These factors include at least the following:

1. The nature of the harm feared[31]
2. The likelihood that the harm will occur in the absence of preemption[32]
3. The source of the harm—deliberate conduct or natural occurrence?
4. The possibility that the contemplated preemption will fail
5. The costs of a successful preemption[33]
6. The costs of a failed preemption
7. The nature and quality of the information on which these decisions are based
8. The ratio of successful preemptions to unsuccessful ones
9. The legality, morality, and potential political consequences of the preemptive steps
10. The incentivizing of others to act preemptively

11. The revocability or irrevocability of the harms caused by the feared event
12. The revocability or irrevocability of the harms caused by contemplated preemption
13. Many other factors, including the inevitability of unanticipated outcomes (the law of unintended consequences)

In light of the complexity, dynamism, and uncertainty of these and other factors that must go into rationally making any preemptive decision, it would be difficult to construct a general formula with which specific decisions could be quantified, evaluated, and tested. At the simple level, any such formula would begin by asking if the seriousness of the contemplated harm,[34] discounted by the unlikelihood that it would occur in the absence of preemption, would be greater than the likelihood of the harms caused by successful preemption, discounted by the likelihood (and costs) of failed (and successful) preemption. This simple formula can be made more complex by the inclusion of other factors, such as the appropriate burdens of action and inaction, the legal and moral status of the intervention, and the likelihood of long-term, unintended consequences. Any formula will necessarily mask subtlety, nuance, and indeterminacy. But a formula that even comes close to approximating reality will help clarify the relationship among the factors that either explicitly or implicitly should be considered by any rational decision maker responsible for taking preemptive actions.

There have been several legal contexts in which judges have tried to construct gross formulas for analyzing decisions with predictive implications. In the First Amendment context, Judge Learned Hand formulated a "clear and present danger" exception to protected free speech in the following terms: "In each case [the judge] must ask whether the gravity of the 'evil,' discounted by its improbability, justifies such invasion of free speech as if necessary to avoid the danger. . . . We can never forecast with certainty; all prophecy is a guess, but the reliability of a guess decreases with the length of the future which it seeks to penetrate. In application of such a standard courts may strike a wrong balance; they may tolerate 'incitements' which they should forbid; they may repress utterances they should allow; but that is a responsibility that they cannot avoid."[35]

That formulation was used (misused) by the Supreme Court to sustain the conviction of the leaders of the American Communist Party in 1951, despite the minuscule likelihood that this weak and unpopular party could actually succeed in overthrowing our government "by force or violence." The "clear and present danger" test was made more speech-friendly by the Supreme Court in its 1969 *Brandenburg* decision, which required that the danger be likely *and* imminent.[36] This is the current view of the First Amendment.

In the context of issuing an injunction, the courts also write about balancing future harms and likely outcomes. Justice Stephen Breyer summarized "the heart of this test" as "whether the harm caused plaintiff without the injunction, in light of the plaintiff's likelihood of eventual success on the merits, outweighs the harm the injunction will cause defendants."[37]

These rather simple formulas do not even begin to capture the subtleties and difficulties of balancing the claims of prevention against those of freedom. Consider the following preemptive decisions, all of which potentially involve life and death choices.

The most far-reaching may be whether a democratic nation, committed to humane values, should go to war before it is attacked in order to prevent an anticipated attack or provide it a military advantage in what it regards as an inevitable or highly likely war.[38] We can call this the preemptive or preventive war decision.[39] Related to that exercise in anticipatory self-defense is the decision to engage in military action to prevent genocide or ethnic cleansing of others within a given country. This can be called the humanitarian intervention decision.

Another may be whether to vaccinate all, most, or some people against a contagious germ that can be, or has been, weaponized under circumstances in which a small, but not insignificant, number of those vaccinated may die or become seriously ill from the vaccination. The decision becomes especially difficult when it is only possible, but not probable, that an attack using the weaponized germ will occur. We shall call this the preventive inoculation decision.

Yet another may involve the decision to try to identify and confine (or otherwise incapacitate) potentially dangerous individuals (rapists, killers, terrorists, child molesters)[40] or groups (Japanese-Americans, Arab-Americans, those who fit certain "profiles," or others). We shall call this the preventive detention decision (or *Minority Report* approach, based on the motion picture about a futuristic law enforcement system that relies on predicting and preventing crime).

A particularly difficult decision may be whether a government should try to prevent certain kinds of speech (or other expression) that are thought to incite, provoke, facilitate, or otherwise cause (or contribute significantly to) serious harms, ranging from genocide to rape to the killing of spies to an overthrow of a government. The causative mechanisms may vary: In some situations the mechanism is informational (revealing the names of spies, the locations of planned military attacks, the instructions for making a nuclear weapon, the names and locations of ethnic enemies, as in Rwanda), in other situations it may be emotional (incitements, degrading the intended victims, issuing religious decrees), while in still others it may contain a combination of elements. We shall call this the censorship or prior restraint decision.

The question is whether decisions as diverse as the above

share enough elements so that there is some benefit in trying to construct a common decision-making formula. Such a formula, with appropriate variations, may help clarify the balancing judgments that must be made before preemptive or preventive action is deemed warranted. Even in the absence of a single formula, comparative discussion of these different but related predictive decisions may contribute to clarification of the policies at stake in each type of decision.

Human beings make both predictive and retrospective decisions every day. Routine predictive decisions include weather reports, college admission decisions, stock purchases, vacation plans, bets on sporting events, and voting choices. Routine retrospective decisions include trial verdicts, historical reconstructions, and punishing children for misbehavior that they deny. Many decisions are of course a mixture of retrospective and prospective elements. These include sentencing, marriage proposals, issuing protective orders against feared abusers, and denying bail to criminal defendants.

In theory we should be no worse at predicting at least some types of future events than we are at reconstructing some past ones, because the accuracy of our predictions (at least our short-term, visible ones, such as weather, stocks, sports, and college performance) is easily tested by simple observations of future events as they unfold, whereas past reconstructions (such as whether a particular crime, tort, or historical event actually occurred) are often not retrievable or observable.[41]

Yet in practice we seem better (or we believe we are better) at reconstructing the past than in predicting the future, perhaps because we fail to learn from our predictive mistakes. It has been argued that prediction is more difficult than reconstruction, because predictive decisions are inherently probabilistic (e.g., how likely is it that it will rain tomorrow?), whereas retrospective decisions are either right or wrong (Booth either assassinated Lincoln or didn't). But this is really a matter of how the issue is put. Predictive decisions are also either right or wrong: It will either rain tomorrow or not. And the question of whether a past act did or did not occur can also be stated in probabilistic terms; jurors are asked to decide "beyond a reasonable doubt" or by "a preponderance of the evidence" if a disputed past event occurred. In either instance, the target event either did or will occur or did not or will not occur, but in the absence of full information, we cannot be sure and must state our level of certainty in probabilistic terms—e.g., it seems highly likely (or 90 percent likely) that X occurred; it seems highly likely (or 90 percent likely) that X will occur.[42] Our ability to predict the future as well as to reconstruct the past has almost certainly improved with developments in science (predictive computer modeling, DNA, etc.), but we are still far from any level of accuracy that eliminates the problems of false positives and false negatives and thus the moral challenge of assigning proper weights to these inevitable errors.

In real life, as distinguished from controlled experiments, most important decisions involve both predictive and retrospective judgments, often in combination. Consider the sentencing decision a judge must make with regard to a convicted defendant. Although the jury has already decided (beyond a reasonable doubt) that the defendant almost certainly committed the specified crime with which he was charged, the judge will generally also consider other uncharged past crimes (his record) as well as the likelihood that he will recidivate.[43] Or consider the decision to hire a lawyer. When a potential client interviews one, he wants to know his past record (which is more complex than simply the ratio of wins to losses because the difficulty of the cases is relevant). He also wants to assess his current status—has he gotten too busy or too old for a long, complex case?—as well as his likely future performance when the case comes before the court. Similarly, with regard to a potential pinch hitter at a crucial stage of a baseball game, the manager looks at past performance—batting average, on base percentage, success against a particular pitcher—and then makes a prospective judgment: How is he likely to do in this specific situation?

Or consider the much more serious, even monumental decision to go to war against Saddam Hussein. The primary considerations were future-looking: What was the likelihood that he would use weapons of mass destruction against the United States, his own people, or one of our allies? What was the likelihood he would sell or otherwise transfer such weapons to terrorist groups? Those future-looking probabilistic judgments had to be based on past and present-looking assessments: What was the probability that he currently had weapons of mass destruction? Did he have them in the past, and if so, what did he do with them? Did he use them against his own people and against Iran? Similarly a decision to target a ticking bomb terrorist for arrest, assassination, or other form of incapacitation will inevitably be based on a combination of past and future-looking probabilistic judgments: What is the likelihood that he has engaged in terrorist activities in the recent past? Has anything changed to make it less likely that he will persist in these activities? Is there current, reliable intelligence about his plans or activities for the future? How many people will he likely kill if he is not incapacitated? How many people (and of what status—other terrorists, supporters of terrorists, innocent bystanders) will likely be killed or injured in the effort to incapacitate him? Will killing him cause others to resort to more terrorism? Or might it deter others?

Asking the broad question of whether preemption is good or bad is as meaningless as asking whether deterrence is good or bad. Preemption is a mechanism of social control that is sometimes good and sometimes bad, depending on many factors. Just as deterrence can be used for bad purposes or in bad ways (in parts of the South in the 1930s any black person who acted "inappropriately" toward a white woman could be lynched), so too preemption can be used for good purposes and in good ways (planting informers within the Ku Klux Klan to learn about and prevent anticipated lynchings). There is, however, something understandably unsettling about giving the government broad powers to intervene in the lives of its citizens before a harm has occurred in an effort to prevent anticipated harm, rather than respond once it has occurred.

Requiring a past harm as a precondition to the exercise of certain governmental powers serves as an important check on the abuse of such powers. But this check, like most checks, comes with a price tag. The failure to act preemptively may cost a society dearly, sometimes even catastrophically. For example, when the United Nations Charter was originally drafted in the wake of World War II, it demanded that an actual "armed attack occur" before a nation could respond militarily. Now, in the face of potential weapons of mass destruction in the hands of terrorists or rogue nations, that charter is being more widely interpreted to permit preemptive self-defense "beyond an actual attack to an imminently threatened one."[44] But acting preemptively also comes with a price tag, often measured in lost liberties and other even more subtle and ineffable values. That is perhaps why deterrence, rather than preemption, is the norm—the default position—in most democracies for the exercise of most extraordinary governmental powers, such as waging war, confining dangerous people, requiring citizens to submit to medical procedures, and restraining speech. More and more, however, this presumption against preemptive actions is being overcome by the dangers of inaction, of not acting preemptively. The stakes have increased for both taking and not taking preemptive steps, as we live in a world of increasing physical dangers and increasing dangers to our liberty. Hence the need for thoughtful consideration of the values at stake whenever an important preemptive action is contemplated.

Because the debate throughout the world has become politicized, it has too often focused on the yes-no questions of whether preemption is a good policy, rather than on the more nuanced issues discussed above. Even for those adamantly opposed to all preemption—or to all preemption of a particular sort, such as preemptive war—the reality is that preemptive actions of different types and degrees are becoming routine throughout the world. These actions are being taken without the careful, rational consideration that carries with it the prospect that this important, if controversial, mechanism of social control can be cabined in a way that maximizes its utility, while minimizing its potential for misuse and abuse. Precise quantification of many of the factors that are relevant to predictive decisions probably exceed our current capacity. Some may indeed go beyond our inherent ability to quantify. A profound observation, made centuries ago and included in the Jewish prayer service, cautions that there are certain things that cannot be measured or quantified, such as helping the poor and doing acts of loving- kindness.[45] Despite this caution, it may still be true that thinking about the costs and benefits of an important mechanism of social control in a roughly quantified manner can be a helpful heuristic.

The elusiveness of any quest for a precise formula capable of quantifying the elements that should govern preemptive decisions must not discourage efforts at constructing a meaningful jurisprudence of preemption. After all, we still lack a precise formula for evaluating retrospective decisions. We have been struggling with efforts to quantify punitive decisions since biblical times, when Abraham argued with God about how many false positives would be acceptable in an effort to punish the sinners of Sodom:

Will you really sweep away the innocent along with the guilty?
Perhaps there are fifty innocent within the city,
will you really sweep it away? . . .
Heaven forbid for you!
The judge of all the earth—will he not do what is just?
YHWH said:
If I find in Sodom fifty innocent within the city,
I will bear with the whole place for their sake.
Avraham spoke up, and said: . . .
Perhaps there will be found there only forty!
He said:
I will not do it, for the sake of the forty.
But he said: . . .
Perhaps there will be found there only thirty!
He said:
I will not do it, if I find there thirty.
But he said: . . .
Perhaps there will be found there only twenty!
He said:
I will not bring ruin, for the sake of the twenty.
But he said:
Pray let my Lord not be upset that I speak further just this one
time:
Perhaps there will be found there only ten!
He said:
I will not bring ruin, for the sake of the ten.
YHWH went, as soon as he had finished speaking to Avraham,
and Avraham returned to his place.[46]

In other words, fifty false positives—innocents punished along
with the guilty—would be too many. So would forty, thirty, twenty,

even ten! But Abraham seems to concede that fewer than ten would not be unjust, since he stops his argument and returns to his place after God agrees that he "will not bring ruin, for the sake of the ten." Even this powerful story does not contain sufficient data on which to base a formula, since we do not know how many false negatives (sinners who deserve punishment) are being spared "for the sake" of the ten, or how many future crimes that could have been prevented would now occur. Despite incompleteness of the data, this biblical account—perhaps the first recorded effort to quantify important moral judgments—almost certainly served as the basis for the formula later articulated by Maimonides,[47] Blackstone, and others that it is better for ten guilty defendants (some have put the number at a hundred, others at a thousand) to go free (to become false negatives) than for one innocent to be wrongly condemned (to become a false positive). That primitive formula is about the best we have come up with in the thousands of years we have been seeking to balance the rights of innocent defendants against the power of the state to punish guilty defendants for their past crimes.

We apply or at least claim to apply the identical formula to suspected murderers, pickpockets, corporate criminals, and drunken drivers. (There are some historical exceptions, such as treason, which our Constitution made especially difficult to prosecute, and rape, which historically was difficult to prosecute because of sexist distrust of alleged victims, a phenomenon that has been undergoing significant change during the past several decades.) A rational, calibrated system might well vary the number depending on the values at stake. The U.S. Constitution contains no specific reference to the maxim that it is better for ten guilty to go free than for one innocent to be convicted, but the Supreme Court has repeatedly invoked it as part of the requirement of proof beyond a reasonable doubt. Although the maxim was first articulated in the context of the death penalty, which was the routine punishment for all serious felonies, over time it came to be applied to imprisonment as well. Many Americans (and many jurors) probably do not prefer to see ten murderers go free in order to prevent the false imprisonment of even one wrongly accused defendant. Nonetheless, the maxim has become enshrined among the principles that distinguish nations governed by the rule of law from nations governed by the passion of persons. The maxim emerged of course from a criminal justice system that dealt with crime as a retail, rather than a wholesale, phenomenon. The guilty murderer who might go free as a result of its application was not likely to engage in future mass murders. The cost of applying the maxim could be measured in individual deaths, terrible as any preventable murder might be. Now, with the advent of terrorists using weapons of mass destruction, the calculus may have to change. It remains true, in my view, that it is better for ten guilty criminals (even murderers) to go free (and perhaps recidivate on a retail basis) than for even one innocent person to be wrongfully convicted. But it does not necessarily follow from this salutary principle that it is also better for ten potential mass terrorists to go free (and perhaps recidivate on a *wholesale* basis) than for even one innocent suspect to be detained for a limited period of time, sufficient to determine that he is not a potential terrorist. It was reported, for example, on November 14, 2005, that a year prior to the suicide bombings of the three American-owned hotels in Amman, Jordan, a man with the same name as one of the suicide bombers had been detained and quickly released by American forces in Iraq. If this was indeed the same man, and if the killing of more than fifty innocent civilians could have been prevented by continuing to detain him (a doubtful conclusion in light of the ready availability of suicide bombers), then it would be fair to question the decision to release him (at least with the benefit of 20/20 hindsight).

These are the sorts of issues that must now be faced squarely as we shift from a primarily deterrent focus to a significantly pre-emptive approach, especially in the war against terrorism.

The terms "preemption," "preemptive war," and "preemptive actions" have recently come into common usage largely as the result of the Bush administration's policies in Iraq and Afghanistan and with regard to global terrorism. But the phenomena are not themselves new. Preemptive and preventive wars have been fought over the centuries, as I shall show in Chapter 2.[48] Other preemptive actions, short of outright war, have been taken since the beginning of recorded history. For example, the killing of heirs to the thrones of deposed leaders to prevent their later ascendancy was common since before the Bible. And preemption as a con-cept has always been an important mechanism of social control, though often called by other names, such as prevention, prior restraint, anticipatory action, *Vorsorgeprinzip* (the precautionary principle), and predictive decision making.

One early, if incomplete, effort at constructing a jurisprudence of preemption was undertaken by the twelfth-century Jewish scholar Maimonides. He began with the biblical rule, "If a thief is caught breaking in and is struck so that he dies, the defendant is not guilty of bloodshed, but if it happens after sunrise, he is guilty of bloodshed."[49] This rule was explained as presuming that a nighttime thief anticipated confronting and killing the home-owner, whereas a daytime thief intended merely to steal property from a vacant house. The Talmud generalized this interpretation into a rule of anticipatory self-defense: "If a man comes to kill you, you kill him first."[50]

Maimonides expanded this rule into an even more general obli-gation: "Whenever one pursues another to kill him, every Jew is commanded to save the attacked from the attacker, even at the cost of the attacker's life."[51] This obligation was called *din rodef*, or the law regarding the pursuer. It was a law of last resort appli-cable only if the danger was imminent and there was no reasonable alternative way to prevent the pursuer from killing.[52] Beyond these broad constraints, however, there was little in the way of a detailed jurisprudence governing the permissible use of anticipatory self-defense. There was no specification of the number of witnesses required to invoke *din rodef* or of the level of certainty that the pursuer intended to kill, nor was there any requirement that a warning be given to the pursuer before lethal force could be directed at him. This contrasts sharply with the laws regulating after-the-fact imposition of the death penalty for such completed crimes as murder. Two witnesses and advance warning were obligatory, and a high standard of proof was required. This difference may be understandable, since *din rodef* is an emergency measure, a law of necessity. Preemptive action, to be effective, must be immediate. This is true, however, of all measures of self-defense. Yet a careful jurisprudence of self-defense has evolved over time. The same cannot be said for anticipatory or preemptive self-defense, for either the individual (the micro level) or the state (the macro level).

The dangers of a generalized doctrine of preventive killing, unregulated by specific jurisprudential constraints, is demonstrated by how the doctrine of *din rodef* was exploited by some extremist right-wing rabbis in Israel to "justify" the assassination of then Prime Minister Yitzchak Rabin, who was trying to reach a compromise peace with the Palestinians. The man convicted of murdering Rabin claimed in court that "Halakhah (rabbinic law) states that if a Jew hands over his people or his land to the enemy he must be killed at once."[53] Several rabbis supported that perverse interpretation of *din rodef*.[54]

Although most rabbis across the spectrum of Judaism rejected that expansive view, the fact that anyone could believe it shows the need for more than a broad statement permitting the killing of those who pose any danger. The same is true today, as advocates of preventive or preemptive self-defense cite general prin-

ciples to justify all manner of anticipatory intervention. The time
has come to develop jurisprudential constraints on the kinds of
preventive and preemptive steps that are now being employed and
considered by governments throughout the world.

For more than forty years, I have focused much of my own
scholarly writing, teaching, and thinking on these ideas and concepts. I have taught courses on the prediction and prevention of
harmful conduct since the 1960s. I have written numerous articles on preventive confinement, predictability, and related subjects from the time I started teaching at Harvard.[55] My interests
have been far broader than the recent policies of the Bush administration. They have included the confinement of predicted sex
offenders, delinquents, criminals, and other allegedly dangerous
individuals.[56] They have also included the preemptive confinement of entire ethnic groups, such as the Japanese-Americans
who lived on the West Coast during World War II.[57] I have written about predictive tests designed to identify future delinquents,
criminals, deviants, and even unethical lawyers.[58] I have criticized
experts, particularly psychiatrists and judges, who were too certain of the correctness of their predictive decisions.[59] I have complained about the unwillingness of our legal system to develop a
jurisprudence of preemption in the face of the reality that we are
employing this mechanism quite extensively.[60] But I have never
confronted the broad issue as a general societal problem. To my
knowledge, no one has. The movement away from deterrence and
toward prevention is an important and largely unnoticed trend that
potentially affects the lives of many people.

The current focus on preemption, resulting from the political
debate over particular preemptive policies and actions, affords an
opportunity to evaluate preemption in its varying contexts and
manifestations. In this book, I suggest how a democratic society
might begin to construct a jurisprudence, a philosophy, of pre-

emption. To put it another way, I shall try to articulate the factors that should go into any process of striking the proper balances between the virtues and vices of early intervention, especially when the intervention involves the use of force, power, compulsion, censorship, incarceration, and death—and especially when the failure to intervene may also involve comparable threats, dangers, and harms. I shall not deal with all these issues, but rather with those that are the most urgent and difficult. When the stakes are high and the available options tend to be "tragic choices" or "choices of evils," the need for thoughtful, calibrated, and nuanced analysis becomes even more compelling. The question, Are you for or against preemption? (or "precaution" or "prevention") thus becomes exposed as a meaningless polemic, as empty of content as the question, Are you for or against deterrence? or, Are you for or against punishment? The costs and benefits of each category of preemptive or preventive decision—indeed of each specific decision—must be carefully weighed and openly debated. I hope to stimulate such debate with this book.

But before we address the more general and specific contemporary issues—both macro, such as preventive war, and micro, such as preventive detention and profiling—we should briefly look to the Anglo-American history of prevention and preemption. We shall see that prevention in general, and preventive confinement of the dangerous in particular, have deep roots and are not as "unprecedented" as some would have us believe. It is to that fascinating, though largely unacknowledged, double-edged history we now turn.

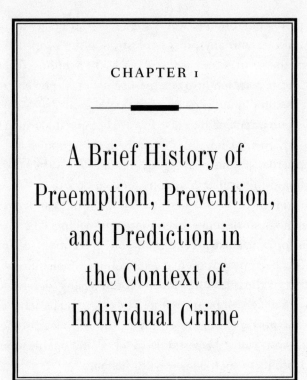

CHAPTER 1

A Brief History of Preemption, Prevention, and Prediction in the Context of Individual Crime

[P]reventive justice is upon every principle, of reason, of humanity and of sound policy, preferable in all respects to punishing justice. . . .[1]

Preventive justice which consists in restraining a man from committing a crime which he may commit but has not yet committed is common to all systems of jurisprudence.[2]

W e all have heard the proverbs "An ounce of prevention is worth a pound of cure" and "A stitch in time saves nine." These quaint expressions of folk wisdom reflect both the human instinct to anticipate and prevent harms and the human limitation on constructing a precise formula for which sorts of preventive actions are justified under what circumstances. In this chapter, I shall explore briefly the history of preventive actions, particularly with regard to efforts at predicting and preventing serious crimes. My focus will be on the Anglo-American legal system because I am most familiar with it and because it is becoming increasingly influential throughout the world.[3]

Consider the following hypothetical case, variations of which have recurred throughout the history of humankind. A man riding his horse accidentally runs down a ten-year-old child, killing him. The father of the dead child swears revenge on his child's killer, threatening to cause "an accident" against the killer's child. What should the society—whether a small, primitive tribe or a large, complex metropolis—do to prevent further bloodshed? Should the threatening blood avenger be preventively confined until his blood cools? Should the family of the accidental killer be placed in protective custody? Should human nature simply be allowed to run its course? If it were to be decided to confine anyone against his will in this situation, what would be the legal or moral basis for doing so? There is no existing jurisprudence that would authorize the involuntary confining of a person on the basis of what we think he might do. Today we do have laws criminalizing overt threats, but in the old days there were no such laws, and even today the threat has to be explicit. This, in a nutshell, is the problem of individualized prevention that, despite the absence of an explicit jurisprudence, has always been practiced and has always generated controversy.

Oliver Wendell Holmes, Jr., in a celebrated passage from *The Common Law*, argued that "prevention" is the "chief and only universal purpose of punishment" and that "probably most English-speaking lawyers would accept the preventive theory without hesitation."[4] William Blackstone, the eighteenth-century British jurist who had considerable influence on the development of American law, in a chapter entitled "Of the Means of Preventing Offenses," observed that "if we consider all human punishments in a large and extended view, we shall find them all rather calculated to prevent future crimes, than to expiate the past."[5]

Other legal authorities have argued in equally categorical terms that prevention has no proper role in the Anglo-American system of criminal justice. Francis Wharton, in his influential nineteenth-century *A Treatise on the Criminal Law of the United States*, dismissed "prevention" as a "proper theoretical justification" for criminal punishment: "If the [prevention] theory be correct, and be logically pursued, then punishment should precede and not follow crime. The state must explore for guilty tendencies, and make a trial consist of the psychological investigation of such tendencies. This contradicts one of the fundamental maxims of English common law, by which not a tendency to crime, but simply crime itself, can be made the subject of a criminal issue."[6]

The debate over the proper role, if any, of prevention in criminal punishment has not been limited to Anglo-American legal writers. The Marchese di Beccaria, one of the founders of modern-day criminology, in his classic eighteenth-century *Essay on Crimes and Punishments*, put forth an essentially preventive justification for the criminal sanction: "It is better to prevent crimes than to punish them. This is the fundamental principle of good legislation. . . . [T]he intent of punishment is not . . . to undo a crime already committed. . . . [It is] no other than to prevent the criminal from doing further injury to society, and to prevent others from committing the like offence."[7]

Immanuel Kant, the eighteenth-century German philosopher, in his *Metaphysical Elements of Justice*, took issue with Beccaria. For Kant, it was intolerable to impose punishment for any future-looking purpose: "Judicial punishment can never be used merely as a means to promote some other good for the criminal himself or for civil society, but instead it must in all cases be imposed on him only on the ground that he has committed a crime. . . ."[8]

Some of the disagreement over the proper role of prevention in a system of criminal justice results from a failure to define precisely what was being considered. "Prevention" obviously meant something very different to Holmes, for example, from what it did to Wharton. The furthest thing from Holmes's mind was any kind of "psychological investigation" for "guilty tendencies" or a system of justice under which "punishment should precede and not follow crime."[9] What Holmes meant by "preventive" was simply a forward-looking approach designed to reduce the frequency of harmful events in the future: "There can be no case in which the law-maker makes certain conduct criminal without his thereby showing a wish and purpose to prevent that conduct."[10]

Blackstone also defined "preventive" in a general way: "[A]ll punishments inflicted by temporal laws may be classed under three heads; such as tend to the amendment of the offender himself, or to deprive him of any power to do future mischief, or to deter others by his example: all of which conduce to one and the same end, of preventing future crimes. . . ."[11]

When prevention is defined as broadly as Holmes and Blackstone defined it, then most authorities, though not Kant, would agree that curtailing future crimes is one permissible function of any legal system.[12]

The issue therefore is not whether prevention should play any role in a system of criminal justice—virtually all commentators (with the exception of strict Kantians) would agree that it should— but how much and what kind of role it should play. There is a considerable difference between a system that confines a youngster who has never committed a criminal act but who is predicted to be a future criminal and one that authorizes confinement only after a consummated harm has been committed, though both may have as their purpose the prevention of future crimes. Prevention, as an element of criminal justice, is best seen as a continuum; some systems authorize preventive intervention of varying sorts relatively early in the process from dangerousness to ultimate harm, while others authorize preventive intervention later.

For the purpose of this historical analysis, it is enough to distinguish three distinct but overlapping approaches to the control of crime that have, with varying emphasis, always been employed in the Anglo-American system of justice.

The Injury or Harm Approach

The first, which has characterized most primitive and simple societies, may be called the injury or harm approach. Cain kills Abel, and God punishes the killer (though perhaps not harshly enough because it was his first offense, indeed the world's first murder according to the Bible). A serious physical injury, such as a death or maiming, is thought to require a response in kind. "Harm is harm and should be paid for. On the other hand, where there is no harm done, no crime is committed; an attempt to commit a crime is no crime."[13] In primitive societies, it is neither the law nor its agents that respond directly to harmful acts; the law simply authorizes those closest to the victim to seek blood revenge. Thus the father of the accidentally killed child was expected to seek revenge against the killer or his family.[14] An "advance [was] marked" when the law moved "towards the suppression of blood-feuds" and private vengeance. This advance, called a "bot," took the form of setting a price on the limbs and life of various victims. This system of compensation was at least in part preventive since its avowed purpose was "the suppression of blood-feuds."[15] The bot did, however, leave many dangerous criminals at liberty since its payment ended the "case."

Another preventive device, employed from the earliest times against criminals who were deemed especially dangerous, was total exclusion from the community and its protection. Exclusion could take the relatively benign form of banishment or the extreme form of outlawry, which was characterized as the capital punishment of a rude age.[16] Indeed, capital punishment (widely viewed today as the vestige of a retributive theory or as an arguable general deterrent) had an important preventive component during an age when the long-term confinement of dangerous offenders was not feasible. As imprisonment came into greater use and dangerous wrongdoers could be locked away, the preventive component of the harm-injury approach became more obvious. But since only those people who had already committed harmful crimes could be locked up, the preventive component of imprisonment was limited by the requirement, inherent in its definition, that no intervention can be authorized until an actual injury has been sustained. Dangerous people, even those who had committed dangerous acts, such as throwing an ax at, but missing, someone, were allowed, at least in theory, to remain free to try again, perhaps this time with better aim. Thus the father of a victim would not be punished until and unless he actually carried out his threat (if it was unlawful to kill the accidental killer of one's child).

The Dangerous Act Approach

This limitation is not inherent in the second approach, which may be called the dangerous or inchoate act approach. It is similar to the harm-injury approach in that it conditions intervention on the commission of a past criminal act. The essential difference is that under this approach the criminal act need not actually have caused any injury or harm; it is enough that the act is deemed dangerous. Thus, throwing an ax, carrying a concealed weapon, driving above the speed limit, creating a fire hazard, and issuing a credible threat all may be made criminal acts without regard to whether an injury actually followed the act in any particular case. The acts themselves, and the situations they create, are considered dangerous enough to warrant preventive intervention. The purpose of the criminal punishment is to reduce the frequency of these acts because it is assumed that the more these acts are committed or the more these situations are permitted to exist, the more likely it will be that injuries will occur.

Included in this approach are the so-called inchoate crimes, such as attempted murder, solicitation to murder, conspiracy to murder, and incitement to kill. Again, no actual injury need be proved; it is enough that the act was culpable and that it evidenced dangerousness. If the father tried to kill his enemy but failed, he could be punished for attempted murder. Thus, the father of the accidentally killed child could be punished for threatening to kill the child's murderer. This approach is considerably more preventive than the harm-injury approach since it authorizes intervention, indeed serious punishment, at a considerably earlier point on the danger-harm continuum.

The Dangerous Person Approach

Finally, the most obviously preventive approach may be called the dangerous person approach. It does not require the commission of any past criminal act as a condition to intervention. A person may be confined because it has been predicted that he may commit a dangerous or harmful act at some future time. Most such predictions will in fact be based upon suspicion that the person committed certain past acts, but these acts generally need not be proved, nor need they have been prohibited by law. Some obvious examples of the dangerous person approach are the confinement of predicted saboteurs or spies during wartime, the commitment of mentally ill persons thought to be dangerous, the pretrial preventive detention of criminal defendants on the basis of likely future criminality, the confinement of material witnesses, and the imprisonment of suspected terrorists. Under this approach, the father might be confined in order to prevent him from taking revenge, even if he has not threatened or tried to kill, so long as it is very likely that he would try.

A related phenomenon is the age-old right of self-defense. John Adams, in his closing argument on behalf of the British soldiers accused of perpetrating the Boston Massacre, invoked what he called "the first and strongest principle in our nature," preventing our own deaths by killing those about to attack us. This too requires a prediction of sorts and an assessment of the dangerousness of the attacker and the imminence of his attack. (As we shall see subsequently, analogies are often drawn to self-defense by those who would justify preemptive military strikes and other preventive measures.)

It is the predictive approach to dangerous persons and the lack of a jurisprudence governing it that is the focus of this chapter.

One important reason why we lack a jurisprudence or philosophy of preventive intervention is that so many intellectual, judicial, and political leaders have denied the legitimacy, even the existence of such intervention throughout our history. If we don't believe in or practice a particular mechanism of social control, then there is no need to construct a jurisprudence or philosophy that rationalizes and regulates it. Indeed, the very act of articulating such a jurisprudence is sometimes believed to lend legitimacy to an otherwise illegitimate mechanism.[17]

Moreover, Anglo-American law has generally evolved pragmatically over long periods of time; a given practice develops over time, is gradually recognized by the courts and commentators, and only then does a jurisprudence emerge. As Roscoe Pound, the former dean of Harvard Law School, put it, "It is true that in Anglo-American law, more than in other systems, juristic theories come after lawyer and judge have dealt with concrete cases and have in some measure learned how to dispose of them."[18] This is partly at least because the Anglo-American legal system is primarily a common law system that relies on cases, with different factual settings, being decided by the courts over the centuries. The Continental system, on the other hand, relies primarily on codification—that is, the enactment of statutes that speak in general terms and must be applied to specific cases as they arise.

Because lawyers and judges have not often "dealt" with preventive intervention—at least not overtly and systematically—and because they have not really "learned how to dispose"[19] of cases involving such intervention, there has been little occasion to develop juristic theories regarding this important and pervasive mechanism of social control. To illustrate this point, let us look briefly at the Anglo-American history of one retail, or micro, mechanism of preemptive intervention, the preventive detention of individuals believed to be likely to cause harm because of their criminal propensities, status, past behavior, profiles, mental illness, or other assumed markers of dangerousness.

Preventive Confinement: A Catalog of Denials

It has been widely assumed and often dogmatically asserted that the very idea of confining someone preventively is antithetical to the principles of the Anglo-American system of criminal justice and virtually unprecedented. As the great American Supreme Court justice Robert Jackson put it more than half a century ago, "[T]he jailing of persons by the courts because of anticipated but as yet uncommitted crimes [could not be reconciled with] traditional American law. . . . [I]mprisonment to protect society from predicted unconsummated offenses [is] unprecedented in this country . . . [and] is fraught with danger of excess. . . ."[20] He was wrong about its being unprecedented (recall the preventive confinement of 110,000 Japanese-Americans during World War II), but he was right about its being "fraught with danger."

Those who would deny the existence and certainly the legitimacy of preemptive intervention as a mechanism to prevent crimes and other harms point to history and its insistence that specific harm must have occurred before the law (or at least the criminal law) is invoked.

Ancient law has as a general rule no punishment for those who have tried to do harm but have not done it. The idea of punishment is but slowly severed from that of reparation, and where no harm is done there is none to be repaired.[21] "[English law] had started from the principle that an attempt to do harm is no offense." There was, of course, one striking exception to the general rule that a harm must already have been done. That exception involved any danger to the King. Not only was any plot against the King a high crime; it was even a crime 'to compass'— that is, to imagine—the death of the King. When it came to defending the King, all bets were off. Prevention was the key, but for all others the principle remained: "The thought of man shall not be tried."[22]

According to the distinguished historians Frederick Pollock and Frederic Maitland, these words "might well be the motto for the early history of criminal law. . . . Harm is harm and should be paid for. On the other hand, where there is no harm done, no crime is committed. . . ."[23] Even attempts to commit violent harms were not generally punished at common law. Professor Hall emphasizes the fact that "Criminal attempt is conspicuous for its absence in early English law. There is not the slightest suggestion of theory or general doctrine. . . . Apparently in those forthright days, a miss was as good as a mile."[24]

These renditions of legal history, ancient and medieval, seem unrealistically wooden to the modern mind. They suggest a society that was willing to tolerate extremely dangerous persons, acts, and conditions in its midst without any effort to prevent future harms—no matter how imminent or certain these harms appeared to be. It is unlikely that "a miss" was ever "as good as a mile," even in "those forthright days." If a man's enemy hurled an ax at him and narrowly missed, it defies common sense to assume that the near victim's attitude was simply to forget it: "For what harm did the attempt cause, since the injury took no effect?"[25] If the father of the accidentally killed child threatened and then tried to kill the person who had killed the child, you can be sure that something would have been done if not by the community then by the potential victim himself or his family. Human nature, even animal nature, reacts to imminent dangers as well as to consummated harms. It is difficult to accept as entirely accurate, therefore, a picture of a society, even a primitive and decentralized society, in which near misses, serious threats, conspiratorial plots, and obvious preparation for harm doing were totally ignored. What of the violently crazy person who had as yet caused no injury? What of the sinister-looking stranger aggressively bearing arms? What of the person suspected of past crimes but not subject to conviction for lack of sufficient evidence? Can it really be the case, as the commentators suggest, that such "dangerous" persons and "inchoate" acts were ignored unless they involved a plot against the king's life?

It may well be true, as Hall argues, that there "is not the slightest suggestion of theory or general doctrine" justifying liability for wrongdoing that "fell short" of actual physical injury. But the history of humankind—even beyond Anglo-American law—is one of pragmatic actions, followed, often only centuries later, by doctrinal or theoretical justifications. Even the Bible begins with stories of crimes, sins, and primitive efforts to prevent them in the Book of Genesis, before moving to the codification of laws in the Book of Exodus. This has certainly been the history with regard to preventive or preemptive warfare, as we shall see in the next chapter. Pragmatically, it is difficult to conceive of a society that ignored serious threats of future harm and always waited for past harms before it intervened.

From the beginning of recorded history, societies have worried about dangerous people who had not "yet" done the harm it was believed—or predicted—they would do. Preventive imprisonment, even in times when places of confinement were primitive, was employed in some systems. For example, the Bible requires two witnesses to convict a murderer. If only one credible witness testified, the defendant had to be acquitted,[26] but that did not necessarily mean that the dangerous killer would be allowed to go free and perhaps murder again. Instead he was placed in a locked room, where he was sometimes fed a lethal concoction of water and grain calculated to cause his stomach to burst.[27] The rabbis justified this extrabiblical punishment as necessary to prevent lawlessness.[28]

I suspect that most societies developed similar informal or extrajudicial mechanisms for dealing with obviously dangerous people who could not be convicted of past crimes.

This ancient example suggests a general rule about the need for preventive mechanisms. The need for preventive intervention becomes more obvious in a society that has circumscribed the formal process of criminal justice with safeguards that make conviction more difficult. Where conviction based upon suspicion (or "bad fame") is relatively easy, then the formal system can effectively play a preventive role: It can convict those who are feared likely to commit future crimes. But as procedural and substantive safeguards are added over time, then one obvious result is that more and more dangerous people will evade the formal criminal process and remain free in society. This will create a perceived need for preventive devices capable of incapacitating the person feared as dangerous but not subject to conviction for past crimes.[29] A close look at the history of the actual administration of justice, both private and public, will corroborate the commonsense conclusion that crime prevention has always played a significant, though largely unarticulated, role in the Anglo-American legal system.

Dual Systems of Criminal Justice: Retrospective and Preventive

Throughout Anglo-American history two criminal justice systems have operated side by side. The more formal system (the one we are most familiar with) has been characterized by high visibility, by progressive common law development through appellate decisions, by frequent legislative revision, and by bookshelves of treatises and other scholarly descriptions and discussions of its philosophy, substance, and procedure. Perhaps most important, it has been characterized by a well-developed jurisprudence imposing principled limits on its employment. Among the most fundamental principles of this system is that criminal punishment must always be based upon a past act or omission, not upon predicted conduct likely to occur at some future time.

Proof beyond a reasonable doubt of a specific criminal act, such as murder or robbery, was the switch that triggered the on-off criminal process that authorized the government to punish the accused, generally by execution, since imprisonment was not yet in wide usage. As more calibrated responses became available, more nuanced uses of the criminal law became feasible. When "moderate" punishments could be imposed, it became morally acceptable to use the criminal law somewhat more preventively—for example, to encourage people to take precautions and not to engage in dangerous conduct that had not yet caused any harm.

Thus, to the extent that those historians and judges were purporting to describe the early formal system, they probably came close to the mark. With a few special and limited exceptions, the formal Anglo-American legal system has not authorized the "jailing of persons by the courts because of anticipated but as yet uncommitted crimes."[30]

There always has been, however, a parallel system that has played a significant role in the Anglo-American legal process. It was less formal and less visible. That is why we know so little about it today, though it was probably well known in its own day. It was characterized by the absence of published opinions and appellate review. It has always been less principled or at least less willing to articulate governing principles. Few treatises or commentaries have been written about it. Most important, it has never developed an articulated jurisprudence that imposes principled limits on its employment. Its primary function has been to fill the gaps that inevitably occur in any formal system of criminal justice. This less visible system has taken on renewed importance because it has been widely employed during emergencies, including the post-9/11 period.

In the earliest times the two systems were essentially merged because the earliest law in general lacked formality, appellate decisions, an articulated jurisprudence, and principled limitations. Thus there was little tension between principle and practice requiring the creation of separate systems.[31]

A more formalized system of criminal justice began to develop in England after the Norman Conquest. By the end of Henry II's reign, near the end of the twelfth century, "there [was] a permanent central tribunal of persons expert in the administration of justice—of sworn judges."[32] There was also the establishment, in primitive form, of trial by jury, formal writs and pleas, the "king's peace," felonies, and the beginnings of a system of fundamental rights (to be solemnized in the Magna Carta in 1215).[33] A time traveler going back to the first millennium would hardly recognize our current legal system, but if that traveler then zipped forward to the thirteenth century, he would see some familiar attributes of the common law system of justice.

It is thus not surprising that at about the same time that the formal law began to develop, serious gaps began to be noted in the increasingly formalized, but "exceedingly inefficient," system of justice.[34] It was necessary therefore to develop a less formal system that could operate with an eye more to efficiency than principle and with the goal of "preventing the breach of the peace (wisely foreseeing and repressing the beginnings therof)"[35] rather than wait until crimes actually were committed.[36] This preventive system, residues of which can still be seen, centered on the office of the conservator of the peace, later called by the more familiar title justice of the peace, a cross between a policeman on the beat and local magistrate.

The Development of a System of Preventive Justice

The development of the special office of conservator of the peace, accomplished by the time of Richard I in the twelfth century, was in large part a measure designed to fill the gaps in the formal system of criminal justice and to check incipient crime.[37] Knights, who were specially assigned to this task, were instructed to summon before them all males over the age of fifteen and "cause them to swear that they would not be outlaws, robbers, or thieves. . . ."[38] These custodians—or keepers—of the peace were instructed to prevent homicide, incendiarism, robbery, and extortion. They were also authorized to prevent the bearing of arms without license, certainly an inchoate offense reminiscent of later gun control laws. As one might expect, among their functions was "to take every precaution to repress" uprisings against the royal authority at the earliest stages before any harm had yet occurred.[39]

The office of conservator of the peace changed names a number of times: guardian of the peace, keeper of the peace, and, eventually, justice of the peace. But the functions of the office, though constantly expanding and taking on more administrative and judicial duties, retained a common core. And that core always included a large preventive component.

In the fourteenth century lawlessness was rampant, and Parliament was convened a number of times to concern itself with problems of law and order. In 1360 a statute empowered the justices of the peace "to enquire of all those that have been pillors [sic] and robbers in the parts beyond the sea, and be now come again, and go wandering, and will not labor as they were wont in times past. . . ."[40] This provision was explicitly preventive in that it authorized inquiry of past malefactors who had been punished but who had returned and were still feared. The justices were authorized "to take and arrest all those that they may find . . . by suspicion, and to put them in prison. . . ." They were also authorized to "take all of them that be [not] of good fame" and to require them to post "sufficient surety and mainprise of their good behavior"[41] (i.e., trusted persons willing to vouch for him and to underwrite a recognizance bond).

By the time of the Tudors, in the sixteenth century, systematic legislation had been enacted against the poor and vagrant classes, which were thought to include a large number of dangerous persons. Poverty, idleness, drunkenness, vagrancy, and the like were seen as early markers of potential criminality.[42] The preamble to a statute enacted in the early sixteenth century declared that idleness among vagabonds and beggars was the "mother and root of all vices, whereby hath insurged and sprung and daily insurgeth and springeth continual thefts, murders, and other heinous offences and great enormities . . . to the marvelous disturbance of the common weal of this realm. . . ."[43]

Later statutes required the justices "to direct night searches for rufflers, vagabonds, and other suspects, and punish all such offenders."[44] If the captured "rogue was a dangerous character," then "two of the justices could commit him to gaol or the house of correction to await quarter sessions." If he was convicted there, banishment from the realm would follow.[45] Vagrancy laws of this kind were in large part preventive in origin and function.[46] These statutes—indeed, the entire jurisdiction of the justice of the peace—filled the interstices of the formal criminal law, which was in large part, though never entirely, retrospective.[47]

The need for preventive law throughout England was apparently great. Crime and violence were rampant, the formal criminal law was cumbersome, the "regular" criminal courts met in many locations at very long intervals, and the penalty structure was relatively inflexible. Thus the need was obvious for a less formal, more flexible, less principled, and more effective mechanism for dealing with those dangerous people who could not adequately, or swiftly, be dealt with under the formal system of criminal justice. The justice of the peace embodied that role.

The Justice of the Peace

Michael Dalton was one of those justices of the peace during the first half of the seventeenth century. He wrote a remarkable diary-treatise of the day-to-day operations of his office that remains the best contemporaneous account of this important job.[48] Dalton outlined the functions of his office as follows:

The conservation of this peace (and therin the care of the Just[ice] of Peace) consisteth in three things, *viz*.
1. In preventing the breach of the peace (wisely foreseeing and repressing the beginnings therof) by taking suretie for the keeping of it, or for the good behaviour of the offendors, as the case shall require.
2. In pacifying such as are in breaking of the peace. . . .
3. In punishing (according to Law) such as have broken the peace.[49]

These important officials combined the functions of today's police, prosecutors, judges, juries, and correctional officials. It is significant to note which of these functions Dalton deemed most specifically allocated to the justices of the peace: "But of the three, the first, the preventing Justice, is most worthy to be commended to the care of the Justices of peace."[50]

Dalton detailed the kinds of people against whom preventive action could be taken by the justices of the peace. It is evident from his listing that the justices exercised a preventive jurisdiction that did not require, as a condition for their intervention, that a crime already had been committed. It was enough if a person "is *minded* to break the peace"[51] or if he "be in a fury *ready* to break the peace."[52] Witchcraft trials may also have had a significant preventive component. The contemporaneous descriptions of the personality types associated with witches would seem to bear this out: "Those who were boastful, illiterate, miserable, lustful, and leading a 'lewd and naughty kind of life,' melancholy—all were likely to be witches. Above all, they were thought to be the type of person who went round begging and those who had vicious tongues. Witches were people of 'ill natures, of a wicked disposition, and spitefully malicious'; 'malicious people, full of revenge, having hearts swolne with rancour.' "

There did not seem to be any requirement of a specific overt act (though it is likely that one was suspected in most cases). It was sufficient if "in the justices conscience [he or she] was a *dangerous* person"[53] or persons "such as are *like* to commit murder, homicide or other grievance to any of the Kings subjects in their bodies" or one "of *evil fame* or *report* generally" or any "*suspicious* person in the night"[54] or any person "suspected to be *inclined* to the breach of the peace."[55] The underlying requirement seems to have been that "there is a fear of some present or future danger, and not merely for a [crime] that is past."[56] Thus, the mere fact that an accused person was "acquitted of a felony" did not eliminate the authority of the justice of the peace: "[I]f he be of evil fame, or of evil behaviour, it seemeth the Justices of Peace upon their discretion, may binde him to his good behaviour."[57] If the "defendant" failed or refused to produce satisfactory sureties, "then the Justice of Peace may commit him to the Gaol."[58]

In today's world this wide discretion to apprehend anyone who looked "suspicious," "dangerous," or "inclined" to commit a crime would be a police officer's dream and a civil libertarian's nightmare. But as we shall see, when the formal and informal systems began to merge, especially during the last half of the twentieth century, the protections of the formal law were extended to preventive police activities, and arrests on "mere suspicion" became impermissible. However, until relatively recently the justices of the peace retained considerable discretion to respond to complaints about dangerous characters wandering about.

Following the attacks of 9/11, this discretion was once again invoked in an effort to prevent terrorism, by casting a wide net around people of Middle Eastern extraction who were suspected of association with terrorism. Some were held as "material witnesses," others were arrested for minor offenses and held without bail, while still others were confined for violating immigration laws. Pursuant to the mandate of the U.S. Justice Department, the law was becoming more proactive and preemptive. It remains to be seen whether these "emergency" measures will outlive the emergencies that generated them.

Even in the days of the justice of peace it was not enough to sit back and wait for complaints to be made against rogues, vagabonds, and others of this sort; the justice's job was to search them out, as illustrated by a document entitled "A warrant for a general search for Rogues."[59] This warrant commanded the constables to "make a general privie search within every of the said

several towns . . . upon (a specified date) at night . . . for the finding out and apprehending of all Rogues, Vagabonds, and wandering and idle persons. . . . And if any of the said rogues shall appear
to be dangerous or incorrigible (they shall be tried and committed
to the house of correction, or gaole)."[60]

———————————

One area of the justice of the peace's role that has been neglected
by historians but that warrants special attention in the context of
crime and terrorism prevention is the control of weapons. This
type of control reflects a kind of prevention different from that
exercised over dangerous persons; this is prevention directed at
dangerous situations (or the combination of dangerous persons
and situations).

The justices of the peace were authorized to take direct action
against "any person [who] shall ride or go armed . . . in Fairs, Mar-
kets, or elsewhere (by night or by day) in affray of the Kings people. . . ." The justices "may cause them to be staid and arrested,
and may bind all such to the Peace or good behaviour (or, for want
of sureties, may commit them to the Gaol)." They were also authorized to "seize and take away their armor, and other weapons, and
shall cause them to be prised, and answered to the King as forfeited."[61] It was not a crime to carry weapons of various kinds, yet
the justices of the peace, in their discretionary power to repress
"the beginnings" of crime, were empowered to "take away" any "gun,
dag[ger], or pistols charged" or any other "armor worn in terrorism"
or weapons that appeared likely to be used against the peace.[62]
There were absolute prohibitions against possession of certain
kinds of weapons or by certain classes of persons: "No person may
shoot in, carry, keep, use or have any hand-gun under one whole
yard in length, nor any other Gun (Dag, or Pistoll) that shall be

under three quarters of a yard in length."[63] (This proscription against concealable weapons seems to be a direct predecessor of modern concealed handgun legislation.) Poor people—anyone who "hath [not] *per annum* 100. li"—were forbidden to have "any Gun, Dagge, Pistoll, Crossbow, or Stonebow. . . ." And any justice of the peace could take such weapons from a poor person found in possession of them. Indeed, every person "having in lands an hundred pounds by the year" was made a "private" justice of the peace for purposes of enforcing the weapons law. Any such person "may from such Malefactors, and to his own use for ever keep" any weapon found in the possession of an ineligible poor person.[64]

Another "dangerous situation" about which the justices of the peace seem to have had special concern was dangerous or unlawful "assemblies." It was believed that in the past such assemblies "began upon very small occasion, yet not being repressed in time, grew to such greatness and height, that they afterwards put in hazard the state and government of this Land." Accordingly, "it is behovefull and good wisdome for all Justices of P. to indeavour by all good meanes to *quench the beginnings and first sparks of such assemblies. . . .*"[65]

Today, of course, the right to assemble is protected by the Constitution of the United States and the common law of Great Britain, but some "assemblies"—lynch mobs, gatherings in certain sensitive locations—can be stopped even today if they are deemed too dangerous to the peace.

Unlawful assemblies were defined by the justices of the peace to include what is today covered by conspiracy laws (except that three persons or more rather than two persons or more had to be involved). These were inchoate crimes that did not require any harm (or substantive crime) to have been committed: "[A]lthough they shall after depart of their own accord, without doing anything, yet this is an unlawfull assembly."[66] Nor was any complaint needed:

"[E]very Justice of peace, hearing of any Rout, or of any intention of a Rout (without . . . tarrying . . .) shall do well to go himself . . . to the place where such persons be so assembled, and to suppress them . . . and to force them to put in surety for the peace . . . and also he may take away their weapons and armour. . . ."[67]

The justices of the peace had a similar preventive role in controlling "affrays. If the affray be 'dangerous,' then the affrayors" may be commanded to "prison for a small time, till their heat be over." If "men shall contend only in hot words, this is no affray," and the constable would have no jurisdiction to intervene. But the justice could still take preventive action, "for from (hot words) oftimes doe ensue Affrays and batteries, and sometimes maimes, yea manslaughters and murders." This approach to "hot words" presages our contemporary approach to what the Supreme Court has called fighting words.[68]

_____

Though the jurisdiction of the justices was predominantly "preventive" and they were authorized to act against persons (even to incarcerate them) who had not "yet" committed any harmful or even criminal act, it seems likely, from what Dalton wrote, that "suspicion" of past misbehavior was often taken into account in deciding if one was to be regarded as a dangerous person. Indeed, the rules of evidence set out by Dalton make it clear that no sharp distinctions were drawn between evidence of past guilt and evidence of future dangerousness.

Among the "circumstances" that were to be "considered" in the "examination of Felons" were the following:

His parents, if they were wicked, and given to the same kind of fault.

His ability of body, if strong and swift, or weak or sickly,
   not likely to doe the act.
His nature . . . a quarreller, pilferer or bloody-minded. . . .
His trade; for if a man liveth idely or vagrant . . . it is a
   good cause to arrest him upon suspicion, if there has
   been any felony committed.
His company. . . .
His course of life. . . .
Whether he be of evill fame or report.
Whether he hath committed the like offense before or if
   he hath a pardon, or been acquitted of felony before . . .
   or beene outlawed for felony. . . .[69]

It is obvious that these items of "evidence," some of which are descriptive of character and not specifically related to any particular past offense, were as probative of future dangerousness as past guilt. They constitute an early form of profiling. Today we employ ethnicity, religion, and race, but in those days virtually every Englishman shared those characteristics and so poverty, heredity, and reputation became the markers. The essential difference between convicting someone of a past crime and preventing him from committing a future crime lay therefore not in the nature of the evidence that could be used but rather in the burden of proof and in the acceptable ratio of false positives to false negatives. There had to be greater certainty that the correct person was convicted of a past crime.[70] Hence, the more stringent requirements of trial by jury, two justices, heavier burdens of proof. Preventive justice, on the other hand, could afford to be overinclusive, to include more "false positives." Dalton candidly acknowledged this and said that it "is no new thing": "There is such a precedent in the old book of justices of peace . . . yea, it is the common practice at this day, and it seemeth to be very serviceable; and of two evils *the lesser is to be chosen*, that an offendor, *or suspected person, should be imprisoned* for a time (though *sometimes wrongfully*) than that *one which hath committed felony should escape unpunished*."[71]

––––––––––––

If the credo that it is better for an innocent person to be wrongfully imprisoned than for a guilty one to escape reflected the actual "practice" of the justices in administering preventive justice during the early seventeenth century in England, it seems strikingly at variance with the famous credo of the formal common law "that it is better that ten guilty persons escape, than that one innocent suffer."[72] This credo refers of course specifically to the burden of proof for a conviction for felonies already committed. Even Blackstone suggested a different standard of certainty with regard to preventing future crimes. In cataloging the kind of person who may be subjected to what he called preventive justice, one who may be required to produce sureties or who "may immediately be committed till he does," Blackstone acknowledged that there is "so great a latitude, as leaves much to be determined by the discretion of the magistrate himself."[73] But he did not seem to object to the possibility that numerous innocent persons may suffer confinement as a consequence of this preventive procedure: "The caution, which we speak of at present, is such as is intended merely for prevention, without any crime actually committed by the party, but arising only from a probable suspicion, that some crime is intended or likely to happen; and consequently it is not meant as any degree of punishment, unless perhaps for a man's imprudence in giving just ground of apprehension."[74]

Blackstone regarded the peace bond (and the analogous good behavior bond) as an innovation unique to English jurisprudence:

"And really it is an honour, and almost a singular one, to our English laws, that they furnish a title of this sort [the title being 'of the means of preventing offenses']: since *preventive* justice is upon every principle, of reason, of humanity, and of sound policy, preferable in all respects to *punishing* justice;[75] the execution of which, though necessary . . . is always attended with many harsh and disagreeable circumstances." Blackstone was reasonably careful in his use of the term "preventive justice." He defined it as a restraint "intended merely for prevention, without any crime actually committed by the party, but arising only from a probable suspicion, that some crime is intended or likely to happen. . . ."[76]

It is still quite remarkable that legal commentators seemed to accept so great a disparity between the preference for one type of error over another, depending on whether confinement was deemed punitive or preventive. It was, after all, still confinement. With regard to the former, the strong preference was for acquitting the possibly guilty over convicting the possibly innocent ("better that ten guilty persons escape than that one innocent suffer"). With regard to preventive confinement, on the other hand, the strong preference was for imprisoning the possibly innocent over freeing the possibly dangerous: "of the two evils, the lesser is . . . that [a] suspected person, should be imprisoned for a time (though sometimes wrongfully) than that one which hath committed felony should escape unpunished."[77] One difference of course was that the punishment for past felonies was often death, whereas the preventive sanction was imprisonment "for a time." But that difference alone would not seem to justify so great a disparity between the highly formalized jurisprudence of punishment and the largely discretionary and ad hoc practice of prevention, especially since imprisonment in English jails carried with it a significant risk of death.[78]

Early English jails were generally designed for short-term,

temporary detention rather than for long-term incapacitation and punishment. The erection of institutions suitable for long-term confinement was probably regarded as needless expense and burden in a land that was still sparsely enough settled that its wandering undesirables could be shunted from isolated community to isolated community and to a people who were still callous enough to tolerate the inexpensive sanction of execution for a wide range of criminal offenses.

Imprisonment was apparently employed, even in America during colonial times, against some persons who could not secure sureties to keep the peace or for good behavior. This institution— the preventive justice administered by the justices of the peace— was transplanted from across the ocean. Justices of the peace were appointed in the colonies and their jurisdiction and powers paralleled those exercised in the mother country. As in Britain, much was left to the discretion of the justices. Their mission was broad: "[T]he prevention of . . . mischief which [persons of evil fame] may be chiefly suspected to be likely to do; and . . . to sever the public from that danger which may probably be apprehended from their future behavior, whether any actual crime can be proved upon them or not. . . ."[79]

The restrictions on their power were few. As an early American commentator said about one of the original statutes empowering justices of the peace to keep the peace, "[I]t is certain it hath been carried much further [than its original purpose] by construction, and the purport of it hath been extended by degrees, until at length there is scarcely any other statute, which has received such a largeness of interpretation."[80]

The available records provide little information on how frequently the peace or good behavior bond was actually employed in the colonies or how often imprisonment was actually ordered for failure to obtain a surety. There is evidence that these devices were employed in certain of the colonies, but it seems likely that actual confinement was not relied on as extensively as in England during that same period."[81]

The authority of the justice of the peace to confine dangerous people on preventive grounds persisted even after the adoption of the Constitution and the Bill of Rights, though the duration of the confinement that could be ordered without a jury trial was generally limited, except in the case of the dangerously mentally ill.[82] This authority lasted until well into the twentieth century, when the courts began to apply constitutional restrictions more aggressively to the police. The events of September 11 and the fear of terrorism may, however, restore some preventive authority to the police, the FBI, and other contemporary keepers of the peace.

Some Tentative Historical Conclusions

This brief history of one type of preventive intervention suggests that the confinement of dangerous persons who cannot be convicted of past criminality but are thought likely to cause serious injury in the future has always been practiced to some degree by every society in history regardless of the jurisprudential rhetoric it has employed. Moreover, it is likely that some forms of preventive confinement, as well as other preventive and preemptive measures, will continue to be practiced by every society.

It suggests that at least some of what has passed for preventive confinement has really been mechanisms for detaining persons who are thought to have committed *past* crimes but who, for one reason or another, cannot be convicted. Thus the original jurisdiction of the justices of the peace, though preventive, often required a "finding" (but a far less rigorous finding) of past criminality.[83]

This historical material suggests an interesting hypothesis: that all other factors being equal, the necessity for and emergence of informal preventive mechanisms will increase as it becomes more difficult to secure convictions against dangerous persons thought to be guilty of past serious crime. Mechanisms of social control, more specifically of confinement and isolation, frequently operate on a balloon principle: If you squeeze the air out of one end, the other will become more inflated. Thus it is a fairly constant phenomenon in most societies that dangerous people will be isolated by one means or another: If banishment is available, imprisonment may be employed less frequently; if there is no law of criminal attempts, then peace bonds may be used against those who attempt, but fail, to do harm; if insane asylums become available, then vagrancy and poor laws will be used less frequently against the insane.[84] This principle is useful, at least, as a caveat: When a particular mechanism of confinement is rendered useless (or less useful), one should at least search to see if the slack has been picked up, in whole or in part, by other mechanisms.

The most disturbing conclusion—and most relevant to this book—is that although preventive confinement has always been and will always be practiced, no systematic and widely accepted jurisprudence of preventive intervention has ever been developed. There were some rules, to be sure, such as those cataloged by Dalton and others. But these rules seem to reflect the ad hoc practices of the justices rather than a fully articulated legal or moral philosophy. It may sound surprising, even arrogant to say that no jurisprudence governing preventive confinement has ever been articulated, but it appears to be true. No philosopher, legal writer, or political theorist has ever, to this writer's knowledge, attempted to construct a systematic theory of when it is appropriate for the state to confine preventively. This is so for a number of reasons. The mechanisms of prevention have been, for the most part, informal; accordingly, they have not required articulate defense or justification. Moreover, there are many scholars who simply deny that preventive intervention, especially preventive confinement, really exists, or if they acknowledge the existence of these mechanisms, they deny their legitimacy, thus obviating the need for a theory or jurisprudence. Finally, it is extremely difficult to construct a theory of preventive confinement that neatly fits into existing theories of criminal law and democracy.

The upshot, however, is that there has always existed a widespread series of practices, involving significant restraints on human liberty, without an articulated jurisprudence circumscribing and limiting its application. People are confined to prevent predicted harms without any systematic effort to decide what kinds of harms warrant preventive confinement, or what degree of likelihood should be required, or what duration of preventive confinement should be permitted; or what relationship should exist among the harm, the likelihood, and the duration.[85] This is not to say that there currently exists a completely satisfactory jurisprudence or theory justifying the imposition of punishment for *past* acts. (Recall Pound's observation that "in Anglo-American law, more than in other systems, juristic theories come after lawyer and judge have dealt with concrete cases and have in some measure learned to dispose of them.")[86] But at least many of the right questions have been asked, and some interesting answers have been attempted. Even the primitive statement that "it is better that ten guilty persons escape than that one innocent suffer" tells us something important about how to devise rules of evidence and procedure. There is no comparable aphorism for preventive confinement: Is it better for X number of false positives to be erroneously confined (and for how long?) than for Y number of preventable harms (and of what kind?) to occur? What relationship between X and Y does justice require? We have not even begin to ask these questions in a systematic way, or to develop modes of analysis for answering them, beyond clichés extolling the virtues of "an ounce of prevention" or "a stitch in time." We must come to understand and acknowledge the harms that could be caused by ounces of preventive warfare or by stitches of preventive confinement.[87]

This brief historical account of one paradigmatic genre of preemption—preventive confinement of individuals believed to be dangerous—is intended to illustrate a more general phenomenon, namely, that preemptive actions of many kinds have been far more common in practice than they appear in theory. Similar historical accounts, though with varying content and rationalizations, could be provided for other preemptive mechanisms as well. For example, as we shall now see, preemptive military attacks on enemies who may themselves be contemplating attack are at least as old as the Bible.

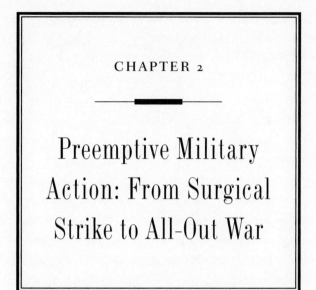

CHAPTER 2

Preemptive Military Action: From Surgical Strike to All-Out War

T he highest-stake preemptive decision faced by a nation may be whether to undertake military action against an enemy who is believed to pose a serious danger. The decision whether to attack an enemy who is planning aggression may make the difference between military victory and defeat. It may save, or cost, untold lives. In some situations it could determine whether a nation survives or is destroyed.

The concept of anticipatory military action is as old as warfare itself. It ranges from a singular surgical preemptive strike to a massive all-out preventive war. It is useful to distinguish between preemptive and preventive wars, with the former limited to *imminent* threats and the latter extending to longer-range but relatively *certain* dangers. The English language distinguishes between these concepts, but as Gareth Evans, the former foreign minister of Australia, has noted, "the English language seems to be unique in having two different words here," while other languages "tend to use the words [preemption and prevention], if at all, interchangeably."[1] I shall discuss both in this chapter and try to draw relevant distinctions between them.

The ancients certainly practiced various forms of each, and philosophers have debated the merits and demerits of anticipatory self-defense in many different contexts. What becomes clear from any review of both the practice and philosophy is that preemptive and preventive warfares are very much matters of degree and that the possible anticipatory steps that can be taken in the context of military confrontation lie across a broad spectrum. What also becomes clear is that as with preventive incapacitation in the individual context, there is little in the way of an accepted jurisprudence or morality of anticipatory self-defense in the military context. What we see instead are a series of ad hoc decisions made over time and place, some of which have been validated by the verdict of history, others condemned. Not surprisingly, history's judgment seems to depend in large part on whether the action that was taken turned out, in retrospect, to be right rather than on whether it was justified on the basis of what was reasonably believed at the time it was taken. Since we can never know for certain how a preventive or preemptive military action will turn out—indeed, we do not even have a shared definition of "success"—these ad hoc verdicts of history provide little in the way of prospective guidance to what sorts of anticipatory military actions are legally or morally justified.

At one extreme is the total annihilation of a perceived enemy who has taken no outward steps toward mounting an attack or even preparing for one. Throughout history, nations and tribes have set out to destroy their enemies before they become strong enough to pose a realistic military threat. (The Book of Genesis tells how two

of Jacob's sons tricked the clan of Hamor into undergoing cir-
cumcision and then killed them when they were still weak from
the operation. The Midrash suggest that Jacob's sons believed that
Hamor, one of whose sons had "humbled" Jacob's daughter, was
planning to kill Jacob's clan at a later time, and so the action was
in anticipatory self-defense. Interestingly Jacob criticized his sons
for "stirring up trouble," fearing perhaps that other clans would
now feel it necessary to take preemptive action against his aggressive clan.)[2] At the other extreme is waiting to be absolutely certain that the enemy is about to attack and simply beating him to
the punch.[3] (That was Israel's claim when it preemptively attacked
the Egyptian and Syrian air forces at the beginning of the Six-Day
War of 1967.) In between these extremes lies a wide range of protective, anticipatory, proactive, preventive, and preemptive actions
against a feared enemy. (The U.S. blockade of Cuba in 1962 following the discovery of nuclear missiles is an example of an intermediate preemptive action.)

"To Kill Him Who Is Making Ready to Kill":
Anticipatory Military Actions throughout History

The Bible contains several instances of preemptive military
action, most famously in the Book of Esther,[4] which recounts how
King Ahasuerus of Persia (sometimes referred to as Xerxes) was
instigated by his adviser Haman to mandate the destruction of the
Jewish people within his kingdom, because their customs were
"different" and they did "not obey the King's laws."[5] Dispatches
were then sent by couriers to all the king's provinces with the order
to "kill and annihilate all the Jews—young and old, women and

little children—on a certain day, the thirteenth day of the twelfth
month . . . and to plunder their goods." After a convoluted plot by
the Jew Mordechai and his niece Queen Esther to turn the king
against Haman, Ahasuerus commanded the execution of Haman,
but the law forbade him to rescind his order to kill the Jews, "for
no document written in the king's name and sealed with his ring
can be revoked." So the King issued another order granting the
Jewish people "the right to assemble and protect themselves"
from anyone preparing to carry out the first order. This order
bestowed on the Jews the right "to destroy, kill and annihilate any
armed force . . . that might attack them and their women and children. . . ." That right of preemptive self-defense came into operation on the thirteenth day of the twelfth month, the same day
specified in the initial order for their destruction. On that day "the
enemies of the Jews had hoped to overpower them, but now the
tables were turned and the Jews got the upper hand over those
who hated them," because "the people of all the other nationali-
ties were afraid of them," knowing that Mordechai "was prominent in the palace." And so "the Jews struck down all their
enemies with the sword, killing and destroying them. . . ."[6]

In this biblical account, the Jewish people acted in anticipatory self-defense against an imminent and certain threat of genocide and were praised for it.[7] The Romans took this principle much
further, according to Edward Gibbon, in his classic account *The
Decline and Fall of the Roman Empire*. He described a preventive
military action that is less praiseworthy:[8] "On the appointed day,
the unarmed crowd of the Gothic youth was carefully collected in
the square or Forum; the streets and avenues were occupied by
the Roman troops, and the roofs of the houses were covered with
archers and slingers. At the same hour, in all the cities of the East,
the signal was given of indiscriminate slaughter; and the provinces
of Asia were delivered, by the cruel prudence of Julius from a

domestic enemy who, in a few months, might have carried fire and sword from the Hellespont to the Euphrates."

Gibbon then assessed this preventive slaughter: "The urgent consideration of the public safety may undoubtedly authorize the violation of every positive law. How far that, or any other, consideration may operate to dissolve the natural obligations of humanity and justice is a doctrine of which I still desire to remain ignorant."

In the account of the "cruel prudence of Julius," the anticipated harm was neither imminent nor certain; the fear was that an enemy "might" have attacked the Romans "in a few months." Moreover, the anticipatory action taken was not limited to neutralizing the men who might attack them: "The signal was given of indiscriminate slaughter." Gibbon seemed to justify this violation of all positive law but insisted on remaining ignorant of how far the dictates of necessity might dissolve *natural* law limitations on what means might justly be employed to prevent a future harm.

Not surprisingly, Machiavelli approved of the Roman approach to preemptive war: "The Romans did in such matters what all wise rulers ought to do. It is necessary not only to pay attention to immediate crises, but to foresee those that will come, and to make every effort to prevent them." He urged his prince to analogize military dangers to medical ones:

> For if you see them coming well in advance, then you can easily take the appropriate action to remedy them, but if you wait until they are right on top of you, then the prescription will no longer take effect, because the disease is too far advanced. In this matter it is as doctors say of consumption: In the beginning the disease is easy to cure, difficult to diagnose; but, after a while, if it has not been diagnosed and treated early, it becomes easy to diagnose and hard to cure. So, too, in politics, for if you foresee prob-

lems while they are off (which only a prudent man is able to do)
they can easily be dealt with; but when, because you have failed
to see them coming, you allow them to grow to the point that anyone can recognize them, then it is too late to do anything.[9]

Machiavelli commended the Romans for always looking
ahead and taking "action to remedy problems before they developed. . . . They never postponed action to avoid war, for they
understood that you can not escape wars, and when you put them
off only your opponents benefit."[10]

More surprisingly, Thomas More included preemption—at
least under certain circumstances—as a tactic agreeable with the
Catholic doctrine of just war: "[I]f any foreign prince takes up
arms and prepares to invade their land, they immediately attack
him in full force outside their own borders. They are the most
reluctant to wage war on their own soil."[11]

Preemptive military action was often analogized to individual
self-defense, which the poet and playwright John Dryden
declared to be "Nature's eldest law."[12] It was also analogized to the
killing of wild beasts in the state of nature. As John Locke put it,
"a criminal, who having renounced Reason . . . hath . . . declared
War against all Mankind. . . ."[13]

Hugo Grotius, one of the founders of international law, argued
that preemptive military action is justified whenever waiting
would impose too high a price. He supported preventive measures
designed "to kill him who is making ready to kill."[14] Other leading
lights of international law "recognized that states were not obli-
gated to 'receive the first blow, or merely avoid and parry those
aimed at [them]' but were rather entitled, at natural law, to engage
in preventive war 'even though [an enemy] has not yet fully
revealed his intentions. . . .'"[15]

Nations, throughout history, have followed this preventive

approach when they believed that to do so served their national interests. Great Britain, for example, initiated a preventive war against Louis XIV, to protect itself against what it regarded as a dangerous union of Spain and France, two of its traditional enemies, under a single Bourbon crown. Britain had not been attacked, nor was an invasion imminent, but it feared a future attack from a powerful combination of its two traditional enemies, so it undertook to attack them while they were still weak and divided. The War of the Spanish Succession was thus a long-range preventive military action. It endured for thirteen years until the Peace of Utrecht was signed in 1713.

In addition to such full-scale preventive wars, there have been throughout history many instances of kings, emperors, czars, sheikhs, and other leaders taking more limited actions to prevent potential threats to their rule. The common law made it a capital crime even to compass—that is, imagine—the death of the king. The theory was that compassing was the first step toward accomplishing, and when it came to the life of the king, all doubts, reasonable or unreasonable, must be resolved in favor of his safety, regardless of the number of false positives. Better a hundred non-plotters against the king be executed than even one plotter remain free to carry out his plot! Similarly British law authorized the use of torture if a judge decided that it was necessary to secure information likely to prevent attacks on the king or the state.[16] Preventive arrests, banishments,[17] and even executions were part of the arsenal used against potential adversaries throughout history.

Nor was prevention limited to protecting those in power. Some seeking to overthrow the incumbent would kill not only the king but sometimes his heirs in order to assure that no claimants to the throne emerged in future years. The Bolsheviks justified the murder of Czar Nicholas II's children with this rationale. It was Lenin's fear of a Romanov restoration that "explains the execution of four grand dukes." The alleged survival of Princess Anastasia did in fact lead some czarists to hold out hope that the little princess might someday regain the throne and restore the monarchy.[18] The Sicilian Mafia sometimes killed the young male children of murdered rivals in order to prevent them from taking revenge in years to come. Even the New Testament recounts Herod's decision to kill all the male children under two years of age in and around Bethlehem because he had been told that the future king of the Jews was among them.[19]

In addition to these and other instances of preventive military action and uses of force, there are examples of the failure to act preventively that have been condemned by the verdict of history and morality. Most notorious was the failure of Great Britain and the other European victorious powers to prevent the remilitarization of Germany following its defeat in World War I despite its open violation of its treaty obligations. British Prime Minister Neville Chamberlain has become the historical poster child for appeasement precisely because he failed to act pursuant to the dictum of former American Secretary of State and War Elihu Root, who advocated "the right of every sovereign state to protect itself by preventing a condition of affairs in which it will be too late to protect itself."[20]

Winston Churchill believed that the rise of Nazi military power could have been prevented, perhaps even without the use of force. Until 1934 Britain, France, and their allies could have "controlled by a mere effort of the will the armed strength of Germany. . . . [T]he strict enforcement at any time till 1934 of the disarmament clauses of the Peace Treaty would have guarded indefinitely, without violence or bloodshed, the peace and safety of mankind," according to Churchill. But they failed to act, and because of their failure, the Germans rearmed. When the Nazis assumed power, democratically at first, the allies failed again.

"Without these follies crime would have found neither temptation nor opportunity."[21]

Even Joseph Goebbels expressed shock that the victorious European governments did not march against the rise of Nazi power while they still maintained military superiority:

> [W]e have succeeded in leaving the enemy in the dark concerning Germany's real goals, just as before 1932 our domestic foes never saw where we were going or that our oath of legality was just a trick. We wanted to come to power legally, . . . but we did not want to use power legally. . . . They could have suppressed us. They could have arrested a couple of us in 1925 and that would have been that, the end. No, they let us through the danger zone. That's exactly how it was in foreign policy, too. . . . In 1933 a French premier ought to have said (and if I had been the French premier I would have said it): "The new Reich Chancellor is the man who wrote *Mein Kampf*, which says this and that. This man cannot be tolerated in our vicinity. Either he disappears or we march!" But they didn't do it. They left us alone and let us slip through the risky zone, and we were able to sail around all dangerous reefs. And when we were done, and well armed, better than they, then they started the war![22]

Britain's failure to intervene in the Spanish Civil War, though more complicated, is also seen by some historians as a show of weakness in what Hitler regarded as an early phase of the impending world war.[23]

These failures are now cited by current proponents of a more proactive military policy, but precise analogies are often misleading in our complex and ever-changing world. Moreover, military attacks by tyrannies are often sought to be justified on preemptive principles. The Nazis tried to justify their invasions of Poland

and, later, the Soviet Union by claiming that they were acting pre-emptively, but nobody believed those transparent lies. Some military historians have justified the Japanese attack on Pearl Harbor as a preemptive attack against the military force of a potential enemy that had positioned its navy in preparation for waging war on Japan and its ally Germany.[24] Had the United States known of the impending attack on its Pacific fleet, it surely would have been justified its attacking the Japanese Air Force first. Indeed, the Roosevelt administration was criticized for its intelligence failures in not anticipating and preventing the devastating Japanese surprise attack. Some have even suggested that Roosevelt had sufficient information to have justified a preemptive attack on the Japanese Air Force but preferred to absorb the first blow and then declare war against both Japan and Germany.[25]

These, and other, costly failures to preempt led to the argument, made in the years between the development of the atomic bomb by the United States and by the Soviet Union, for a preventive attack by the United States against the nascent Soviet nuclear facilities.[26] Those who favored such an attack believed that it was only a matter of time before the Soviet nuclear arsenal would be directed at American cities and military bases. Quoting Franklin Delano Roosevelt's famous analogy to Nazism—"when you see a rattlesnake poised to strike, you do not wait until he has struck before you crush him"[27]—they argued that it would be better to take out the Soviet nuclear threat before it was capable of being deployed than to wait for a first strike by Stalin. Those who opposed a preemptive strike argued that because the Soviets already had some atomic capability, it was already too late, too risky, and too difficult. Better to threaten nuclear retaliation as a deterrent against potential Soviet attack. In the end, a policy of deterrence prevailed over a policy of preemption, and nuclear war was averted by the mutual threat of massive destruction (mutual assured destruction, or MAD).

Deterrence as the Alternative to Prevention

In its editorial quoted in the Introduction, the *New York Times* cited the Soviet example as evidence of the preference for deterrence over preemption when dealing with nation-states. It then argued that while preemption may be appropriate against terrorists, it was a far more questionable strategy in dealing with Iraq.

It is true of course that in retrospect the "brutally simple idea" of mutually assured destruction succeeded in deterring an attack by the Soviet Union during the Cold War. But if the Soviets had in fact launched a first-strike nuclear assault against the United States, those who argued against a preemptive attack would almost certainly have been condemned by the verdict of history. We now know, with the benefit of hindsight, that the Soviet military capacity was weaker than many believed, even after it had acquired an offensive nuclear capability,[28] but at the time of the debate over a preemptive attack, the risks of a Soviet nuclear first strike seemed plausible.[29]

Even years later, in 1962, the United States came close to waging a preventive war, or at least a preventive attack, against Cuba after American intelligence had discovered that Soviet nuclear rockets were being installed ninety miles from our shores. There was no evidence of any intention to fire these rockets imminently, but their presence so close to American population centers was thought to shift the balance of power and to pose too great a potential threat. Tough diplomacy, including a naval blockade (or quarantine), ultimately resolved the crisis, but not without a credible threat of military action by the United States if the nuclear weapons were not removed.[30] Even more recently the United States, according to some reports, "considered attacking North Korea before agreeing to seek a peaceful solution to the standoff over nuclear weapons."[31] In the end the Clinton administration decided in 1994 not to act preventively against the Korean threat. For the most part the superpowers relied on mutual deterrence to prevent nuclear warfare during the Cold War, which finally ended in 1991.

Though the *New York Times* and others have praised the use of MAD as a deterrent threat—certainly when compared with the use of preemptive war or preventive military action—there is considerable doubt whether a democratic nation, committed to the rule of law, can lawfully carry out or even threaten mutually assured destruction in retaliation against a nuclear attack upon its own population centers. International law seems clear—or at least as clear as international law ever is—that a nuclear attack that specifically targets enemy population centers is not permitted. In other words, if the Soviet Union had dropped a bomb on New York City, killing millions of Americans, it might have been unlawful for the United States to retaliate by dropping a nuclear bomb on the center of Moscow. We could have attacked Soviet nuclear facilities and other *military* targets, even if some were close to population centers. But we could not lawfully do precisely what we had threatened: tit-for-tat nuclear annihilation of a Soviet civilian population center. This is not to say we would not have done precisely that. After all, we dropped atomic bombs on Hiroshima and Nagasaki without the Japanese having bombed our cities. And we and the British dropped conventional bombs on Dresden and other German cities, after Germany had bombed British cities. But following the nuclear attacks on Japanese cities—attacks on *civilians* that America sought to justify as necessary to save the lives of American *soldiers*—the rules of international law made it relatively clear that civilians could not be targeted even in retaliation for attacks on civilians.[32] Despite this prohibition, both the United States and the USSR promised—threatened—mutually assured destruction as a deterrent to a first strike by a nuclear weapon.

In 1996 the International Court of Justice issued a decision and a series of opinions in a case challenging the lawfulness of using, or threatening to use, nuclear weapons. The majority decision was anything but clear. It declined "to pronounce . . . on the practice known as 'the policy of deterrence.'"[33] Nor was it willing to "reach a definitive conclusion as to the legality or illegality of the use of nuclear weapons by a State in an extreme circumstance of self-defence, in which its very survival would be at stake."[34] It did rule unanimously, however, that any "threat or use of nuclear weapons" must "be compatible with the requirements of the international law applicable in armed conflict, particularly those of the principles and rules of international humanitarian law. . . ."[35] These rules of course generally forbid the targeting of civilian population centers and require proportionality even in the bombing of military targets.[36] Since nuclear weapons are by their nature virtually incapable of destroying military targets without also inflicting countless civilian casualties, it would seem to follow that they could not be used except against remote military targets, such as ships and submarines on the high seas or armies in isolated deserts or mountains. In a hotly divided vote "by seven to seven, by the President's casting vote,"[37] the court ruled that "the threat or use of nuclear weapons would generally be contrary to the rules of international law applicable in armed conflict, and in particular the principles and rules of humanitarian law. However, in view of the current state of international law, and of the elements of fact at its disposal, the Court cannot conclude definitively whether the threat or use of nuclear weapons would be lawful or unlawful in an extreme circumstance of self-defence in which the very survival of a State would be at stake."[38]

Since states generally fear that their survival would be at stake in the event of a nuclear attack, the decision gave little practical guidance in the most difficult case.

The court's vice-president, an American named Stephen Schwebel, wrote a stinging dissent, castigating the majority for ducking the most important issue: "This is an astounding conclusion to be reached by the International Court of Justice. . . . [That i]n 'an extreme circumstance of self-defence, in which the very survival of a State would be at stake,' the Court finds that international law and hence the Court have nothing to say. After many months of agonizing appraisal of the law, the Court discovers that there is none."[39]

He then cited the American experience during Desert Storm (the First Iraq War, of 1991) as presenting "a striking illustration of a circumstance in which the perceived threat of the use of nuclear weapons was not only eminently lawful but intensely desirable." According to Judge Schwebel, Iraq was preparing to use weapons of mass destruction, "notably chemical, perhaps bacteriological or nuclear weapons—against the coalition forces arrayed against it." Secretary of State James Baker described what he had done to deter this possibility: "I then made a point 'on the dark side of the issue' that Colin Powell had specifically asked me to deliver in the plainest possible terms. 'If the conflict involves your use of chemical or biological weapons against our forces,' I warned, 'the American people will demand vengeance. We have the means to exact it. With regard to this part of my presentation, that is not a threat, it is a promise. . . .'"

Judge Schwebel then quoted a chilling account from the *Washington Post*:[40]

> Iraq has released to the United Nations new evidence that it was prepared to use deadly toxins and bacteria against U.S. and allied forces during the 1991 Persian Gulf War. . . .
>
> Iraqi officials admitted to [a UN investigator] that in December 1990 they loaded three types of biological agents into roughly 200 missile warheads and aircraft bombs that were then distributed to air bases and a missile site. . . .
>
> [T]hey decided not to use the weapons after receiving a strong but ambiguously worded warning from the Bush administration on Jan. 9, 1991, that any use of unconventional warfare would provoke a devastating response.
>
> Iraq's leadership assumed this meant Washington would retaliate with nuclear weapons. . . .
>
> [T]he Iraqi side took it for granted that it meant the use of maybe nuclear weapons against Baghdad, or something like that. And that threat was decisive for them not to use the weapons. . . .

Judge Schwebel concluded therefore that the Iraqis might in fact have been deterred from "using outlawed weapons of mass destruction against forces and countries arrayed against its aggression at the call of the United Nations by what the aggressor perceived to be a threat to use nuclear weapons against it should it first use weapons of mass destruction against the forces of the coalition." He then asked the following rhetorical question: "Can it seriously be maintained that Mr. Baker's calculated—and apparently successful—threat was unlawful?" He answered it with a clarity absent from the majority opinion: "Surely the principles of the United Nations Charter were sustained rather than transgressed by the threat. 'Desert Storm' and the resolutions of the Security Council that preceded and followed it may represent the greatest achievement of the principles of collective security since the founding of the League of Nations. . . ." He concluded therefore that "in some circumstances, the threat of the use of nuclear weapons—as long as they remain weapons unproscribed by international law—may be both lawful and rational."[41]

Judge Schwebel acknowledged that international law prohibits reprisals against "civilians" but permits "belligerent reprisal" in general, including nuclear reprisal in appropriate situations. But he did not say whether in his view, "belligerent reprisal" included the targeting of civilian population centers, such as Baghdad, for nuclear annihilation.[42] If it did not, then the deterrent threat of nuclear retaliation was greatly diminished. If it did, then the force of rules prohibiting the targeting of civilians was greatly diminished. Nor did Judge Schwebel indicate whether the American threat of nuclear reprisal against Iraq, which he credited with deterring the use by Iraq of biological and/or chemical weapons against American forces, was intended to include, or understood as including, a nuclear attack on Iraqi cities. Studied ambiguity with regard to this critical question seems to lie at the heart of most discussions of the deterrent impact of nuclear retaliation. Antiseptic legalisms, such as "belligerent reprisal," "deterrence," and "collateral consequences," are used as masks for what would actually be done if mutually assured destruction were ever to be carried out.*

The International Court of Justice's decision, with its four separate opinions, gives little guidance on the most important issues

---

* On November 25, 2005, the *New York Times* carried a story headlined "Nixon Was Torn by Prospect of Nuclear War, Papers Show" (p. A26). The story reported that "American officials worried that their nuclear threat lacked credibility because it was so awful that adversaries questioned whether the United States would ever use it."

regarding nuclear deterrence. Nor does it provide any guidance on possible alternatives such as prevention or preemption. Rather it proposes the utopian solution of nuclear disarmament, akin in some ways to the utopian hopes of the post–World War I period— hardly a realistic prospect in the age of nuclear proliferation.

This history makes it clear that both deterrence and prevention will remain in the arsenals of nations facing threats from their perceived enemies. This history also demonstrates the need for a coherent jurisprudence of prevention alongside our existing, if imperfect, jurisprudence of deterrence. This becomes particularly relevant as the world seeks to confront the development of nuclear weapons by such "rogue" states as Iran and North Korea and the potential acquisition of such weapons by terrorist groups like al-Qaida.

These, and other historical successes and failures of prevention, preemption, and deterrence, constitute a brief background for any review of the contemporary uses of preventive war and preemptive attacks, a narrative that unfolds largely, though not exclusively, in and around the sands of the Middle East.

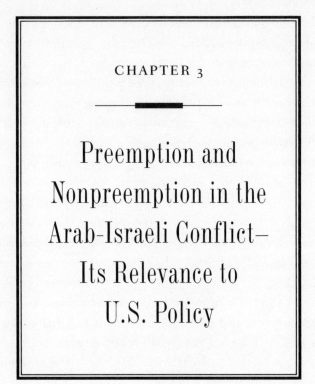

CHAPTER 3

Preemption and Nonpreemption in the Arab-Israeli Conflict— Its Relevance to U.S. Policy

B ecause of the lack of a widely accepted international jurisprudence governing preventive and preemptive wars, the United States tends to look to experience—our own and that of other democratic nations—with regard to such military actions. Before the invasion of Iraq in 2003, the United States had not initiated a full-scale preventive war.[1] Our military had carefully studied the actions of other nations, especially Israel, because it was one of the few modern democracies that had employed pre-emption successfully, particularly at the beginning of the Six-Day War in 1967, and had then employed prevention in its successful attack against the Iraqi nuclear reactor in 1981. Moreover, Israel had adopted preemption and prevention as important elements in its overall defense strategy.

Perhaps because of its small size, the nature of the threat posed by its surrounding neighbors, and its inability to secure the assistance of the United Nations, Israel, more than any other modern, democratic nation, has served as a laboratory for contemporary preventive and preemptive actions. Some have been widely approved by objective scholars, while others have been condemned.[2] Many fall into intermediate categories. A review of some of Israel's anticipatory actions—the good along with the bad—will provide insights into the challenge of constructing a jurisprudence of preemption.[3]

From the very beginning of its history, Israel has recognized both its inability to absorb a first blow and the absence of a credible deterrent capacity to persuade some of its enemies that they will lose more than they will gain from striking such a blow.[4] It has also understood that it cannot expect the United Nations to protect it from enemy attack,[5] and that with regard to international law and international organizations, it lives in a "state of nature."[6] It has operated under Dean Acheson's dictum "[T]he survival of states is not a matter of law,"[7] especially when the law has not been fairly applied to a nation that has been virtually excluded from the law-making and law-applying processes.[8] Accordingly, preemption has been an important part of Israel's strategic policy since at least 1956, with little regard for UN condemnations, which have been plentiful. Israel has sought, however, to operate within the rule of law, as defined by its own legal system, and in the process has contributed to an emerging jurisprudence of anticipatory self-defense. What the late Justice William Brennan said about Israel's contribution to the jurisprudence of civil liberties may well be applicable to the jurisprudence of preemption:

It may well be Israel, not the United States, that provides the best hope for building a jurisprudence that can protect civil liberties against the demands of national security. For it is Israel that has been facing real and serious threats to its security for the last forty years and seems destined to continue facing such threats in the foreseeable future. . . . The nations of the world, faced with sudden threats to their own security, will look to Israel's experience in handling its continuing security crisis, and may well find in that experience that expertise to reject security claims that Israel has exposed as baseless and the courage to preserve the civil liberties that Israel has preserved without detriment to its security. . . .

I [should not] be surprised if in the future the protections generally afforded civil liberties during times of world danger owed much to the lessons Israel learns in its struggle to preserve simultaneously the liberties of its citizens and the security of its nation. For in this crucible of danger lies the opportunity to forge a worldwide jurisprudence of civil liberties that can withstand the turbulences of war and crisis.[9]

In the coming pages I shall consider Israel as a case study in the uses and misuses of preemptive and preventive types of action. As with nearly all such actions, they generally included both proactive and reactive elements, with the former dominant.[10]

The first war fought by Israel was largely reactive. On the day it declared statehood, May 14, 1948, the new nation was invaded by the armed forces of Syria, Iraq, Lebanon, Egypt, Transjordan, and Saudi Arabia. Attacks from Palestinians, which had been ongoing, persisted. Israel responded and prevailed, but with an enormous toll of "5,682 dead, 20 percent of them civilians."[11] By the time the armistice was signed, the new nation had lost "about 1 percent of the total Jewish population."[12]

Attacks on Israel continued after the armistice, and between

1948 and 1956 hundreds of Israelis were killed in cross-border terrorist attacks. Israel adopted a policy of retaliation and deterrence, which had only limited success.[13] In 1956, the Egyptian president Abdul Gamal Nasser announced that he had decided to nationalize the Suez Canal and to close to all Israeli shipping the Strait of Tiran, a recognized international waterway. Egyptian military forces had previously fired on and detained commercial shipping headed toward the Israeli port of Eilat, but Nasser's announcement of a new policy constituted, in the words of Israeli Prime Minister David Ben-Gurion, a casus belli, a cause of war, entitling Israel to open the strait to its shipping by use of military force.[14]

Despite Egypt's provocation, it is unlikely that Israel would have acted alone. But Britain and France also regarded Nasser's decision to nationalize the Suez Canal as an act of aggression warranting a military response. On October 29, 1956, in a plan coordinated with Great Britain and France, Israel invaded the Sinai and easily captured it. Although the Suez Canal attack was in reaction to Egyptian provocation, the war—or campaign, as it was called—was largely preventive in nature: It was designed to stop the Egyptians from exercising control over two international waterways and to keep the Egyptian Army from using the large shipment of weapons it was scheduled to receive from the Soviet bloc.[15]

The results of the joint invasion were decidedly mixed: a clear military victory for Israel, which enhanced its deterrent capacity; condemnation of Israel's actions by much of the international community, including the United States; and a diplomatic defeat for Great Britain and France, which suffered both domestic and international condemnation.[16] The Strait of Tiran remained open to Israeli shipping, and relative peace prevailed across the Egyptian border for more than a decade.

As a result of its decisive military success in the Sinai Cam-

paign, coupled with the enormous civilian casualties it had suffered during the 1948 war, the Israeli armed forces adopted a "doctrine of warfare [that] was based on two principles: first, a
preemptive strike by the air force, and second, the transfer of the
war into the enemies' territories."[17] This preemption doctrine was
tested during Israel's next two wars.

To Preempt or Not to Preempt:
A Comparison between the Six-Day and Yom Kippur Wars

In both 1967 and 1973 Israel faced the decision whether to preempt an expected imminent attack or to absorb the first blow and
then respond. Each decision has, with the benefit of hindsight,
been criticized as wrong,[18] but at the time the decisions had to be
made both may well have been correct. A comparison between
them affords unusual insight into the appropriate criteria for preemption in the military context.

The Six-Day War
Israel had to decide whether to attack preemptively in 1967,
when Egypt, in coordination with Syria, again closed the Strait of
Tiran, expelled UN peacekeepers, massed its regular army on the
border, and threatened a genocidal war. According to Nasser, the
war was to be not over the Strait of Tiran but over Israel's "existence," and "The objective will be Israel's destruction."

Hafiz al-Assad ordered his Syrian soldiers to "strike the
enemy's [civilian] settlements, turn them into dust, pave the Arab
roads with the skulls of Jews. Strike them without mercy." He
characterized the forthcoming attack on Israel as a "battle of annihilation." Damascus Radio incited its listeners: "Arab masses, this

is your day. Rush to the battlefield. . . . Let them know that we shall hang the last imperialist soldier with the entrails of the last Zionist."[19]

Israel attacked preemptively, destroying the Egyptian and Syrian air forces on the ground, and went on to win a decisive victory in six days. Although it also feared an attack from Jordan, it did not act preemptively against that enemy to the east. Indeed, on the morning of June 5, 1967, it passed to Jordan through a UN envoy a message that it would not attack Jordanian forces if Jordan did not attack first. Instead it absorbed the first blows from Jordanian artillery against civilian targets in West Jerusalem and military targets near Tel Aviv and Ramat David.[20] Jordanian ground forces also took control of Government House in Jerusalem, threatening Mount Scopus. Israeli authorities believed that "if [the Jordanian Army] could take Mount Scopus and encircle Jewish Jerusalem,"[21] it would hold a strong military position. Israel then responded with ground and air attacks. It defeated Jordan as well, though with considerable casualties.[22]

Much of the world accepted the necessity of, and justification for, Israel's preemptive attack of 1967, because Israel was seen as an underdog surrounded by hostile Arab nations threatening its destruction. Moreover, Egypt had been the first to commit a casus belli, an act of war, by denying Israeli shipping access to an international waterway and then threatening a large-scale attack by expelling UN peacekeepers, and by massing its troops on the border. The Egyptian Air Force also flew over Israel's nuclear facility in Dimona, raising the specter of an aerial attack on Israel's nuclear capacity.[23] Nasser had earlier threatened that "the Arabs would take preemptive action" in order to stop Israel from developing nuclear weapons.[24] It was Israel, however, that fired the first shot, because as Israeli Prime Minister Levi Eshkol told his cabinet, a war in which "the first five minutes will be decisive" was inevitable, and "[t]he question is who will attack the other's air-fields first."[25] The Israeli Air Force attacked the Egyptian airfields first, and Israel's air superiority was assured. Its swift and decisive ground victory resulted in fewer civilian casualties than in any comparable modern war.[26] The number of Israeli civilians and soldiers who might have been killed in an initial attack from the combined Arab armies was estimated to be quite high.[27] It is not absolutely certain, however, that the Egyptians would necessarily have attacked despite their provocative actions.

In his influential book *Just and Unjust Wars*, Michael Walzer has noted that Nasser intended to make Israel believe that a catastrophic attack was imminent, so as to require it to call up its reserves and destroy its economy as well as its self-confidence. He cited Egyptian documents captured by Israel during the war that suggested a plan by Nasser to maintain "his army on Israel's border without [actual] war." This would have achieved "a great victory" because it would have kept the Strait of Tiran permanently closed to Israeli shipping and because "of the strain it would have placed on the Israeli defense system."

Walzer pointed to the "basic asymmetry in the structure of forces: [T]he Egyptians could deploy . . . their large army of long-term regulars on the Israeli border and keep it there indefinitely; the Israelis could only counter their deployment by mobilizing reserve formations, and reservists could not be kept in uniform for very long. . . ."[28] He also pointed to the failure of international diplomacy that made clear "the unwillingness of the Western powers to pressure or coerce the Egyptians. . . . Day by day, diplomatic efforts seemed only to intensify Israel's isolation." Finally, he cited the psychological factors: "Egypt was in the grip of a war fever, familiar enough from European history, a celebration in advance of expected victories. The Israeli mood was very different, suggesting what it means to live under the threat: rumors of coming disasters were endlessly repeated; frightened men and women raided food shops, buying up their entire stock, despite government announcements that there were ample reserves; thousands of graves were dug in the military cemeteries; Israel's political and military leaders lived on the edge of nervous exhaustion."[29]

Despite the after-the-fact uncertainty whether Egypt would actually have attacked, Walzer believed that Israeli leaders experienced "just fear" and that Egyptian leaders intended "to put it in danger."[30] Accordingly, Walzer concluded: "The Israeli first strike is, I think, a clear case of legitimate anticipation."[31]

The Six-Day War ended with the capture and subsequent occupation of the West Bank, Gaza, and the Golan Heights, a situation that changed international opinion and made future preemptive actions more problematic.

Walzer is plainly correct as a matter of law. In the context of both domestic individual self-defense and international military preemption, the action must be judged by what was known and reasonably believed at the time the action was taken, not by what was later learned or even what was "objectively" true.[32] By that criterion Israel's preemptive attack was a lawful instance of anticipatory self-defense in response to a deliberate provocation and threatened attack by Egypt and Syria.

The Yom Kippur War

In 1973 Israel again faced a coordinated attack from Egypt and Syria. The intelligence concerning its enemies' intentions was not as good as in 1967, and the threat was not perceived as so grave because of the buffer provided by the territories conquered in 1967 and because the threat was not as overt. Perhaps the knowledge, obtained in the aftermath of the Six-Day War, that Nasser may not have intended to attack in June 1967, led some to believe that Sadat did not intend to strike. Moreover, in this case Sadat intended to make Israel believe that it was *not* planning to attack. Nonetheless, there was a brief opportunity for a preemptive attack against the Egyptian and Syrian air forces, despite the reality that they were better protected than they had been in 1967. At 4:00 A.M. on October 6, 1973, Israeli intelligence received a report from a high-level Egyptian official who was spying for Israel that an Egyptian-Syrian attack was imminent. Several military leaders proposed preemptive action. Indeed, Israel's Chief of Staff David Elazar "ordered the commander of the air force . . . to prepare a preemptive strike and issued a standby order to attack at 11:00 in the morning."[33] But Defense Minister Moshe Dayan "adamantly opposed a preemptive strike," observing that "we're in a political situation in which we can't do what we did in 1967."[34]

In the hours leading up to the Egyptian-Syrian attack, the proposal for preemption was debated in front of Israel's prime minister, Golda Meir. The case for preemption was presented by General Elazar, who argued that it would save many lives: "Elazar entered Mrs. Meir's office on that Saturday morning with some persuasive arguments in favor of a pre-emptive air-strike, namely, that a first strike could disrupt and retard the enemy offensive, allow Israel's army more time to mobilize, destroy at least part of the enemy air-defense systems, and limit Israeli casualties."[35]

The negative case was argued by Dayan, who said that a preemptive attack by Israel would make it more difficult to secure American support if needed. He believed that the "political damage Israel would incur by striking first would be far greater, and accordingly he opposed pre-emption."[36] When the presentations were completed, "the prime minister hemmed uncertainly for a few moments but then came to a clear decision. There would be no preemptive strike. Israel might be needing American assistance soon and it was imperative that it not be blamed for starting the war. 'If we strike first we won't get help from anybody,' she said."[37]

At the close of the war, U.S. Secretary of State Henry Kissinger told Dayan that Israel "had been wise not to stage a preemptive strike on Yom Kippur. If it had . . . it would not have been received so much as a nail from the United States."[38] Because Israel was willing to absorb the first blow, and because it suffered enormous losses—in both life and in equipment[39]—the United States agreed to supply it with considerable replacement armaments. Most of the American weapons arrived too late for actual use in the war, but the knowledge that they were on the way allowed the Israeli Army to use all available weapons and ammunition without fear of running out.[40]

The immediate military cost to Israel of having not preempted is impossible to calculate, but some experts have estimated that the number of casualties suffered by Israel—2,656 dead and 7,250 wounded—would have been considerably lower.[41] During the 1967 war, fewer than 800 Israeli soldiers were killed and approximately 2,500 wounded.[42] More significant, the ratios of dead and wounded between Israel and its enemies was very different in the two wars. The ratio in the Yom Kippur War was between four to one and seven to one in Israel's favor, depending on whose figures are credited,[43] whereas the ratio during the Six-Day War was "approximately 25 to 1 in Israel's favor."[44]

Military historians and analysts have studied the Israeli decision not to preempt and have concluded that the cost of not preempting was high. U.S. Air Force specialists estimated that "had the air force been permitted to pre-empt, the destruction of 90 per cent of the SAM [surface-to-air missile] sites could have been accomplished in a period of three to six hours for the loss of under ten aircraft." This would have reduced "Israeli losses on the ground" considerably: "Pre-emptive air strikes on front-line missiles and troop concentrations could certainly have been expected to disrupt the enemy offensive and its communications. Some authoritative writers have argued that the IAF [Israeli Air Force] could have delivered three thousand tons of bombs on enemy targets before the Arab attack reached full strength."[45]

One reason why it is impossible to come up with precise estimates of how many lives might have been saved by a preemptive attack is that such an attack could have changed the entire course of the war, perhaps even prevented the attack by Egypt and Syria.[46] This must remain highly speculative, especially with regard to the Yom Kippur War because Egypt's goal was not to win a full-blown military victory in traditional terms but rather to restore its honor by inflicting heavy casualties on the Israeli Army and regaining some of its lost territories before a cease-fire could be imposed. That is why, despite its eventual military defeat, "for Egypt, the war was a towering accomplishment,"[47] and its president, Anwar el-Sadat, the man who started the war, emerged as "the clearest victor."[48] Egypt's "victory" in the Ramadan War (as the Yom Kippur War is called in the Arab world) is still celebrated, despite massive military losses.

It is precisely with regard to wars that are not subject to the usual deterrent calculi of military costs and benefits that preemption becomes an attractive option. Deterrence, at least in theory, is always a preferable way of preventing a war since it relies on the sword of Damocles's hanging rather than dropping. However, for enemies who do not fear the sword dropping, preemption may be the only realistic option. It will probably always be a matter of degree since almost no enemy is completely oblivious to the threat of retaliation.

The calculations that went into the decisions regarding the Yom Kippur War went well beyond short-term military advantages and disadvantages. Israel would almost certainly have gained considerable short-term military benefits from a preemptive strike against Egypt and Syria.[49] But the longer-term risks would have been considerable, especially in regard to its relations with its major ally, the United States.[50] One important reason why the risks of preemption would have been so high for Israel was that it had successfully employed that tactic six years earlier and had won an overwhelming victory. Because it now was perceived as so strong, and because it had been criticized in some quarters for starting the shooting in the Six-Day War, Israel was in a difficult position with regard to preempting once again. It feared—understandably, as it turned out—that the international community would not believe that it was in fact acting preemptively once again to ward off an inevitable and imminent attack, but rather that it was using the excuse of preventive self-defense to wage an aggressive war.

This suggests another important potential cost of preemption: that once done—even successfully—it becomes difficult to repeat. This is so for a variety of practical reasons. First, an enemy who is aware of the prior preemptive act can better prepare for a repetition. Sadat went to great efforts to mask his intentions on the eve of the Yom Kippur War so as to deny Israel the opportunity to take effective preemptive measures. (We shall see how Israel's preemptive attack against Iraq's nuclear reactor in 1981 caused Iran to take precautions against a similar attack later.) Second, a successful preemptive attack makes it difficult to justify—on moral, legal, political, and diplomatic grounds—a subsequent attack. We saw this in Dayan's argument against a repeat in 1973 of what Israel had done successfully in 1967. Finally, and related to the second reason, if a nation repeatedly preempts following an initial successful preemption, the propriety of its initial preemption will be retrospectively challenged. This too was part of Dayan's concerns. We shall see that the United States' preventive attack on Iraq in 2003 (and its subsequent occupation) have made it more difficult to justify a preventive attack against Iran's nuclear facilities, even though Iran appears to be much closer to developing nuclear weapons than Iraq was.

Another related factor that may have contributed to Israel's decisions to preempt in 1967 but not in 1973 is that in 1967 Nasser was overtly threatening to attack and took action designed to make Israel, and the world, believe that an attack was imminent (even if it was not). The world would thus be more likely to accept Israel's preemptive justification than it would in 1973, when Sadat intended that Israel, and the world, believe that he was *not* planning an attack (even though he was). Accordingly, a preemptive attack may be more acceptable in the face of an overt threat, even if intended as a bluff, than in the face of a well-concealed sneak attack.

In sum, therefore, an analysis of the Six-Day and Yom Kippur wars suggests that a major factor in deciding whether to undertake a preemptive attack will generally be the short-term military advantage secured by striking the first blow. As Shimon Peres, the former prime minister and defense minister of Israel, has written, it is the duty of a leader to "meet [war] under the least dangerous conditions," which necessarily must include the option of a preemptive attack.[51] But there will be other considerations as well, including political, diplomatic, legal, moral, humanitarian, and prudential. Moreover, there is always the possibility that firing the first shot—even on the basis of the best intelligence and with the highest of motives—may turn out to provoke a war that would not otherwise have begun.

The burden of justification should always be on the nation that acts preemptively or preventively. In satisfying that burden, the anticipatory actor can point to the certainty of an attack, its imminence, and the extent of the damage it would suffer from absorbing the first blow, both militarily and to its civilian population. Other critical factors include the nature of the preemptive action (a single decisive first strike against a military target as distinguished from a full-scale war with massive casualties and a long-term occupation); the limited damage to noncombatants it would inflict with its preemption (especially as compared with absorbing the first blow and then retaliating); the likelihood of a shorter, less damaging war, if it preempts; and other ineffable factors. In the end the decision will always be dependent on the quality of intelligence and an assessment of probabilities.[52] It will also turn on the comparative values placed on the lives of a nation's own civilians and soldiers and those of its enemies. It will always be a matter of degree and judgment. But no law or rule of morality will ever succeed in prohibiting all preemptive military actions. Nor should it.[53]

The Rescue of Hostages at Entebbe

In June 1976 Palestinian terrorists hijacked an Air France commercial jet flying from Athens to Paris. This flight had originated in Tel Aviv. The terrorists then flew the airplane to Entebbe, Uganda, where they threatened to kill the Israeli passengers unless their demand for the release of prisoners was met. Although the Israeli decision to attempt to rescue the hostages was not strictly a preemptive action since it was taken in response to an ongoing act of aggression, it was designed to prevent the killing of the passengers. It thus included preemptive elements. Moreover, the decision to authorize a military attack on foreign soil was based on the same kinds of complex factors that frequently inform purely preventive actions. And some critics of Israel within the international community accused Israel of waging an unlawful preventive aggression against the territorial integrity and sovereignty of Uganda.[54] It is thus useful to include this military action among the preemptive decisions to be evaluated. Moreover, the type of military action Israel took—precise, targeted, and singular—will probably have to be reprised by other countries as hostage taking increases, as it is in Iraq, Chechnya, and other hot spots around the world. The United States now has well-trained teams, modeled on the team sent into Entebbe, ready to rescue hostages in the right circumstances. Its most visible effort—the attempt to rescue its embassy personnel held captive by Iranian radicals in Tehran—failed as the result of technical problems.

The prime minister of Israel at the time was Yitzhak Rabin. His daughter, Dalia, told me that prior to the commencement of the rescue operation Rabin wrote a letter in which he offered to resign if the mission failed. He defined failure as twenty or more deaths. Obviously these did not include the deaths of the terrorists or the Ugandan soldiers who were protecting the terrorists. I do not know whether the figure of twenty included Israeli soldiers, Ugandan civilians, or only the hostages, but it probably was limited to Israelis and other innocents.[55]

Whether or not Rabin and the others who made the risky decision engaged in an explicitly quantitative and qualitative cost-benefit analysis, it seems likely that they weighed several factors, including the likelihood that some or all of the hostages would be killed if nothing were done; the likelihood that Israel would be forced to make concessions if some of the hostages were killed and the others threatened; the probability that some or all of the hostages, plus some or all of the rescuers, would be killed or injured if the rescue was attempted and failed; the likelihood that some of the hostages and rescuers would be killed or injured even if the rescue "succeeded"; the benefits to the prestige and deterrent credibility of Israel in the event of "success"; and the loss of deterrent credibility and prestige in the event of failure.

The daring military action, a secret flight by a large transport loaded with jeeps full of well-trained Israeli commandos who caught the Ugandans and the terrorists by surprise, succeeded and almost certainly prevented the deaths of more hostages, but at some cost in terms of the deaths of three hostages and one Israeli soldier.[56] Among the benefits, in addition to the lives probably saved, was Israel's enhanced deterrence against terrorism outside its borders.

There was also some loss in terms of diplomatic criticism of Israel for violating "Ugandan sovereignty," despite hard evidence that Uganda's murderous leader, Idi Amin, was actively assisting the hijackers. The secretary-general of the UN, Kurt Waldheim, condemned Israel. France, whose plane had been hijacked, did not even thank Israel. And many UN member nations joined a chorus of one-sided criticism directed against the successful efforts of the Jewish state to rescue 103 of its citizens who had been threatened with execution. An "Afro-Arab resolution condemning Israel's alleged violation of Ugandan sovereignty and territorial integrity" did not, however, garner sufficient votes and was ultimately withdrawn, but not before Israel was absurdly accused of invading Uganda as part of a plot to implement an old plan, dating to 1903, to establish a Jewish state in Uganda.[57]

Several years after the successful rescue mission, an interesting analysis of the decision-making process was published in the *Journal of Conflict Resolution*.[58] It disclosed that Israel had considered several options, including negotiation with the terrorists, who were demanding release of Palestinian prisoners in Israel, Germany, France, and Kenya. At the beginning Israel also considered trying to persuade Idi Amin to secure release of the hostages, but it soon became clear that he was fully cooperating with the terrorists and would not help Israel. It was also clear that the specific group in charge of the hostages would not hesitate to kill them all; they had previously killed hostages, including an

American diplomat, and they had separated Israelis from the others in preparation for beginning to kill the Israelis.[59]

Rabin was initially opposed to a rescue operation because the chief of staff of the army told him that none of the military options "had a good chance to succeed, due to lack of information regarding some critical details." He decided instead to begin negotiations with the hijackers on the release of Palestinian prisoners. Defense Minister Peres strongly disagreed, arguing that "Israel could not afford to capitulate in the face of blunt blackmail. Such an exchange would severely damage Israel's capacity to fight terrorism in the future and would lead to an increased number of terrorist attacks on Israeli citizens."[60]

A decision to begin negotiations was made, while the Israelis were preparing for a military option. Israel intelligence soon began to fill the information gaps, and the new information led Israeli military planners to raise the likelihood of a successful outcome, especially after they learned that the terminal in which the hostages were being held had not been wired with explosives, as originally feared. Rabin then changed his opinion and told his advisers: "We now have a military option with a high probability of success. . . . I ought to stress, however, that success cannot be assured with certainty. Even if the military force can overcome the terrorists, we should expect between 15 to 20 fatalities among the hostages and the raiding forces." He acknowledged the "grave consequences" of failure, including a very high death toll and diplomatic condemnation, but he recommended that "we take the military option, because I believe that it has a good chance of success."[61]

Although the author of the article in the *Journal of Conflict Resolution* acknowledged that the Israeli decision makers did not perform a precise cost-benefit analysis, he found that an "analysis of individual and intraorganizational revision suggests that both individuals and planning teams closely approximated, in an intuitive fashion, Bayesian approach[*] to revision of opinion in light of new information."[62]

The author then provided his own explicit Bayesian analysis, replete with numbers and complicated formulas, and determined that the intuitive decisions actually made were remarkably close to the Bayesian decisions that would have been made had an explicitly mathematical model been employed. He concluded, therefore: "The Entebbe case demonstrates that individuals can be vigilant explorers of multiple options, competent information processors, and comprehensive evaluators of multiple values under the most stressful circumstances. The evidence suggests awareness of and willingness to accept highly sensitive value tradeoffs and efficient revision of opinion in light of new information."[63] He then offered a caveat: "These findings run contrary to most of the evidence regarding choice processes under crisis conditions, and may suggest that decision-making in the Entebbe crisis is the exception rather than the rule."

The Destruction of the Iraqi Nuclear Reactor in 1981

The Israeli military action most frequently cited in the current debate over preemption is the one-strike destruction of Iraq's nuclear reactor in 1981. As Professor Michael Reisman put it in the *American Journal of International Law*, "[I]nternational law has been grappling with the claim of preemptive self-defense for decades. . . . The Israeli destruction of the Osirak reactor near

---

[*] Bayesian logic "deals with probability inference: using the knowledge of prior events to predict future events." TechTarget Network, "Bayesian logic," http://whatis.techtarget .com/definition/0,,sid9_gci548993,00.html.

Baghdad in 1981 was a quintessential preemptive action."[64] Although the UN Security Council unanimously condemned Israel's attack as "in clear violation of the Charter of the United Nations and the norms of international conduct," as we shall see, Israel's preemptive action has—over time—become accepted as a proper and proportional example of anticipatory self-defense in the nuclear age. It is extremely relevant therefore to current options under consideration, especially with regard to Iran's efforts to become a nuclear power discussed in detail in Chapter 6.

Five years after Israel's successful rescue at Entebbe, a new government faced an even more daunting preventive decision: whether to bomb and destroy Iraq's nuclear reactor. That decision is a paradigmatic example of a pure preventive (or preemptive, as we shall see) attack short of full-scale war. It also illustrates the limitations of the "imminence" and "certainty" requirements. The reactor was not yet completed or operational. Iraq possessed no nuclear devices, yet it was threatening to produce one and to deploy it against Israel.

Following a failed Iranian attack on the Iraqi nuclear reactor on September 30, 1980, the official Baghdad newspaper *al-Jumhuriya* assured the Iranian people that the nuclear reactor posed no threat to Iran: "The Zionist entity is the one that fears the Iraqi nuclear reactor [which] constitutes a grave danger for 'Israel.' " Another Iraqi newspaper was even clearer: "The Iraqi nuclear reactor is not intended to be used against Iran, but against the Zionist enemy."[65] Iraqi Deputy Prime Minister Tariq Aziz repeated the threat in an interview with a Jordanian journalist.[66]

The threat to use nuclear weapons against Israel, though clear, was neither imminent nor certain. Israel, with its own well-developed nuclear weapons, certainly had a significant deterrent capacity despite its official unwillingness to confirm its status as a nuclear power.[67] Moreover, Saddam Hussein's Iraq was a secular tyranny that was amenable to material threats (as distinguished from a fundamentalist religious regime whose leaders claim to welcome death as a prelude to a better world). Because Iraq was still technically "at war" with Israel—it had adamantly refused to sign on to the various cease-fires between Israel and its immediate neighbors—it proclaimed the right to continue the ongoing war at a time and place of its choice, as it subsequently did during the First Gulf War when it rained Scud missiles on Tel Aviv. Israel believed therefore that it too was legally free to attack Iraqi military targets at will.[68] Politically and diplomatically, however, there were significant risks associated with any attack, since Iraq had not engaged in any casus belli against Israel for eight years (since 1973). There were also military and other risks involved in any decision to bomb a target seven hundred miles away and separated by hostile enemy territory.

In spite of the lack of imminence and certainty to the threat posed by the Iraqi reactor, the Israeli government after much consideration concluded that the potential benefits outweighed the risks because the magnitude of the threat (even discounted by the lack of imminence and certainty) was so cataclysmic.[69] Israel's prime minister, Menachem Begin, who had lost much of his family during the Holocaust, feared that "another Holocaust would have happened in the history of the Jewish people." He pointed to intelligence estimates that Saddam Hussein could develop "between three and four Hiroshima-type nuclear bombs" and warned that "we shall not allow any enemy to develop weapons of mass destruction turned against us."[70]

In other words, even if there was only a 5 percent likelihood that Iraq would deploy a nuclear weapon against Israel in the succeeding ten years, the magnitude of the potential harm—hundreds of thousands, perhaps even millions of deaths and injuries to its civilian population—was more than enough to justify a pre-

emptive strike. Moreover, a dirty bomb might have made significant portions of Israel's tiny landmass unlivable for generations.

The timing of the strike also involved careful calculations of
the costs and benefits of waiting until the Iraqi reactor was closer
to completion and the threat therefore more imminent and certain. As the reactor moved toward activation, the risks to Iraqi civilians became greater in the event of an Israeli bombing. The
window of opportunity was quite narrow for destroying the reactor before the risks to civilians became too great. Prime Minister
Begin stated unequivocally that Israel would not have bombed the
reactor once it became "hot," which, according to intelligence
sources, was expected to occur in July or September 1981: "No
Israeli government could contemplate bombing [when] such an
attack would have brought about a massive radioactive fallout over
. . . Baghdad [in which] tens of thousands of innocent residents
would have been hurt."[71] The commander in chief of Israel's armed
forces apparently told Begin that he would not have obeyed an
order to bomb the reactor under such circumstances.[72] Begin
went so far as to say he did not think that if Tel Aviv had been
destroyed by an Iraqi nuclear bomb, he could agree to a retaliatory attack against Baghdad: "That is our morality." As he put it in
a related context, "The children of Baghdad are not our enemy."[73]

Michael Walzer has observed that: "The Israeli attack on the
Iraqi nuclear reactor . . . is sometimes invoked as an example of
justified preventive attack that was also, in a sense, preemptive:
the Iraqi threat was not imminent, but an immediate attack was
the only reasonable action against it."[74]

Imminence, according to this view, involves more than merely
the temporal immediacy of the threat itself; it is a function of the
temporal opportunity for carrying out the preventive action, as well
as the seriousness of the feared harm. For many pragmatic international law scholars, the Israeli strike against the Iraqi nuclear

reactor represented both a paradox and a challenge: It produced what many believed was a positive result, but it was difficult to square with existing international law. Indeed, Kenneth Adelman, who was part of the American delegation to the UN when the condemnation occurred, described the U.S. vote as a "big mistake" about which he was "mortified." He now regards the Israeli attack as "the most wonderful example of preemption in the modern era."[75] "Thank God Israel did that, looking back at it [sic]. The idea of Saddam Hussein being the main Arab leader with nuclear weapons since 1985 is frightful."[76]

The debates over whether to condemn Israel for its bombing of the Osirak reactor, both within the U.S. administration and at the UN, evidence the changes in attitudes about anticipatory self-defense that have occurred within less than a quarter century. Immediately after the bombing, hawkish Republicans, some of the same people who now support the invasion of Iraq, took the lead in denouncing Israel. They were led by Secretary of Defense Caspar Weinberger and included Attorney General Edwin Meese.[77] *

Leading the chorus of European criticism of Israel was former British prime minister Margaret Thatcher who declared: "Armed attack in such circumstances cannot be justified. It represents a

---

* The same Caspar Weinberger enthusiastically supported the preventive invasion of Iraq in 2003 and condemned those who would have "ignored" reports "about Iraq's efforts to acquire biological and chemical as well as nuclear weapons." Yet he would have required Israel to "ignore" much more solid intelligence not only about Iraq's "efforts" to acquire nuclear weapons but also about its stated intention to use them against Israel. As far as I can determine, he has never tried to reconcile these apparently inconsistent positions. Nor has Meese reconciled his hawkish support for the U.S. attack on Iraq with his condemnation of Israel for its attack. Even before the U.S. invasion Meese argued that al-Qaida's terrorist attack of September 11, 2001, justified "going after [Hussein], certainly going after his headquarters, going after his military establishment and if in the course of that we have to hit him, I think that's very appropriate." (Fox News, *Hannity and Colmes,* March 11, 2003.)

grave breach of international law." She apparently forgot about that reading of international law when she urged President Bush not to "go wobbly" on Saddam Hussein. Prior to the joint U.S.-British attack on Iraq, Thatcher advocated "a major deployment of ground forces as well as sustained air strikes."[78] Her article was subheadlined: "Saddam must go. It's bad enough that India and Pakistan have nukes."[79]

The defense of the Israeli action was led by such Democratic senators as Edward Kennedy and Alan Cranston but included several Republican senators as well. One Republican senator, Larry Pressler of South Dakota, changed his mind after hearing the evidence and concluded his statement with a prescient observation: "I began in these hearings to be somewhat of a critic of Israel. But as time has passed, I have come to believe, based on the information Israel had, it probably did the only thing that a country could do, and *probably something our country down the road will do at some point.*"[80]

Some experts on international law offered analogies to other preemptive actions, such as the U.S. blockade of Cuba and the Israeli rescue of the hostages at Entebbe. They pointed to Israel's limited purpose of destroying a nuclear reactor that would have placed the very "existence of a small state such as Israel . . . in jeopardy" and distinguished this attack from one on "a plant that manufactured tanks or conventional artillery, because of the enormous destructive potential of nuclear weapons."[81]

Former Supreme Court Justice Arthur Goldberg weighed in with an influential legal analysis that justified the Israeli attack not only as preemptive, but also as part of an ongoing war: "In light of the fact that by its own decision Iraq deems itself to be at war with Israel, the State of Israel, under established rules of international law, has the right to take military action, including bombing, against installations in Iraq which potentially may assist Iraq in its proclaimed war-like designs. It is not necessary, in my under-standing of applicable rules of international law, for Israel to prove that the nuclear installation in question is producing nuclear bombs. It is sufficient that this nuclear installation potentially may be of assistance to Iraq in its announced program designed to undermine the security of the State of Israel."[82]

Notwithstanding these and other arguments, both the U.S. administration and the UN condemned the attack on the reactor in what Israel characterized as a "festival of hypocrisy." Perhaps the most hypocritical of the arguments was that Israel could not be absolutely certain that delaying the attack until after the reactor became hot would actually have killed thousands of Iraqi civilians.[83] It was answered by Congressman Jonathan Bingham: ". . . the crit-ics of Israel are now arguing that the danger to Baghdad, if the reactor was bombed while operational, was not so great. If Israel had waited until that reactor was hot and had then bombed it, those same critics would have increased the decibels of their criticism by about tenfold, for the heartlessness of Israel in bombing a live, hot reactor."[84]

The decision to bomb the Osirak reactor demonstrates that preemption, if implemented cautiously, often carries the prospect of killing fewer innocent civilians than does deterrence. By its nature, preemption is generally directed against military targets (with the ever-present possibility of inadvertent civilian casual-ties), whereas deterrence is by its nature often directed at civilian targets. The Cold War concept of mutually assured destruction promised tit-for-tat retaliation: If you bomb our population cen-ters, we'll bomb your population centers. The deterrent threat would be far less effective if it merely promised retaliation against military targets for an attack on civilian targets. Moreover, mutually assured destruction gives an advantage to amoral totalitarian states over moral democracies. The former would not hesitate to retaliate against a first strike by dropping a nuclear bomb on an enemy city. A moral democracy, on the other hand, might hesitate on ordering such tit-for-tat retaliation, as evidenced by Menachem Begin's statement about the children of Baghdad's not being his enemy. The threat of mutually assured destruction worked for the United States during the Cold War because it had proved its willingness to drop nuclear bombs on enemy cities at the end of World War II. It might work less well for Israel, because the Israeli Air Force has never deliberately targeted a large civilian population center,[85] and its leaders have said its morality would not permit it to do so.[86]

Deterrence, however, has the virtue of greater certainty and fewer false positives. The retaliation does not occur until after the enemy attacks, thereby reducing the risk of error. Preemptive action, on the other hand, must always be based on predictions, and predictions always carry with them the risk of false positives. Thus preventive attacks may well occur in situations in which what is sought to be prevented might never have occurred.[87] Moreover, the line between prevention and deterrence in the context of military action will not always be clear, since the threat of acting preventively may itself serve as a deterrent. It may also serve as a stimulus to belligerent action. The issues are extraordinarily complex, as we shall soon see.

The Invasion of Lebanon in 1982

Following Israel's successful use of a decisive, single-strike preemptive attack against a uniquely dangerous potential weapon,

Israel engaged in a very different sort of preventive action, the large-scale, long-term occupation of southern Lebanon in an effort to prevent terrorist attacks against its northern towns and to end the Palestinian Liberation Organization (PLO) presence in Lebanon. The war in Lebanon, which began in June 1982, is among Israel's most controversial military actions, both domestically and internationally. It remains controversial within Israel because many Israelis believe that Ariel Sharon, who was the defense minister, misled his own prime minister, Menachem Begin, as well as the Israeli people, about the intended scope and duration of the invasion. The original mission, as approved by the cabinet, was extremely limited:

"(a) The IDF is entrusted with the mission of freeing all the Galilee settlements from the range of fire of terrorists, their Headquarters and bases concentrated in Lebanon. (b) The operation is called 'Peace for Galilee.' (c) During the implementation of the decision the Syrian army should not be attacked unless it attacks our forces. . . ." The goal, according to Sharon, was "to remove the 'terrorists' from firing range of Israel's northern border, 'approximately 45 kilometres.' " Beirut was "out of the picture." The entire operation was supposed to last forty-eight hours.[88]

It turned out very differently, with Israeli troops surrounding Beirut. The siege of Lebanon's capital lasted seventy days. The Israeli Air Force also engaged the Syrian Air Force, first destroying its ground-to-air missile system and then shooting down ninety-six Syrian F-15s and F-16s, without the loss of a single Israeli plane. The PLO eventually abandoned Beirut, with nearly fifteen thousand Palestinians, along with Yasser Arafat, departing by the end of August 1982. At the same time Bashir Gemayel, a Lebanese Christian, was elected president of Lebanon and signaled his intention of signing a peace treaty with Israel following his scheduled inauguration on September 23, 1982.

Up to this point Israel's (or Sharon's) preventive war seemed to be achieving all its goals—and more. Then, on September 14, 1982, Gemayel was assassinated, and Sharon's plans unraveled. Israeli troops poured into Beirut to prevent a civil war, and "the Maronite [Christian] Phalangist militia entered the [Palestinian] refugee camps of Sabra and Shatilla to 'clean out' the 2,000 PLO guerrillas who, according to reports, were still hiding there."[89] But the Falangists went beyond cleaning out the guerrillas. They exacted revenge for the murder of their elected leader by massacring between six and seven hundred Palestinians, including civilians. Although the Israeli armed forces did not participate in the massacre, a commission of inquiry imputed responsibility to Sharon for not stopping the Falangists, who he knew, or should have known, would—in the long tradition of Lebanese blood feuds—seek revenge against those they believed responsible for the murder of their leader.

Following the events at Sabra and Shatilla, the situation in Lebanon deteriorated. Israeli attitudes toward this war were different from those toward any previous war because this was widely viewed as a war of choice, rather than as one forced on Israel by impending aggression. It was the first war that provoked conscientious objections from some soldiers and widespread demonstrations throughout the country.[90] This war was different because it was almost entirely preventive rather than preemptive in nature, designed to strengthen Israel's position in the event of future attacks. The 1967 war had been preemptive, and the 1956 campaign, though also largely preventive, had come at a time when Israel reasonably believed that an attack by a well-armed Egypt was only a matter of time. Moreover, the 1956 war had reactive elements, since Egypt had blocked access to an international waterway and was, at the very least, facilitating cross-border attacks against Israeli civilians by fedayeen. The 1982 war was also at first reactive to terrorist attacks from southern Lebanon, but its scope and duration exceeded by far any reasonable response to these threats.

Summarizing the Israeli-Arab War Experience: A Swinging Pendulum of Preemption

The 1982 war was the last of Israel's wars against foreign enemies. The remaining "wars" have been against terrorists, primarily from within the occupied territories of the Gaza Strip and West Bank. These wars did not involve large-scale attacks by regular armed forces, with airpower and artillery. Combating terrorism requires different kinds of responses, many of which are also preventive or preemptive in nature, but on a more micro rather than macro scale. Before we turn to this somewhat different, though related, set of issues, it may be useful to draw some conclusions with regard to the Israeli's uses and misuses of prevention and preemption in fighting its external enemies.

This history can be represented by the image of a pendulum with wide swings. Israel's first war, the War of Independence, was largely reactive. Israel fought back against a multinational aggression and in the process suffered large numbers of civilian and military casualties. Israel's next large-scale military operation, conducted in cooperation with Great Britain and France, was undertaken in response to Egypt's blockading of an international waterway and its facilitation of cross-border fedayeen attacks, but it also had preventive aspects, though there was no real preemptive justification. As the result of these initial experiences, the Israeli military developed a strategy that emphasized two elements: preemption, when appropriate, and fighting battles outside its territory and away from civilian population centers. This strategy was tested in the 1967 war and succeeded beyond all expectations. But despite its success, perhaps because of it, this strategy could not be employed when Israel received several hours of warning before a planned attack by Egypt and Syria in 1973. It fought an entirely reactive war after being attacked on Yom Kippur and suffered considerable casualties. In 1976 it reacted to the hijacking of an Air France commercial airliner with Israeli passengers who were threatened with execution by proactively sending in a rescue team. In 1981 it took preemption to a new level, by attacking and destroying the Iraqi nuclear facility just before it was likely to become "hot" and thus no longer vulnerable to preemptive attack. Despite unanimous condemnation by the Security Council, virtually all Israelis regarded the Osirak attack as a great success that was both morally and legally justified. Then, a year later, Israel overplayed its hand and engaged in a purely preventive large-scale war and occupation of Lebanon, which had some immediately positive but many long-term negative results and which is more difficult to justify either morally or legally.

This decidedly mixed history suggests that the distinction between preventive and preemptive military action is important. When Israel had little choice but to attack or face potential devastation, its preemptive actions were justified and generally successful. Its one failure to take preemptive action when faced with an imminent attack in 1973 proved costly and militarily wrong, though diplomatically understandable. But when it engaged in preventive wars, in 1956 and 1982, the results were more questionable and the condemnation was more warranted.

CHAPTER 4

Preventive Measures against Terrorism

Preventive and Preemptive Actions against Terrorists

Fighting against terrorism is different from fighting conventional wars against nation-states. The difference may be a matter of degree, especially when the terrorism is large-scale and state-sponsored or state-supported, as it often is. But it is real nonetheless, especially when the terrorists are willing, sometimes even anxious to die for that cause.[1] Deterrence is less effective under these circumstances, and preventive mechanisms must assume a larger role. In the following pages we shall consider several preventive strategies that have been employed, with varying success, against individual terrorists and terrorist groups. We shall also examine some measures that are likely to be tried if the threat of terrorism increases, as it almost certainly will. Since the threat of terrorism has driven much of the current debate and even changed its terms, it must be a central focus in any attempt to construct a jurisprudence of preemption and prevention.

Preventive Detention of Potential Terrorists

One preventive mechanism that has been widely used during "emergencies" has been the preventive detention of individuals or groups believed likely to engage in future acts of terrorism. Although the decision to detain a particular individual on preventive grounds represents the sort of micro action discussed in Chapter 1, sometimes it is made in the context of macro actions, such as the war against terrorism, and can thus be seen as part of an overall preventive strategy, particularly when it involves large groups of detainees, as distinguished from individual suspects.

Before we return to the Middle East, we should briefly touch on the experiences of Great Britain and the United States, especially since the British approach to preventive detention has served as the basis for similar actions by Israel, Jordan, and other Middle Eastern nations.

The English Experience Great Britain has long practiced preventive detention during wartime and other national security emergencies. During both world wars the British government promulgated regulations explicitly authorizing the preventive detention of certain dangerous persons. In 1915 Regulation 14B was proclaimed. This wartime grant of extraordinary power authorized the home secretary to detain anyone of hostile origin or association whose internment was deemed expedient to the securing of "public safety and defence of the realm."[2] During the Second World War a similar regulation was enacted. Pursuant to this power, thousands of people, ranging from Jewish refugees who had escaped Nazi Germany to homegrown British fascists, were interned. Special retention powers were also granted to the government in its fight against Northern Irish terrorism, and hundreds were interned in accordance with this power.[3]

Following the 9/11 attacks, Britain enacted an antiterrorism law that authorized the indefinite preventive detention of foreign nationals designated as terror suspects. In December 2004 the House of Lords ruled that such unlimited detention without trial was incompatible with the European Convention on Human Rights, but the British government refused to release the nine Muslim detainees it was holding without having pressed criminal charges on the ground that they were "a significant threat to our security."[4] (The details of the reason for detention are secret.)[5] The detainees are now appealing to the European Court of Human Rights.[6]

The terrorist attacks in London on July 7, 2005, stimulated the British Government to reconsider its antiterrorism laws. As Prime Minister Tony Blair asserted following the London bombings: "We have, in my judgment, not been tough enough or effective enough in sending a strong signal across the community that we are not going to tolerate people engaging in extremism or propagating it or inciting it."[7] Blair noted that after the bombings the public awareness of terrorism changed: "I tried for several months before the election to get tougher on terrorism legislation through. People said this was scaremongering and so on. People don't say that now."[8] He observed that "[v]irtually every country in Europe, following terrorist acts, has been toughening up their legislation."[9]

The prime minster's current twelve-point antiterrorism plan includes the deportation and detention of terror suspects, as well as a ban on organizations supporting terrorism. Blair stated that deportation will be ordered against "those fostering hatred, advocating violence and validating such violence."[10] Acknowledging that his plans on the issue of deportation might conflict with current human rights laws, Blair stated that the human rights acts should be "amended if necessary"[11] to facilitate deportations.

Under the Blair proposal, the detention extensions would be issued by judges with "special security clearance" who are authorized to consider evidence that is "currently inadmissible in normal courts,"[12] such as from certain phone-taps. The director of a British civil rights group reported: "The thought of secret hearings where once again the accused will never hear the case against them fills me with dread."[13] Defending the proposed piece of legislation, Britain's lord chancellor, Lord Falconer, stated: "We need to debate the three months and we need to try to build a consensus around what the right period of time is. . . . But what is being suggested is not any form of internment, just a sensible period to detain suspects while sensible investigation is going on."[14]

Finally, the plan to criminalize "indirect incitement" and "glorification of terrorism" was criticized by human rights groups as an infringement of peaceful expression. Holly Cartner, Europe and Central Asia director at Human Rights Watch, said: "Directly inciting violence is already a crime in Britain. . . . These overly broad new offenses will have a chilling effect on free speech in the classroom, the newsroom and the mosque."[15] (Australia has begun to follow suit; its prime minister has urged the passage of a law that would expand the definition of sedition "to include statements that 'urge disaffection' toward the government, or that promote 'ill will or hostility' among groups.")[16]

The American Experience In the United States too preventive detention was practiced on a relatively small scale prior to World War II. During the Civil War, President Lincoln suspended the writ of habeas corpus, thereby making it possible for his military advisers to confine individuals believed to be dangerous.[17]

When the Supreme Court ruled that "the writ could not be suspended, except by Act of Congress," Lincoln persuaded Congress to give him the authority to detain dangerous enemies.[18] In a subsequent case, the military decided not only to detain a civilian named Lambdin Milligan, who was arrested for organizing an uprising against the Union, but also ordered his execution. In an appeal that came before it after the war had ended, the Supreme Court held that the civil courts of the Union state of Indiana had been open and "needed no bayonets" to protect them, meaning that it had been unconstitutional to try Milligan before a military commission. Recognizing that Milligan was arrested in wartime, when passions run high and "considerations of safety" are deemed all-important, the Court concluded that the framers of our Constitution "foresaw that troublous times would arise, when rulers and people would become restive under restraint, and seek by sharp and decisive measures to accomplish ends deemed just and proper; and that the principles of constitutional liberty would be in peril, unless established by irrepealable law. . . ."

It went on to say: "This nation . . . has no right to expect that it will always have wise and humane rulers, sincerely attached to the principles of the Constitution. Wicked men, ambitious of power, with hatred of liberty and contempt of law, may fill the place once occupied by Washington and Lincoln, and if this right [to suspend provisions of the Constitution during the great exigencies of government] is conceded, and the calamities of war again befall us, the dangers to human liberty are frightful to contemplate."

Having delivered itself of this bold rhetoric about "irrepealable law," the Supreme Court then proceeded to suggest that the right to bail could be suspended during emergencies: "If it was dangerous, in the distracted condition of affairs, to leave Milligan unrestrained of his liberty, . . . the *law* said to arrest him, confine

him closely, render him powerless to do further mischief; and then
. . . try him according to the course of the common law."[19]

This view of preventive confinement during emergencies
was reaffirmed and strengthened by Justice Oliver Wendell
Holmes in a case growing out of a private war between Colorado
coal miners and owners, which led to a declaration of local martial law by the governor. In addition to suppressing newspapers,
deposing civil magistrates, and closing all saloons, the governor
suspended habeas corpus and ordered the arrest of certain
"objectionable characters." One of these "characters," a leader
of the miners, was detained without bail for two and a half
months and sued the governor after his release. Though Holmes
need never have reached the legality of the detention, the Civil
War veteran went out of his way to justify the governor's action.
Employing "logic" for which he surely would have chastised
first-year Harvard law students, Holmes argued that since a governor can order soldiers to "kill persons who resist" efforts to put
down a rebellion, it certainly follows that "he may use the milder
measure of seizing the bodies of those whom he considers to
stand in the way of restoring peace."[20]

That is where the law stood on December 7, 1941, when
Japanese forces bombed Pearl Harbor, throwing Hawaii into tur-
moil and generating fear of attack in our West Coast cities.
Within hours the governor of Hawaii, at the insistence of the army,
declared martial law, suspended habeas corpus, ordered the civil
courts closed, and empowered military tribunals to try all criminal cases.[21] It wasn't until after the war (and the restoration of
habeas corpus by the president) that the Supreme Court decided
that Congress, in authorizing martial law in Hawaii, had not
intended to permit the "supplanting of courts by military tribunals."[22] By that time thousands of person-days of illegal imprisonment had already been served.

Martial law in Hawaii, with all its abuses, did not include mass detention on racial grounds of the kind employed on the West Coast between 1942 and 1944. At that time there were about 110,000 Americans of Japanese ancestry living on the West Coast, of whom 70,000 were American citizens.[23] A virulent anti-Japanese hysteria followed the attack on Pearl Harbor. Rumors were circulated that Hawaiians of Japanese ancestry were signaling enemy pilots and submarines, that Japanese-Americans had intentionally infiltrated the power and water companies, and that they had formed sabotage and espionage rings numbering in the thousands. None of these stories proved true. The records of "the Federal Bureau of Investigation and Army and Navy intelligence indicate that there was not a single instance of espionage or sabotage by a resident of Japanese ancestry before, during, and after World War II."[24] The absence of such activities did not, however, satisfy a hysterical population with deep-rooted racial antagonisms. Indeed, the attorney general of California, Earl Warren, expressed the Alice in Wonderland view that it was the very absence of sabotage that was "the most ominous sign in our whole situation." It convinced him, he said, "that the sabotage . . . the fifth-column activities that we are to get, are timed just like Pearl Harbor" and that the present inaction by the Japanese-Americans was designed to lull us "into a false sense of security."[25]

The various intelligence agencies—the FBI and army and navy intelligence—preferred to approach the problem of potential terrorism and espionage "on the basis of the individual, regardless of citizenship, and not on a racial basis." This was what was done with people of German and Italian extraction on the East Coast. Thousands of aliens "regarded by the Attorney General as dangerous to the national security if permitted to remain at large" were preventively detained on an individual basis. But on the West Coast the prevalent attitude was reflected by General John

DeWitt, head of the Western Defense Command: "A Jap's a Jap. There is no way to determine their loyalty." Earl Warren agreed: "We believe that when we are dealing with the Caucasian race we have methods that will test their loyalty. . . . But when we deal with the Japanese . . . we cannot form any opinion that we believe to be sound."[26] The decision was made to confine the entire West Coast population of Japanese-Americans: Accordingly, 109,650 men, women, and children were put in detention camps, where they remained for nearly the entire war.[27]

The mass confinement of West Coast Japanese-Americans constitutes one of the "purest" examples of preemptive incapacitation in history. The alleged harms sought to be prevented by the massive confinement included espionage and sabotage. It was also claimed that the detention of entire families in isolated camps was designed to prevent attacks *against* Japanese-Americans by "real" Americans who were angered by Japan's attack on Pearl Harbor and its continuing war against America.

The preemptive incapacitation was "pure" in the sense that it was based entirely on predictions of the future since none of the detainees had any prior history of espionage or sabotage

Many, though not all, civil libertarians were extremely critical of the detention of the Japanese-Americans on racial grounds.[28] Prominent leaders of the American Civil Liberties Union urged President Franklin D. Roosevelt to "constitute a system of hearing boards to test the loyalty" of individual citizens and noncitizens. The justices of the Supreme Court who dissented from the judicial approval that was given to the exclusion and detention orders faulted the government for not treating "these Japanese-Americans on an individual basis by holding investigations and hearings to separate the loyal from the disloyal as was done in the case of persons of German and Italian ancestry." (Virtually no criticism was ever leveled against the individualized preventive

detention of the latter.) Academic criticism centered on our failure to detain Japanese-Americans "on the basis of individual suspicion" and on our unwillingness to adopt a system of graded
restrictions—as the British and French did—whereby only the
most dangerous were detained and others "were subjected to certain continuing restrictions especially as to their travel."[29]

There is no hard evidence that even a single case of espionage
or sabotage was actually prevented by the massive detentions,
though it is of course possible that there may have been such cases.
It is in the nature of preventive confinements that it is difficult to
prove that they constituted false positives, especially if the confinement is pervasive and coextensive with the duration of the
threat. Since confined people cannot engage in the predicted conduct, it is easy to claim that it worked. And it is difficult for its critics to prove that the same result would have been achieved in the
absence of the confinement. The verdict of history, however, is on
the side of the critics, and detention of the Japanese-Americans
must be counted as perhaps the largest-scale false positive confinement in the history of American preemptive incapacitation.[30]

It was also the largest-scale racial profiling case in American
history, differing in both kind and degree from other instances of
racial profiling. By confining all West Coast Japanese-Americans,
the U.S. government was essentially saying that all Japanese-
Americans were potential spies or terrorists. This is quite different from what happened after September 11, 2001. Following that
attack on America, many law enforcement officials came to a quite
different conclusion—namely, that all suicide bombers were Muslim extremists, but that very few Muslims were potential terrorists. This led law enforcement officials to focus their attention on
Muslims, rather than on Christians, Jews, or atheists, but it did
not result in the confinement of all or even a significant percentage of Muslims or even Islamic extremists. Despite the Supreme

Court's ill-advised approval of the Japanese detentions, or perhaps because of it, our nation has never again made the mistake of pre-emptively confining an entire ethnic or national origin group on the basis of a generalized prediction that it might do harm.[31]

The Israeli Experience

Since its establishment in 1948 Israel has followed a model similar to the one suggested by many of those civil libertarians who disagreed with Franklin Roosevelt's policy of mass detention based solely on ethnicity: namely, individualized determinations of dangerousness (not loyalty). Israel faced terrorist attacks even before it became a state. During the 1920s and 1930s bands of terrorists attacked Jewish settlements in Palestine, killing hun-dreds of Jewish civilians, and between 1948 and 1967—before the occupation of the West Bank and Gaza Strip—more than fifteen hundred Israelis were killed by fedayeen terrorists. Since the end of the Six-Day War more than two thousand Israelis have been killed in terrorist attacks. Only a fraction of the terrorist attacks planned by Palestinian terrorists have succeeded because Israel has managed—through intelligence and other preventive meas-ures—to preempt or thwart thousands of such attacks, thereby saving tens of thousands of lives.[32]

Although these preventive measures have saved many Israeli lives, they have been costly, in terms of Palestinian lives, liberty, property, and dignity. They have entailed preventive detention, tar-geted killings, the taking of property for the building of security barriers, and the erection of checkpoints. Even more important, they include the reoccupation of large parts of the West Bank fol-lowing the renewal of the intifada, beginning in 2000 and 2001, with its spate of suicide bombings against Israeli civilians.[33]

One preventive mechanism used by Israel since its inception has been preventive (or administrative) detention. Between 1948 and 1979 it operated an individualized system of preventive detention based on British mandatory law. Most, but certainly not all, of those detained under this approach were Arabs suspected of complicity with terrorism. In 1979 Israel's Knesset enacted the Emergency Powers (Detention) Law. Both the old and current laws required individual proof of dangerousness and provided some procedure for challenging the government's allegations, though the procedures were a far cry from those required for criminal prosecution. Under current Israeli law a person suspected of complicity with terrorism can be detained for a renewable period of six months on the basis of a finding of "reasonable cause" by the minister of defense that his detention is required by reasons of "state security or public security." These vague criteria provide little legislative guidance to the appropriate balance to be struck between false positives and false negatives. Nor do they provide much in the way of evidentiary guidance beyond authorization to "deviate from the rules of evidence" if the president of the court is satisfied that this will be "conducive to the discovery of the truth and the just handling of the case."[34]

There are several distinct but often overlapping reasons why a democracy, committed to the rule of law, would employ preventive detention instead of (or in addition to) the traditional criminal process. The first involves individuals who the intelligence agencies are convinced have been guilty of past acts of terrorism, ranging from actually planting bombs to organizing terrorist attacks, but for whom the information on which these conclusions of past guilt are based cannot be introduced at a public trial without compromising ongoing intelligence operators. For example, the evidence may come from an undercover operative who is deep inside the terrorist network. If he were to be revealed as the source, he would likely be killed, or at the very least his continuing value as a spy would be endangered. It may also come from electronic or other high-tech means of surveillance not yet known to the terrorists.[35]

A closely related situation involves individuals who are believed to be planning a future terrorist attack. Since planning a future attack is already a crime (at least if the planning has reached a certain stage), such future criminals are generally also past criminals and therefore fall within the first criterion discussed above. The difference may be only a matter of degree: In the first category, the individual may be suspected of having already caused multiple deaths, whereas in the second category, the past crime may be inchoate in nature, but the future crimes may risk massive loss of life.

In the above cases, a democratic society has essentially four options: It can continue to rely exclusively on the conventional criminal law, an option that will require it to choose in every case whether to reveal the secret information or to forgo prosecution. No democracy faced with significant threats of mass victimization has selected this "pure" option.

The second option is to change the existing criminal law and adapt it to the new reality. This could entail, for example, a watering down of the hearsay rules, which generally require testimony by the person who claims to have firsthand knowledge of the events, so that he can be cross-examined. The hearsay rules could be changed to allow an intelligence operative to testify that a secret informer who has proved reliable in the past told him that the individual at issue had committed specified past acts of terrorism or was in the process of planning future terrorist acts. This is currently permitted in applications for search warrants and in grand jury and some other proceedings, but not at criminal trials. (Even hearsay testimony could in some cases endanger secret intelligence sources because the nature of the information might provide a clue to its source.) In 1970, while studying Israel's system of preventive (or administrative) detention, I put this option to a high-ranking Israeli legal official. This is what he said in response: "We are very proud of our civil liberties. It would be absurd to wreck our entire judicial system to accommodate a few wartime security cases." But would you really have to wreck the system? I asked. Couldn't you just change some of the rules of evidence? "The rules of evidence lie at the center of our civil liberties, and the right to confront your accuser is the heart of any fair system of evidence. If we created a rule allowing into evidence [hearsay testimony regarding] the invisible-ink message and the agent's report,[36] there would be virtually nothing left to the right of confrontation. I would rather see us act completely lawlessly in a few security cases than a little lawlessly in every case." This official felt strongly enough to say that he would "resign in protest" if Israel ever changed its rules to allow hearsay evidence in the general run of cases.[37]

A variation of this option would be to change the existing criminal law *only* in terrorist cases while preserving the hearsay and other protections in all other cases. One problem is that the U.S. Supreme Court recently held that at least certain aspects of the hearsay rules are mandated by the confrontation clause of the Sixth Amendment, which provides that in all criminal prosecutions, the accused must "be confronted with the witness against him." This constitutional protection could not be changed without amending the Bill of Rights, though the Supreme Court has also sustained watered-down protections in the case of terrorists captured abroad and held as enemy combatants.[38]

The third option is to do what Great Britain and Israel have done—that is, to enact an explicit preventive detention law authorizing the noncriminal detention of individuals who are thought likely to engage in future acts of terrorism. This option has the virtue of explicitness. A good preventive detention law—and neither Great Britain's nor Israel's is particularly well crafted—should provide specific and narrow criteria for permitting this extraordinary remedy. It should also provide procedural safeguards that are as rigorous as the reality of fighting terrorism permits. Finally, it should provide assurances that this mechanism, which is vulnerable to abuses, can never be used to serve the political or ideological ends of those in power. In May 2005 the Israeli government ordered the preventive detention of several Jewish extremists who were opposed to the scheduled unilateral withdrawal from the Gaza Strip. Although the authorities claimed that the detention was justified by the threat of violent opposition to the controversial withdrawal, some Israelis, especially on the hard right, believed it was as much a political attempt to silence the opposition.[39] Without a specific past criminal act to point to, those who administer preventive detention, especially against political enemies, will always be subject to charges of misuse of this antiterrorist measure.

The British-Israeli approach, despite its explicitness and accountability, still requires a compromise of the principle articulated by Justice Robert Jackson: "[T]he jailing of persons by the courts because of anticipated but as yet uncommitted crimes" cannot be reconciled with "traditional American law."[40]

In order to avoid compromising this oft-stated (and, in practice, oft-compromised) principle, the United States has selected the fourth option. Our government does not explicitly acknowledge that we are employing preventive detention. Indeed, a federal law enacted in reaction to the detention of Japanese-Americans explicitly provides that "[n]o citizen shall be imprisoned or otherwise detained by the United States except pursuant to an act of Congress."[41] To avoid this prohibition, our government stretches existing law to achieve the same result, but with far less accountability. In the aftermath of 9/11 we dusted off the anachronistic material witness law that was designed to permit the short-term detention of crucial witnesses to a crime who were proved to be likely to flee the jurisdiction. Federal law enforcement agents swept up hundreds of foreign nationals,[42] many of them Arabs and Muslims, and declared each to be a "material witness." But to what crimes were they alleged to be witnesses? Often, it was the crimes they themselves were suspected of committing or planning![43] This misuse of the material witness law was plainly designed to circumvent the absence of an explicit preventive detention law.

Another existing set of laws that was stretched to achieve preventive detention was the immigration rules, which authorize the short-term detention of aliens who are out of status or do not have proper papers. These laws were designed to facilitate the quick deportation of such aliens in cases in which that was the appropriate remedy. But in the aftermath of 9/11 they were used to effectuate the preventive detention of specific individuals—almost all Muslims and Arabs—who were thought to pose a future danger.

In 1971 I wrote an article entitled " 'Stretch Points' of Liberty."[44] In the process of researching the article, I interviewed the deputy attorney general of the United States—the person then responsible for planning any response to a national emergency. I asked whether if terrorism were to strike the United States, he would recommend invoking "extraordinary powers of temporary detention." He told me, "We wouldn't have to. There is enough play at the joints of our existing criminal law—enough flexibility—so that if we really felt that we had to pick up the leaders of a violent uprising, we could. We would find something to charge them with, and we would be able to hold them that way for a while."

He was right, at least as a factual matter. Every legal system has its "stretch points," its flexible areas capable of expansion and contraction depending on the exigencies of the situation. The stretch points in our system include broad police and prosecutorial discretion, vaguely defined offenses (such as disorderly conduct), inchoate crimes (which may also be vaguely defined, like conspiracy), denial of pretrial release (which can sometimes result in confinement exceeding a year), and the material witness and immigration laws previously mentioned. Some systems employ such devices as common law (judge-made) crimes, ex post facto (after the fact) legislation, and emergency powers, to achieve similar results.

It is typical of the U.S. government, in this area and in others, to opt for what one commission labeled "the way of the hypocrite."[45] We loudly proclaim our commitment to maintaining certain restrictions on governmental action—in this case the prohibition against preventive detention—while at the same time accomplishing the ends of this mechanism by discreetly stretching existing law.

Another reason why a democracy might employ preventive detention is to provide for a period of detention outside the restrictive criminal process sufficient to permit interrogation of the detainee for purposes of obtaining crucial intelligence information about future terrorist acts being planned by others. Interrogation within the criminal process is closely regulated by statutory and constitutional law, most particularly the so-called Miranda rule. In theory, no interrogation of a confined criminal suspect may occur in the absence of his lawyer.[46] In practice, this restriction is often avoided by a number of well-known subterfuges. Moreover, the Supreme Court recently ruled that the privilege against self-incrimination does not come into play until the prosecution seeks to introduce evidence against a defendant at a criminal trial.[47] At that point—and only at that point—must the court decide if the evidence was the product of an improper interrogation. This decision provides intelligence-gathering agencies with considerable leeway in interrogating individuals in order to secure intelligence information that they have no intention of ever using in a criminal trial. Still, there must be time to conduct the interrogation, and under current law a criminal suspect may not be detained for purposes of interrogation beyond a relatively brief period of time. Preventive detention seeks to remedy that problem by authorizing noncriminal detention for much longer periods of time, thereby enabling the kind of interrogation that would not be permissible in the criminal process.[48]

The preventive detention of suspected future terrorists is likely to continue wherever terrorism is perceived as a serious threat.[49] It is essential that democratic nations committed to the rule of law begin to develop a jurisprudence regulating this increasingly important preventive mechanism. It is fair to say that to date no nation has satisfied this important need.

Targeted Preemption of Terrorists Detention (preferably after a full-blown criminal trial) is the tactic of choice against suspected terrorists, but it is not always feasible to capture suspected, or even self-proclaimed, terrorists or others who pose an immediate and serious danger to a state. Many states have opted, under these circumstances, for a more drastic form of preventive incapacitation—namely, targeted killing. Again, Israel has been among the most public in its willingness to address this issue (which it calls focused preemption) directly and to try to incorporate it within the rule of law. The United States has also employed targeted killings, but thus far without any real attempt to justify it under the law.

Over the past several years, nearly all those who have been targeted for killing by Israel have been terrorists or terrorist commanders and leaders, but in earlier years, preemptive or preventive assassinations were also directed against scientists, weapons providers, and others who were in the business of harming Israel by providing its enemies with weapons of mass destruction.

In an earlier microversion of its later macroattack against the Iraqi nuclear reactor, Israel tried by various means to prevent German scientists, some of them former Nazis, from helping Egypt develop weapons of mass destruction for use against the Jewish state. According to a historical account of Israel's intelligence services by Ian Black and Benny Morris:

> [The Mossad] believed that the German scientists were working on weapons that threatened the very existence of Israel. . . . The Mossad in that period [1956–1961] conducted only intelligence-gathering. . . . In September 1961 . . . a first assessment on the development of ground-to-ground missiles in Egypt [was produced]. A second Intelligence Branch evaluation in October 1962 predicted that about 100 rockets could be operational within a year to eighteen months. . . . The worrying reports about the scale of the Egyptian programme were reinforced catastrophically when a [defector] claimed that the Egyptians were preparing to fit their missiles with warheads containing radioactive waste in an operation codenamed Ibis I. Even more seriously, a project called Cleopatra was geared to producing nuclear warheads.[50]

Several targeted attacks on individuals who were working on these weapons of mass destruction ensued, and the Egyptian program never really got off the ground.[51]

In the leadup to the attack on the Iraqi nuclear reactor, some targeted attacks were also tried, but without success. Diplomatic efforts failed as well, leading Israel to conclude that its only realistic option was the air assault on the Osirak reactor.

In at least one case, bribery and threats were tried first. But when they failed, the weapons maker was killed. Dr. Gerald Bull, a leading expert in barrel ballistics, was helping the Iraqis develop "a supergun capable of launching shells containing nuclear, chemical, or biological warheads from Iraq directly into Israel. The supergun's barrel was 487 feet long, composed of thirty-two tons of steel supplied by British firms to Iraq. Late in 1989 a prototype had been test-fired at a gunnery range at Mosul in northern Iraq. Saddam Hussein had ordered three of the weapons to be built at a cost of $20 million. Bull was retained as a consultant at $1 million. The project was code-named Babylon."[52] First Israel tried "to buy his expertise." But each time "Bull had made clear his distaste for the Jewish state."[53] Threats followed, but also to no avail. Finally, Bull was killed, and the supergun project ended.

In addition to these targeted attacks against weapons providers, Israel used targeted killings against terrorist leaders, especially following the attack against Israeli athletes at the Munich Olympics of 1972 and the decision by the West German government to free the captured terrorists.[54] This decision was one of many by European governments to free captured terrorists or not to apprehend them in the first place. This led Israel to conclude that the only effective measures it could take against terrorist leaders operating in foreign countries was to kill them.

Some of these killings were explicitly preventive—the targets were directly involved in the ongoing planning of future terrorist attacks, and their deaths would abort or at least confound these plans—but others were carried out for deterrent purposes. According to Black and Morris, "The Munich massacre marked a turning-point in Israel's war against Palestinian terrorism. Golda Meir decided that the time had come for a wholesale vengeance, not just for its own sake but as a deterrent."[55]

These operations provided the background for the controversial Israeli decision to employ targeted killings during the Palestinian terrorism campaign that began in the fall of 2000. Targeted killings were adopted as a tactic, especially in the cities, towns, and refugee camps of the Gaza Strip, where Israeli soldiers did not operate freely. Hamas did, however, have a relatively free hand in Gaza. Many terrorist acts originated in Gaza, and Israel had good intelligence about terrorist groups and individuals in that area. Sometimes, but only rarely, it was feasible to arrest terrorists who were planning or implementing imminent attacks. In most cases, however, capture was not feasible because the terrorists deliberately hid among civilians in densely populated urban areas, where Israeli soldiers could not safely operate without massive military support and at great risk to themselves as well as to Palestinian civilians. In those cases, Israel opted for another preventive measure, the targeted killing of terrorists, including commanders, operatives, and suicide bombers. Generally the attacks took place from the air, but sometimes they employed exploding cell phones and other technological ways of delivering a lethal explosive against a terrorist combatant, like the Engineer, a man named Yehiya Ayash, who was the chief bomb maker for Hamas until Israeli agents targeted him by planting an explosive charge in his cell phone. If these combatants—and they are combatants, under any reasonable definition of that term—had been captured, arrested, or otherwise detained, there would be no basis for criticism since every government is empowered to take reasonable and proportional steps to protect its civilians and soldiers from terrorist attacks. The criticism arises because this preventive mechanism involves the targeting and killing of suspected terrorists. Since targeting, no matter how carefully implemented, can never be perfect, especially in the large urban centers where terrorists hide, innocent bystanders are sometimes killed or injured along with the terrorists. The complaint is therefore twofold: First, even if, as is often the case, the only ones killed are suspected terrorists (sometimes along with their bodyguards, who are also combatants), they are being "executed" without the "due process" of a trial; second, innocent people are too often killed or injured along with suspected terrorists.

As for the first complaint, critics of this practice argue that ter-

rorism is a law enforcement issue, since terrorists are not technically at war with Israel. It would follow from this argument—were
it sound—that suspected terrorists must be treated precisely the
same as suspected rapists or robbers. They must be arrested and
tried, not hunted down and killed. They may be killed only in self-
defense—if they pose an immediate danger to the arresting officers. If they are killed, this constitutes extrajudicial execution,
which is illegal.

The extrajudicial execution argument is flawed, however,
since all military killings are by their nature extrajudicial. Indeed,
it is judicial executions that I, and many other civil libertarians,
strongly oppose, precisely because there is always the alternative
of lengthy, even life imprisonment. The person to be judicially executed is, by definition, already in captivity and no longer a direct
danger. With regard to targeted killings, there is generally no other
viable option other than allowing the terrorist to continue killing
without any effort to stop him. Targeted killings of terrorists are
more akin to the killing of a dangerous felon who is fleeing from
arrest or to killing in self-defense, both of which are extrajudicial
but entirely lawful. The relevant question to be asked of targeted
killings is whether they are lawful and moral, not whether they are
extrajudicial. This involves a number of factors, including the evidence that the targeted suspect is in fact a terrorist involved in
ongoing operations, the imminence and likelihood that these terrorist operations will succeed, the availability of other less lethal
alternatives, and the possibility that others will be killed or injured
in the targeted attack (in other words, how well targeted will the
attack be).

As for the question of whether terrorists are to be treated as
ordinary criminals or as combatants who are violating the laws of
war, it is interesting to note that when terrorists are captured, many
refuse to be treated as ordinary criminals, demanding POW sta-

tus and insisting that they are part of a military or paramilitary insurgency. On the flip side, those who capture them often refuse to treat them as combatants entitled to prisoner of war status. The reality is that terrorists involved in an ongoing insurgency or campaign of terror are in a hybrid status that may well justify treating them as combatants for purposes of targeted killings but not as prisoners of war once they are captured.[56] As Professor Yoram Dinstein has put it, "However, a person is not allowed to wear simultaneously two caps: the hat of a civilian and the helmet of a soldier. The person who engages in military raids by night, while purporting to be an innocent civilian by day, is neither a civilian nor a lawful combatant. He is an unlawful combatant. He is a combatant in the sense he can be lawfully targeted by an enemy, but he cannot claim privileges appertaining to lawful combatancy."[57]

The second major criticism of targeted killings focuses on the risk to what Israel calls uninvolved individuals. Because terrorists and their commanders deliberately hide among civilians (often, but not always, with the consent or even encouragement of these "uninvolved individuals"), there is almost always some risk of "collateral damage" (to use an antiseptic term calculated to diminish the suffering of innocent civilians). This is a legitimate concern in evaluating the costs and benefits of targeted killings of terrorists, and it is a concern that Israel takes very seriously. According to Israeli military authorities, approximately two hundred terrorists have been successfully targeted, while approximately one hundred uninvolved civilians were unintentionally killed during these operations.[58] Palestinian authorities obviously disagree with these figures, but they provide some rough quantification of the ratio between true and false positives. Israel also claims that hundreds, perhaps thousands of deaths to its own citizens have been prevented by these targeted killings.

In December 2003 I studied this issue at close range during a three-week visit to Israel. I met with many of those responsible for implementing the policy, as well as with critics. I watched as a high-intensity television camera, mounted on a drone, zeroed in on the apartment of a terrorist. The Israeli commander had been given authorization by the government to kill the terrorist if he got into his car alone or with other terrorists, provided that the street was empty and the likelihood of killing or injuring uninvolved civilians was minimal. The commander could easily have killed the terrorist by blowing up the house he was in, but the decision had been made not to target the house or even the apartment because there may have been others in the house and their status as combatants or noncombatants was uncertain. I watched as the camera focused on the house and the nearly empty streets. People could be seen as large dots, but it could not be determined (at least by my untrained eye) whether they were men or women, children or adults. Cars could easily be identified, and even their type—jeep, small car, large car, truck—could be determined. It was early evening, and infrared cameras could pick up the heat from the engines of moving vehicles and determine whether an engine was in the front or the back of the vehicle. I was permitted to watch for only a few minutes, and no action was taken while I was watching because the target remained in the house. He could not be arrested because Israeli soldiers and police could not safely enter Gaza City, as they could certain cities and towns on the West Bank, where arrests are used more frequently than targeted preemptions.

The next day I learned that the terrorist target did leave his home and got into his car later in the evening with another terrorist and that a missile was fired at the car, but the terrorist escaped with only minor injuries. Several others were injured as well. There were no deaths.

Earlier that day I watched a video of a previous successful attack in which two terrorists, on their way to plant explosives, were targeted and killed. The video showed a clean attack on their car in an isolated area. Two explosions can be seen. The first is of the Israeli rocket hitting the engine in the front of the car; the second is an explosion from the trunk of the car, where the explosives were being kept.

A few days before the failed preemptive attack, I had been allowed to meet with the several members of a high-level committee that had been established to consider policy questions regarding the technique of targeted preemption. The committee members included men and women with varying expertise. Among them were an eminent professor of philosophy at Tel Aviv University, a distinguished professor of international and human rights law at Bar-Ilan Law School, several lawyers of the IDF, a general who headed the military college, and a few field commanders in charge of implementing the policy of preemptive targeting in the Gaza Strip. Sometimes a mathematician specializing in probability theory attended the meetings. These men and women considered various possible scenarios, some real, others hypothetical, and discussed the policy options. Typical and not so typical cases were discussed.

The simplest case involves the ticking bomb terrorist who, alone, is on his way to a civilian population center with a suicide bomb belt strapped around his waist. Hard, confirmed intelligence makes it almost certain that unless he is stopped before he reaches his target, he will blow himself up in a crowd, killing and injuring dozens. He is in a car driving toward the target. In half an hour he will reach the population center, with its heavy traffic.[59] The decision must now be made whether to blow up his car with an air-to-ground missile. Trying to stop him in any other way—say, by arrest—will endanger the arresting officers and will almost surely cause his death anyhow since he is likely to detonate himself rather than disarm the bomb.

What are the possible objections to ordering the rocket attack under these circumstances? First, the intelligence may be wrong, and an innocent person may be killed. Error is always a possibility, even in classic self-defense cases. The man coming at you with a gun may be an actor; the gun may be unloaded; he may decide not to fire, or he may miss. The classic response to this possibility compares the likelihood of a false negative error to the likelihood of a false positive error. If the self-defense action taken appeared reasonable under the circumstances, if the person claiming self-defense had a reasonable apprehension of imminent harm and had no other reasonable way to avoid it, he should prevail in a claim of self-defense even if it turns out he was mistaken. If the alleged attacker is culpable, if he in fact was intent on harming the alleged victim, then society prefers a false positive error (mistakenly killing the culpable assailant) to a false negative error (mistakenly allowing the culpable assailant to harm the victim). Even if it turns out that the alleged assailant was not culpable (he was an actor pretending to be a killer), we excuse the mistake if it was reasonable under the circumstances because we recognize the right of a person to defend his life against reasonably perceived risks (though it cannot be said that we actually prefer a false positive to a false negative error in the context of two nonculpable people, one of whom unintentionally appears to be culpable).

Self-defense is appropriate even if the risk of death is less than certain, as the following hypothetical case illustrates. An assailant points a six-shooter at your head and tells you that there is only one bullet in the barrel and that he is going to play Russian roulette with you. If the gun fires a bullet, you are dead, but if it does not, then you are free. You believe he is telling the truth. (Perhaps you have seen him play this dangerous game with others.) Surely you should have the right to kill him if that is the only way to prevent him from exposing you to a nearly 17 percent chance of being killed.

In the context of armed conflict, the law is even more supportive of lethal action. All that is required under the laws of war is a reasonable basis for concluding that the target is a combatant, as distinguished from a noncombatant. In a traditional war, a combatant is defined as a uniformed soldier. Under the accepted laws of war, once the target's status as a combatant is reasonably determined, he can be killed even in his sleep and regardless of his role in the military.[60] This would seem highly immoral, especially in extreme cases. If the soldiers of Nation A come upon a group of unarmed and sleeping army cooks from Nation B, under existing law they can slaughter them without even giving them a chance to surrender. No moral army would actually do this, but the traditional laws of war are based on clear lines and sharp demarcations between combatants and noncombatants.

These lines become blurred in the context of terrorism, but a ticking bomb terrorist headed toward a city with the bomb strapped around his waist certainly should qualify as a combatant under any reasonable standard. He is armed, intent on engaging in imminent lethal action, and his intended targets are noncombatants. Nor is he simply an individual criminal in the traditional sense of that word. He is part of a military, quasi-military, paramilitary, or insurgency group that is functionally closer to a military unit than to a criminal gang. He is an unlawful combatant engaged in military conflict. In the context of military conflict, there is no requirement of imminence or of the absence of other alternatives, such as arrest. As we shall see, preemptive self-defense is generally deemed more acceptable in the military than in the civilian context. Only an absolutist who believes that preemption should never be permissible (or a selective moralist with a political ax to grind against the nation employing preemption) would argue that blowing up the car of this ticking bomb terrorist should be deemed a violation of the laws of war, of human rights, or of morality. Reasonable people could argue against this action by reference to policy considerations, such as "It will only cause more terrorism," or "It will only contribute to the cycle of violence." But equally reasonable people could argue that taking the life of one probable terrorist to prevent the probable deaths of more than one innocent civilian is a good policy. In a democracy such decisions are properly made by the government, so long as they are lawful and reasonable. Nearly every democracy would opt for the preventive killing of a probable terrorist over a probable terrorist attack on its civilians.[61] So would any reasonable moralist.

This first, relatively simple case is not typical of the difficult situations faced by the Israeli military, though there have been many such cases (including the one involving the explosives in the trunk of the car).[62] More complex cases involve difficult variations on this paradigm. Consider the following case that was presented to the Israeli government in 2002. Salah Shehada, the leader of the military wing of Hamas, who was known to be responsible for planning and ordering numerous successful suicide bombings, was in the planning stages of yet other attacks that were "unprecedented in size and scope," according to Israeli intelligence.[63] They included at least the following: "rigging a truck with 600 kilograms of explosives to blow up the recently constructed Gush Katif bridge, the sole route used by hundreds of Israelis daily to travel to and from their communities . . . massacr[ing] residents of Gush Katif communities by carrying out an attack during the celebrations currently under way there, and . . . planning to have suicide bombers infiltrate Israel for a number of bomb attacks to be carried out in populated areas in Beersheba. . . . abduct[ing] soldiers and civilians to gain the release of Palestinians in Israeli jails, and plann[ing] to rig a boat with explosives to be blown up on one of the beaches used by residents of the Gush Katif communities."

He was also using "young Palestinian children" to "carry out

suicide attacks against Israeli targets, arming them with home-
made weapons." This intelligence was gathered "from Palestinians affiliated with the Hamas in the Gaza Strip, who operated
under Shehadeh's command."[64] At least one of the massive
attacks was believed to be imminent. He was "the ultimate ticking time bomb," according to an Israeli spokesman.[65] "We did not
target him simply to retaliate or as punishment. We did it as a preemptive operation. . . . He planned to send people to carry out a
massacre tonight in Gaza."[66] Arresting him was not feasible. If it
were, it would have been the option of choice." 'The optimal move
is to arrest a terrorist, because then you get information out of
him,' a senior Prime Minister's Office official said. 'The next
option is to kill him, because we would rather prevent terror
attacks than react after the fact.'"[67]

Killing him, it was reasonably believed, would thwart the
planned future attacks. The government therefore decided that
he was an appropriate target under the principles of the first case,
so long as he could be killed without undue risk to other noncombatants. The problem was that "he constantly changed his living quarters, moving from safe house to safe house, chosen
purposely in densely populated residential areas, from where he
continued to give orders for attacks to be carried out."[68] He often
traveled and slept with his wife at his side. Although his wife was
fully aware of, and presumably supported, his activities, she was
regarded as an "uninvolved person." The military commanders
sought permission from the government to attack him with a rocket
when he was alone with his wife, arguing that he was a sufficiently
important military target to justify the killing of *one* noncombatant, especially since that particular noncombatant was far from a
"total innocent," having allowed herself to be used as a "human
shield" by her combatant husband. After considerable debate, the
decision was made to authorize the "hit," but only if it was clear

that he could not be found alone and only if there would likely be no other casualties among noncombatants. Three days before they ultimately bombed him they had "called off a strike . . . when they discovered he was with family members."[69] When they did bomb him, they were not aware that there were civilians close by. The rocket killed not only the terrorist commander and his top aide but also his wife, his fourteen-year-old daughter, two other relatives, and several neighbors who were noncombatants. The undue number of civilian casualties was apparently caused by a breakdown in intelligence, and the reaction from the Israeli media and public was extremely critical of the action." We did not intend to cause this number of civilian casualties," an Israeli military official was reported as saying. "If we had known this would be the result, we would not have taken this action today."[70] Yossi Sarid, who at the time chaired the "dovish" Meretz Party, said that though the assassination was justified, "the timing was inappropriate, the assassination method was wrong, it was a kind of act of terror."[71] But if the intelligence that he was planning a massive attack that very night was accurate, a postponement might have cost the lives of even more Israeli civilians than the number of innocent Palestinian lives that were lost by the preemptive killing. Such is the nature of tragic choices caused by ticking bomb terrorists who deliberately hide among their own civilians.

Another variation on the theme of targeting suspected terrorists involves the targeting of individuals who are the religious or political leaders of terrorist groups. In 2004, Israel killed two Hamas leaders in quick succession. One was Sheikh Ahmed Yassin, and the other was Dr. Abdel Aziz Rantisi. Both were killed with minimal "collateral damage," yet their targeting was controversial and widely condemned. I wrote the following article about these targeted killings, comparing Israel's action with those of the United States and Great Britain:

The United States Army was recently given a highly specific military order. According to the top U.S. commander in Iraq, Lt. General Ricardo Sanchez, the mission is to kill radical Shi'ite Cleric Muqtada al-Sadr.

This order to target al-Sadr for extrajudicial killing is perfectly legitimate and lawful under the laws of war. Al-Sadr is a combatant, and it is proper to kill a combatant during an ongoing war unless he surrenders first. It doesn't matter whether the combatant is a cook or bomb-maker, a private or a general. Nor does it matter whether he wears an army uniform, a three-piece suit, or a kaffiyeh. So long as he is in the chain of command, he is an appropriate target, regardless of whether he is actually engaged in combat at the time he is killed or is fast asleep. Of course, his killing would be extrajudicial. Military attacks against combatants are not preceded by jury trials or judicial warrants.

Al-Sadr fits squarely into any reasonable definition of combatant. He leads a militia that has declared war on American and coalition forces, as well as on civilians, both foreign and Iraqi. He is at the top of the chain of command, and it is he who presses the on-off button for the killings. Like Osama bin Laden and Mullah Omar Mohammed, he is a proper military target, so long as he can be killed without disproportional injury to noncombatants.

If American forces can capture him, they are permitted that option as well, but they are not required—under the laws of war—to endanger the lives of their soldiers in order to spare al-Sadr's life. Indeed, unless al-Sadr were to surrender, it is entirely lawful for American troops to kill him rather than to capture him—if it were decided that this was tactically advantageous.

Although U.S. commanders mentioned capture along with killing as an option, it may well be preferable not to capture al-Sadr, for fear that his imprisonment would stimulate even more hostage-taking in an attempt to exchange hostages for al-Sadr. The order to kill or capture al-Sadr may well be a euphemism for "kill him unless he surrenders first" (as Saddam Hussein did).

The world seems to understand and accept the American decision to target al-Sadr for killing, as it accepts our belated decision to try to kill bin Laden and Mullah Omar Mohammed. There has been little international condemnation of America's policy of extrajudicial killing of terrorist leaders. Indeed, the predominant criticism has been that we didn't get bin Laden and Mullah Omar Mohammed before September 11.[72]

How then to explain the world's very different reaction to Israel's decision to target terrorist leaders, such as Sheikh Ahmed Yassin and Dr. Abdel Aziz Rantisi, the former leaders of Hamas. Surely, there is no legal or moral difference between Yassin and Rantisi on the one hand, and al-Sadr and bin Laden on the other. Yassin and Rantisi both personally ordered terrorist attacks against Israeli civilians, approved them in advance, and praised them when they succeeded.

Each was responsible for hundreds of civilian deaths and was involved in ordering and planning more terrorist attacks at the times of their timely deaths. They were terrorist commanders, just as al-Sadr was. They were both killed, along with their military bodyguards, in a manner that minimized civilian casualties, despite the fact that they generally—and unlawfully—hid among civilians, using them as human shields. Israel waited until they, and their fellow terrorist guards, were alone and then targeted them successfully. There was no realistic possibility of capturing them alive, since they had sworn to die fighting; and any attempt to extirpate them from the civilians among whom they were hiding would have resulted in numerous civilian casualties. (Israel does try to capture terrorist commanders in the West Bank, where it has large numbers of troops on the ground, but it employs targeted killings in Gaza, where it has a far more limited military presence.)

Reasonable people can disagree about whether the decision to target Yassin, Rantisi, al-Sadr, bin Laden, or any other terrorist is tactically wise or unwise, or whether it will have the effect of reducing or increasing the dangers to civilians. But no reasonable argument can be made that the decision to target these combatants—these terrorist commanders—is unlawful under the laws of war or under international law.

British Foreign Secretary Jack Straw was simply wrong when he declared that targeted assassinations of this kind—specifically referring to the killing of Yassin and Rantisi—are unlawful and in violation of international law. And he knows it, because his own government has authorized the killing of terrorist leaders who threaten British interests.

I challenge Straw to distinguish Israel's killing of Yassin and Rantisi from the coalition's targeting of al-Sadr, Saddam Hussein and his sons, Osama bin Laden, and Mullah Omar Mohammed.

He could not do so. Any claims that Hamas is divided into military and political (or religious) wings is belied by the fact that Yassin and Rantisi both ordered the military wing of Hamas to engage in acts of terrorism and approved specific murderous acts in advance.

If Straw cannot distinguish these situations, then does he disapprove of the American policy of killing al-Sadr? If British troops were to have al-Sadr—or, for that matter, bin Laden—in their sights, would they have to hold their fire because Straw has told them it would be illegal to pull the trigger?

We have a right to know the answers to these questions, since American and British troops are supposedly operating under the same rules of engagement. Or would Straw simply (and honestly) say he is not applying the same rules to Israel as he is to his own nation and its military allies?

The international community cannot retain credibility if it

continues to apply a different, and more demanding, standard to Israel than it does to more powerful nations.*[73]

The debate over targeted killings persists. As is typical of the Israeli legal system—unlike the American system—the issue of targeted killings of suspected terrorists, like so many other contentious ones, has been brought before the courts[74] by Israeli human rights groups. The case had been fully briefed when Israel, as part of its cease-fire with the Palestinians, decided to suspend targeted killings, and the case is now on hold, but the controversy— within Israel and around the rest of the world—persists. Russia announced, following the hostage takings and deaths in the Beslan school in September 2004, that its military would henceforth engage in preemptive actions against Chechnyan terrorists, presumably including targeted killings of their leaders and commanders. Both candidates in the American presidential election of 2004 pledged to kill Osama bin Laden and other terrorists who endanger the United States.

In October 2004 a debate erupted following the publication in the British medical journal *Lancet* of a study suggesting that approximately a hundred thousand Iraqi civilians had died as a result of the American invasion of Iraq. These numbers were hotly disputed, and the actual figures will never be known.[75] An organization called Iraq Body Count has placed the number of civilian dead at between 27,115 and 30,559 as of November 28, 2005. It is beyond dispute that a large number of collateral deaths were caused by American and British bombings and other military actions—far greater than the number of deaths caused by Israel's policy of targeted killings. Some of the coalition bombings were

---

* On December 4, 2005, the *New York Times* reported the targeted killing, apparently by the CIA, of Hamza Rabia, the number-three man in al-Qaida. Mohammed Khan and Douglas Jehl, "Attack Kills a Top Leader of Al Qaeda, Pakistan Says," *New York Times*, December 4, 2005, p. 24.

precisely targeted; others less so. The issue should not be framed in terms of whether targeted killings should ever be permitted—clearly they should under some circumstances—but rather in terms of the proper criteria for employing this extraordinary means of preventive self-defense. It also should be framed by reference to the available alternatives.

A report issued in November 2004 by a group under the direction of Professor Philip Heymann of Harvard Law School proposed that targeted killings of terrorists who pose a real and imminent threat should be authorized by the law, provided that specified rigorous criteria and procedures are satisfied. The report concluded:

> [T]argeted killings against known terrorists have become a real and accepted option within the United States as the only reasonably effective way of reaching a hostile target. The targeted killing of a terrorist could prevent a planned attack and could serve as a deterrent to terrorist groups or to individuals who may be inclined to join them. Targeted killing, in some contexts, would also improve domestic morale because it shows progress against a specific terrorist enemy. One can readily imagine the impact of the known death of Osama bin Laden on the sense of security in the United States. Still, the most basic purpose is trying to stop the next attack. The targeted killing of a leader or a critical member of a terrorist group may temporarily incapacitate the organization and at least delay terrorist activity. Given the other options available, killing a terrorist receiving shelter in a hostile state would be far less costly in terms of lives and money than invading that state. Where a threat is imminent, targeted killing—which does not require extensive evidence gathering for trial or preparation for full-scale invasion—also provides needed speed.[76]

The report observed that the existing executive order, which again represents the "way of the hypocrite," mandates an absolute prohibition on anyone "acting on behalf of the United States" participating in any assassination. Despite this paper prohibition, the United States has targeted Osama bin Laden and several other terrorist leaders for assassination. We actually assassinated the terrorist Qaed Salim Sinan al-Harethi by bombing a car in which he—along with five others, including an American citizen—was driving in Yemen. The current executive order is, according to the report, "basically no standard at all."[77]

Accordingly the report proposes a "three-pronged test" for targeted killings: "[T]o be 'necessary' means that there is no other reasonable alternative, that targeted killing is a practice of last resort; to be 'reasonably imminent' means that the development of an alternative (capture, arrest, etc.) would not eliminate a real likelihood of imminently threatened, lethal attack or would be inordinately dangerous to U.S. or allied personnel; and, finally, to be preventive, the targeted killing can only be for prospective purposes, rather than as retribution for previous bad acts under those standards."[78]

These criteria, while generally sensible, lack the specificity that is required to focus accountability on decision makers at various levels of responsibility. I propose some such specificity in Chapter 7.[79]

On January 25, 2005, Israel announced that it would stop the targeted killings of Palestinian terrorists as part of a truce or cease-fire.[80] Hamas agreed in turn to suspend its attacks against Israeli civilians. Both sides reserved the right to resume their actions if the other side broke the cease-fire. In late September 2005, following the Israeli withdrawal from Gaza, Hamas conducted rocket attacks against the town of Sderot, resulting in several injuries. In response, Israel launched air strikes in Gaza against Hamas targets. Shortly thereafter, Hamas announced that it was ending the rocket attacks—at least for the time being. On

November 14, 2005, Hamas threatened to renew its terrorist attacks against Israel after the Israeli Army shot and killed a Hamas commander in a raid in Nablus.

Preemption and Prevention of Biochemical Attacks In January 2005 it was reported that a CIA-affiliated think tank was "predicting that America is 'likely' to be hit by bio-terrorist attacks at some point in the next 15 years. 'Bioterrorism . . . appears particularly suited to the smaller, better-informed groups. Indeed, the bioterrorist's laboratory could well be the size of a household kitchen, and the weapon built there could be smaller than a toaster. Terrorist use of biological agents is therefore likely, and the range of options will grow. Because the recognition of anthrax, smallpox or other diseases is typically delayed, under a "nightmare scenario"an attack could be well under way before authorities would be cognizant of it.' "[81]

A leading expert on bioterrorism, who serves as a consultant to the Pentagon, warned that although biological agents have the "potential to be much more life-threatening [than nuclear weapons], we are not prepared to prevent or control this threat." Nor is America's "fragmented and stressed" health care system prepared for a biological attack because it is "structurally unfit" for any adequate response.[82] According to a feature article, "Remain Calm," in the November 14, 2005, issue of *New York* magazine, Dr. Irwin Redlener, head of the National Center for Disaster Preparedness at Columbia, has observed that "[f]our years after 9/11, we are, as a nation, extraordinarily, inexplicably unprepared to deal with a major catastrophic event." The inadequate response to Hurricane Katrina in September 2005 only confirms these concerns.[83] On November 1, 2005, President Bush announced a $7.1 billion plan to prepare for a possible avian flu pandemic, following the death of sixty-two people in sixteen countries from this disease. "Our country has been given fair warning of this danger . . . and time to prepare," the president said. "It's my responsibility . . . to take measures now to protect the American people." We may receive no warning, however, of a secret biological attack.

The strategy for anticipating a biological or chemical attack, from an enemy nation or a terrorist group, is in some respects the same as for other weapons of mass destruction or conventional mass casualty attacks: effective intelligence; preventive destruction of the capacity to develop, deploy, and deliver the weapons; deterrence by threat of massive retaliation; and other diplomatic, economic, political and military options. But there are important differences as well. Steps can be taken to neutralize or diminish the threat of at least some biological and chemical weapons. These steps include a program of widespread inoculation capable of preventing much of the damage sought to be wrought by those contemplating a biological or chemical attack. Other more reactive steps, which, as we shall see, also have prevention components, would focus on developing plans and procedures for an immediate and effective first response, including the use of gas masks and sealed rooms to protect against the deadly chemicals, a quarantine program designed to stanch the spread of contagious disease, a pharmaceutical response designed to minimize the effects of the germ or chemical weapons, the widespread availability of detoxification facilities capable of cleaning the body of toxic materials, and other combinations of public health and conventional medical and pharmaceutical responses.

Some of these steps, such as the construction of detox facilities, are relatively cost-free, at least in terms of human life. They simply require expenditures of money. Israel has already begun to construct facilities that include powerful cleansing showers in the event of a chemical attack.[84] New York City has installed "extensive monitoring systems to catch problems before they occur."[85]

These problems include chemical attacks. A BioWatch system registers biological dangers. Wind patterns are checked to determine the likely paths of anthrax if it were to be released into the air. One expert recently concluded that "an outdoor anthrax release over a city would not be difficult at all."[86] Other steps, such as widespread availability of injections or pills for use following an attack, may cost some lives, since almost any powerful drug produces some serious side effects, including death. Even gas masks can create a hazard to life when improperly used, as they inevitably are by some. When Iraqi Scuds rained down on Israeli cities during the First Gulf War, and it was feared that they contained chemical warheads, several people died from putting on their gas masks. It turned out that the Scuds contained only conventional explosives and preventive measures were unnecessary, but more Israelis died from the gas masks than from the missiles.[87]

If a biological or chemical attack is confirmed, then the benefit of a pharmaceutical response outweighs the costs, since the number of lives to be saved by the injections, pills, or other measures will greatly exceed the number of lives lost from the pharmaceuticals themselves.

The same cannot necessarily be said for a program of widespread or universal inoculation in anticipation of a biological or chemical attack. If the attack is relatively certain and immediate, and if the inoculation is very effective, the benefit will exceed the cost. But if this attack is uncertain and distant, the number of people who will inevitably die from receiving the inoculation may well be greater than the risk of attack discounted by the unlikelihood that it will actually occur.

Much useful thought has gone into the calculation of costs and benefits in the context of the feared weaponization of smallpox.[88] It is uncertain whether any of America's enemies actually have access to the smallpox virus and are capable of weaponizing it. But recent advances in synthesizing long molecules of DNA have made it more likely that "the technique might be used to make the genome of the smallpox virus"[89] and weaponizing it. What is known is that if terrorists can manage to introduce smallpox into our borders, the devastation may be catastrophic since most Americans are not currently immunized against that killer disease. What is also known is that an extremely effective inoculation that could neutralize the threat with a high degree of success is available. But that success would come at a considerable cost, since a small but not insignificant number of people who receive the inoculation will suffer serious permanent and devastating medical consequences, and a smaller number will die.[90]

According to a recent report by a group of doctors at the University of Michigan, "We estimate that a vaccination strategy directed at people aged 1 to 29 years would result in approximately 1600 serious adverse events and 190 deaths. Vaccinating people aged 1 to 65 would result in approximately 4,600 serious adverse events and 285 deaths."[91]

Because the threat of a smallpox attack is deemed to be small— despite the catastrophic effect of such an attack were it to occur in the absence of widespread inoculation—the current approach apparently taken by public health and terrorist experts is to prepare for the possibility that inoculation may be prudent at some point in the future if the likelihood of an attack were to increase, but that no program of widespread preventive inoculation is warranted now.

An alternative to widespread inoculation, with its inevitable costs in human life and health, would be more limited targeting for preventive inoculation only of specific categories of such people as first responders, soldiers, public health workers, those assigned to handle any quarantines, and others. It might also include much larger groups, such as all medical personnel, all residents of particularly vulnerable cities, all residents of an entire nation, and all people with particular susceptibilities, such as the very old and the very young, or even only those who chose to accept the risks and benefits of being inoculated (though if the germ is highly contagious, individual choice might not be a viable option). For each such group, the balance of risks might be somewhat different, but for each such category a probabilistic determination would have to be made and an appropriate balance struck. Whether this balance should be struck by legislative, judicial, administrative, or other institutions and whether it should be a matter of federal or local decision making involve important issues of democratic theory.

Another alternative is the quick availability of inoculation, coupled with quarantine, at the first sign of a smallpox attack. Public health experts have devised a ring strategy for reducing the spread of smallpox or other highly contagious dangerous diseases. An appropriate balance must be struck between too much and too little inoculation.[92]

Whether inoculation is employed either before or after a biological attack, quarantine will be part of any effective response to a highly contagious disease. The United States, however, has no quarantine law on the books designed to cope with a biological attack. Most state laws are anachronistic both medically and legally. They were enacted in response to natural outbreaks of such contagious diseases as tuberculosis, which no longer pose significant public health hazards.

Were a highly contagious and deadly virus to be transmitted through the air filtration (or air-conditioning or heating) system of a large, fully occupied skyscraper (such as the Empire State Building), a terrible choice of evil problems would be presented. Should the building be sealed off and all the people in it be quarantined (at least until they can be tested)? If the decision to do so were to be the best public health response to the crisis, there might be no legal basis under any specific statute for issuing and enforcing such an order, especially against those who would argue that they had not yet been exposed to the virus, but who reasonably feared exposure if required to remain in quarantine alongside exposed and contagious individuals.[93] I have little doubt that the courts would in fact sustain any reasonable public health order, citing the emergency and perhaps martial law as declared by the proper authorities. But, to paraphrase an old saw, "Martial law is to law as martial art is to art."[94] It is essentially a lawless assertion of power labeled as "necessity," and to quote an ancient aphorism, "Necessity knows no law." (In every jurisdiction, there is at least one judge known to the bar as "necessity" because he too "knows no law.") It would be far better to enact specific quarantine laws in advance of any biological attack. They should address the issues likely to be faced in the event of such an attack. A leading scholar of quarantine laws has concluded that "both law and science have changed since the time when quarantine was a standard tool against infectious disease. A court giving unquestioning approval to quarantine in modern circumstances would be utilizing an anachronistic rationale." But this was written in 1985, in the context of the AIDS epidemic. It did not take into account the weaponization of contagious disease. The time has come for experts to rewrite the laws of quarantine, making them both more responsive to current needs and more protective of civil liberties.[95]

On a broader level, the legal structure for dealing with biological or chemical warfare or terrorism is woefully inadequate. It must be addressed before an attack occurs if chaos is to be reduced and the role of law preserved, and the criteria for requiring people to accept costs and risks—whether of inoculation, quarantine, or any other burden—must become part of an overall approach to or jurisprudence of preemptive and preventive governmental actions.

Prior Restraint of Expression

Throughout history, expression—speech, writing, religious practices, art, and assembly—has been restrained on the basis of predictions that if not prevented, it would lead directly, or indirectly,
to harms ranging from undercutting the authority of the church
to overthrowing the government, rape, even genocide. Opponents of prior restraint or censorship often argue that there is no
empirical relationship between the restraining expression and
the predicted harms. For example, many civil libertarians point
to the absence of evidence that pornography causes (or con-
tributes substantially to) the incidence of rape (or related sexist
evils).[96] Others argue that even if there is a direct causal relationship between certain kinds of pornography (for example, violent
sexual portrayals) and certain evils (such as rape, harassment,
and devaluation of women), the cost of prior restraint or censorship is too high.[97]

There can be no question that some kinds of expression contribute significantly to some kinds of evils. The International
Criminal Tribunal for Rwanda found a direct causal relationship
between certain radio broadcasts and genocide,[98] just as the
Nuremberg Tribunal had found a relationship between the anti-
Semitic diatribes of *Der Stürmer* and the genocide against the
Jews. The International Criminal Tribunal for Rwanda convicted
three men of genocide, conspiracy to commit genocide, and other
crimes for allegedly inciting violence against the Tutsis. One of the
defendants was charged with helping "to set up the Radio Télévi-
sion Libre des Mille Collines (RTLM) in order to promote the ideology of Hutu extremism. The programmes broadcast by RTLM
allegedly promoted ethnic division and incited the murder and
persecution of persons of Tutsi origin." Another was accused of
"broadcasting messages on national radio that incited ethnic

hatred and murders of the Tutsi people." A third was "alleged to have consented to the publication of material in the Kangura Newspaper which promoted ethnic hatred and incited mass killings and/or serious bodily or mental harm to the Tutsi." In convicting the three, the court noted that the case "raises important principles concerning the role of the media, which have not been addressed at the level of international criminal justice since Nuremberg. The power of the media to create and destroy fundamental human values comes with great responsibility. Those who control such media are accountable for its consequences." Two of the defendants received life sentences, and the third thrity-five years in prison. All three have appealed.[99]

There are various mechanisms by which the relationship between expression and action can operate. Sometimes it is simply informational. Facts that facilitate previously decided-upon goal are communicated. For example, one nation that wishes to attack another is given secret information. It could be anything from attack plans to vulnerable areas to the recipe for producing a nuclear weapon. Sometimes the information is largely emotional: incitements to kill; dehumanization of the enemy; religious commands to kill. For example, the material that appeared in *Der Stürmer* or in some of the sermons that are commonly broadcast on Arab and Islamic television stations may well have contributed to the willingness of readers or listeners to kill. Sometimes there is a combination of factors. For example, the media in Rwanda combined emotional incitements to kill Tutsis, with precise information about the whereabouts of particular Tutsi leaders. Some accounts of the genocide suggest that it was common for members of militias in search of Tutsis to set up roadblocks and listen to their transistor radios, which broadcast messages to try to rile up listeners' hatred.[100]

The constitutional law of the United States generally prohibits governmental censorship of "speech,"[101] but various exceptions have always been recognized. Within five years of the ratification of the First Amendment, Congress enacted the Alien and Sedition Laws, which punished seditious speech that was critical of the administration of President John Adams.

Prior restraint of speech, as contrasted with subsequent punishment of speech, has rarely been authorized by the courts. In the famous *Pentagon Papers* case, the Supreme Court drew a sharp distinction between the two mechanisms of controlling speech that is alleged to be dangerous."Prior restraints require an unusually heavy justification under the First Amendment," Justice Byron White wrote in his concurring opinion, "but failure by the Government to justify prior restraints does not measure its constitutional entitlement to a conviction for criminal publication. That the Government mistakenly chose to proceed by injunction does not mean that it could not successfully proceed in another way."[102]

The rationale of the court was that distinguished newspapers like the *New York Times* and the *Washington Post* would remain accountable *after* publication for violating any laws that would result from publishing impermissible material. In other words, because they could be deterred, there was no basis for seeking to prevent violation of the law by the extraordinary and disfavored mechanism of prior restraint. But those who publish on the Internet might not be as amenable to deterrence since many of them are not traditional publishers, with return addresses and deep pockets. For purposes of deciding whether deterrence or prevention is the more appropriate mechanism of control, these "fly-by-night publishers" have been compared with nondeterrable terrorists.

At the Practising Law Institute's Communications Law 2002 Conference, panelists "struggled to reconcile recent court decisions allowing speech restrictions with their notions of prior restraint doctrine, finding new issues arising as more and more communication is accessed through the Internet." One case the panel examined arose after the American Coalition of Life Activists "distributed posters and posted on the Internet names and other identifying information of doctors who perform abortions, crossing out those who had been killed or injured."[103]

Recently there have been efforts at self-policing by Web logs and other Internet operators, particularly in the context of assuring credibility: "There have even been fledgling attempts to create ethical guidelines, like the ones found at Cyberjournalist.net. Defenders of the status quo argue that ethics rules are not necessary in the blogosphere because truth emerges through 'collaboration,' and that bias and conflicts of interest are rooted out by 'transparency.' But 'collaboration' is a haphazard way of defending against dishonesty and slander, and blogs are actually not all that transparent. . . . Bloggers may need to institutionalize ethics policies to avoid charges of hypocrisy. But the real reason for an ethical upgrade is that it is the right way to do journalism, online or offline."[104]

These efforts do not, however, address the problems of *irremediable* harms that could be caused by irresponsible bloggers, such as death and disclosure of state secrets or terrorist targets. If terrorism were to increase, and if the Internet were to become an important tool for the communication of dangerous information, and if those employing the Internet were deemed undeterrable by after-the-fact sanctions, then the push for preventive tools, including expanded notions of prior restraint, would increase. This is the time to begin serious consideration of the conflicting claims of liberty and security in this important context.

As terrorism increases, I predict that there will be increasing calls for prior censorship of speech that is believed to incite suicide bombers and others who target civilians. The American constitutional law of incitement as an exception to the First Amendment has always varied with the perceived dangers of the times. During

World War I, handing out leaflets against the draft was analogized to falsely shouting fire in a crowded theater. During the McCarthy era, being an active member of the Communist Party was deemed to be prohibited advocacy of violent overthrow of the government. These were unjustified constraints on freedom of speech since there was no reasonable basis for concluding that these expressions constituted a clear and present danger of serious harm.

The same cannot necessarily be said about charismatic imams inciting young believers to become suicide bombers.[105] The competitive marketplace of ideas is not always open to these zealots, who are often not exposed to the general media and live controlled religious lives in which the imam's word is law. The culture of death coupled with the promise of a glorious afterlife for martyrs may be irresistible to some.

It is only a matter of time before serious proposals for prior restraint of this kind of direct incitement will be offered.[106] Already some imams have been threatened with deportation from France, Australia, and Britain for their incitements.[107] Deportation is one form of preventive restraint on speech. Others will not be long in coming. We must be prepared to confront this challenge to freedom of expression and religion.

Other Preventive Mechanisms

There are other mechanisms of prevention that are more specific to particular locations or disputes and warrant only brief mention. The military "occupation" of an area from which terrorism originates may have preventive components. The U.S. presence in Afghanistan and Iraq, and the Israeli occupation of the West Bank and Gaza, were sought to be justified on terrorist prevention grounds. Opponents claim that it is the occupations that stimulate, or at least contribute to, the terrorism. Israel points to the fact that it largely ended its day-to-day occupation of the major West Bank cities shortly after the Oslo agreements were signed in 1993 and that it reoccupied some, but not all, only after the onslaught of suicide bombing that followed Arafat's refusal to agree to the offers made at Camp David and Taba in 2000 and 2001. Reoccupation became necessary as a means of controlling and preventing the terrorism that was emanating from the West Bank cities. The Palestinian perspective is of course quite different, and this is not the place to try to resolve these differences. I mention this dispute only to point out the allegedly preventive nature of the reoccupation.

Related to the above is the construction by Israel of the security fence that it claims is also designed to prevent terrorist attacks and that it sees as a more passive substitute mechanism for occupation. It is, of course, the location of the fence rather than its construction alone that has generated so much controversy. Again, this is not the place to address that controversy, but rather to list the mechanism of a security fence within the catalog of preventive tactics that have been employed in an effort to control terrorism.

Either with or without security fences, checkpoints control the flow of human and cargo traffic and can serve as a preventive measure against terrorism. But these same checkpoints impede legitimate traffic and make it difficult for innocent people to get to work, to hospitals, and to families. Striking the proper balance between the legitimate preventive needs and the illegitimate harassment effects of such checkpoints is never without considerable controversy. Fences and checkpoints are of course part of the larger issue of border controls. In the United States there are large, uncontrolled borders to both the north and the south, as well as large stretches of unpatrolled shorelines. Efforts to control these vulnerable borders, both by the government and by citizens' groups, generate considerable controversy because it is never easy to separate legitimate concerns over terrorism with less legitimate concerns about limiting the influx of Mexicans and others seeking to come to the United States for better lives.

Another controversial preventive tactic is the sting or the scam, in which law enforcement agents pretend to be terrorists, arms dealers, or other facilitators of terror. They actively seek to encourage the members of terrorist cells who are in deep cover to surface by offering their services and wares. Related to this tactic is the recruitment of informers from within the ranks of terrorists. A more passive variation on this mechanism is the planting of spies or electronic spying devices among terrorists or potential terrorists.

Other preventive mechanisms include mass roundups of suspects; sweeps for weapons; profiling; random stops, frisks, and searches; preventive arrests; material witness detentions; dog sniffs; and sophisticated chemical detection devices.

Only the human imagination, current technology, the law, and morality limit what steps could be taken in an effort to prevent terrorism.[108] The mechanisms described above are intended to be illustrative of those currently in use and those likely to be tried if terrorism increases. Each of these preventive mechanisms presents perils and prospects that must be thoughtfully considered on an ongoing basis. But they should not be considered only on an ad hoc, case by case basis. They must become part of a developing jurisprudence of early intervention, not only in the context of terrorism but in the context of other serious harms as well. Only the greatest of these harms can ever justify resort to the preventive mechanism of full-scale war—such as that which the United States waged against Iraq in March 2003—since such a war imposes the highest of costs on those attacked and often on those attacking. It is to that war that we now turn.

CHAPTER 5

Bush Doctrine on Preemption, the U.S. Attack against Iraq

The Bush Doctrine

A testing case for the doctrine of preventive war, and for any jurisprudence of prevention, is the Bush administration's decision to attack, invade, and occupy Iraq in March 2003. In December 2002—three months before we attacked Iraq and fifteen months after the September 11 attacks on us—the administration published a major policy paper entitled "The National Security Strategy of the USA," in which it tried to make the case for employing "preemptive actions to counter a sufficient threat to our national security."

The paper, which outlined what has come to be known as the Bush Doctrine, began with a discussion of deterrence as the major strategy in dealing with the Soviet Union and its allies during the

Cold War. It emphasized that the nature of this cold war, confronting a "risk-averse" nuclear power adversary, reasonably led the United States "to emphasize deterrence of the enemy's use of force, producing a grim strategy of mutual assured destruction. . . ."[1] The paper went on to argue that the type of deterrence that proved successful against the risk-averse Soviet Union was insufficient in dealing with international terrorism because "the threat of retaliation is less likely to work against leaders of rogue states more willing to take risks, gambling with the lives of their people, and the wealth of their nations. . . ."

It contrasted our enemy during the Cold War, in which "weapons of mass destruction were considered weapons of last resort whose use risked the destruction of those who used them," with today's enemies—terrorists and rogue states—who see "weapons of mass destruction as weapons of choice." They also see these weapons as capable of blackmailing the United States and its allies "to prevent us from deterring or repelling the aggressive behavior of rogue states." For example, if Saddam Hussein's Iraq had had nuclear weapons when it invaded Kuwait in 1990, it would have been far riskier for the United States to force it back. Nor would deterrence work "against a terrorist enemy whose avowed tactics are wanton destruction and the targeting of innocents; whose so-called soldiers seek martyrdom in death and whose most potent protection is statelessness." This new reality, concluded the paper, "compels us to action."

The action contemplated by this analysis included preemptive military attacks against stateless terrorists and the states that harbor and support them: "We must be prepared to stop rogue states and their terrorist clients *before* they are able to threaten or use weapons of mass destruction against the United States and our allies and friends. . . . The inability to deter a potential attacker, the immediacy of today's threats, and the magnitude of potential harm that could be caused by our adversaries' choice of weapons, do not permit [the] option [of merely reacting]. We cannot let our enemies strike first."

The paper then sought to justify the use of preemptive military measures in select situations by adapting existing international law to the new reality of international terrorism: "For centuries, international law recognized that nations need not suffer an attack before they can lawfully take action to defend themselves against forces that present an imminent danger of attack. Legal scholars and international jurists often conditioned the legitimacy of preemption on the existence of an imminent threat—most often a visible mobilization of armies, navies, and air forces preparing to attack."

But this limited concept—preemption in the face of an "imminent" threat—would not justify preventive wars designed to head off longer-range and less certain, but still serious, threats. To address this problem, the paper recommended adapting the traditional concept of imminence "to the capabilities and objectives of today's adversaries." Therein lie the leap that is so controversial and the leap that lacks a firm jurisprudential basis in international or domestic law. The paper tried to bridge this gap by invoking the danger of terrorism, pointing to our new enemies' reliance "on acts of terror and, potentially, the use of weapons of mass destruction—weapons that can be easily concealed, delivered covertly, and used without warning." The paper pointed to 9/11 as proving that the infliction of "mass civilian casualties is the specific objective of terrorists and these losses would be exponentially more severe if terrorists acquired and used weapons of mass destruction." It then extrapolated from precedent: "The United States has long maintained the option of preemptive actions to counter a sufficient threat to our national security. The greater the threat, the greater is the risk of inaction—and the more compelling the case for taking anticipatory action to defend ourselves, even if uncertainty remains as to the time and place of the enemy's attack. To forestall or prevent such hostile acts by our adversaries, the United States will, if necessary, act preemptively." By using the words "preemptive" and "preventive" interchangeably, the paper papered over real differences between these concepts and differences in the jurisprudential basis for employing them.

Finally, the paper assured friends and enemies alike that the United States will "always proceed deliberately, weighing the consequences of our actions. To support preemptive options, we will":

- build better, more integrated intelligence capabilities to provide timely, accurate information on threats, wherever they may emerge;
- coordinate closely with allies to form a common assessment of the most dangerous threats; and
- continue to transform our military forces to ensure our ability to conduct rapid and precise operations to achieve decisive results.

The purpose of our actions will always be to eliminate a specific threat to the United States or our allies and friends. The reasons for our actions will be clear, the force measured, and the cause just.

Although these cautionary, prudential assurances are useful, they are a far cry from any carefully thought-out jurisprudence or even specific guidelines for action. Nor has historical precedent provided these missing elements. The paper was correct in observing that the United States "has long maintained the option of preemptive action" in extreme cases. President Clinton had considered several preemptive military actions during his administration and had, in fact, authorized at least three such actions and threatened one more.[2] But until the Bush Doctrine was officially propounded, this option had not been publicly articulated as a central aspect of our National Security Policy.[3] Nor was it used, prior to the attack on Iraq, as a justification for a full-scale war designed to prevent an enemy from securing weapons of mass destruction, disseminating such weapons to terrorists, and producing other evil and dangerous results at unspecified future times[4]—in other words, for a preventive war, as distinguished from a preemptive attack.

Because the war in Iraq has been so controversial, especially in light of the failure to find weapons of mass destruction (WMDs) or proof of a clear link to international terrorism, the current discussion regarding preemptive or preventive military action has been understandably skewed by our nation's first major use (some would argue misuse) of the doctrine. For the most part, the debate over preemption, and especially over preventive war, has become a debate over the legitimacy of the attack on Iraq and its subsequent occupation. Moreover, the very different issues of singular surgical preemptive attacks (such as Israel's bombing of the Osirak reactor), as contrasted with full-scale preventive war (such as the invasion of Iraq) have become conflated in at least some of the discussion growing out of the invasion of Iraq. Thus, although the invasion of Iraq is indeed *a* testing case for the doctrine of preventive war, it should not be regarded as *the* testing case for that important and controversial doctrine. A far wider array of potential situations must be evaluated before an acceptable general jurisprudence can be articulated.

The Prewar Debate over Prevention and Preemption

In the months leading up to the attack on Iraq, and in the months since, there has been a close association in the minds of many between the policy of preemptive or preventive military action and the implementation of that policy in Iraq. Though this association is understandable, since the attack was justified in preemptive terms as part of an ongoing "doctrine," and since it is the first and only example of a full-scale preventive war fought by the United States, it is important to delink the general issues of preemption and prevention from the specific application of these policies in the one controversial case of Iraq. It is also important to recall the important differences in degree between a preemptive surgical strike and a full-scale preventive war. It is certainly possible that a preventive policy of some kind may be sound if properly implemented in appropriate situations and that the attack on Iraq did not fit the criteria for appropriate use. On the other hand, it is impossible to ignore or downplay the Iraq experience, since it has been the primary testing case and it may well demonstrate the dangerous potential for misuse of any doctrine of military prevention or preemption.

In the run-up to the invasion of Iraq, the debate over the Bush Doctrine in general and its preemptive aspect in particular took on a polemical quality because of the immediacy of the threat of a dangerous and controversial war in Iraq and the strong opposition to this prospect by many in religious, academic, and peace communities. The questions were often posed in either/or terms: Are you for preemption or against it? Do you favor preventive war or do you oppose it? Would a preventive or preemptive attack be legal or illegal under international law? Would it be just or unjust under principles of "just warfare"? Is a policy of deterrence preferable to a policy of preemption?

With an invasion of Iraq at stake, the answers to these over-broad questions tended to come in rather absolute terms, often reflecting the ideological or political predisposition of the writer. Professor Robert A. Pape of the University of Chicago insisted: "Preventive war by the United States would violate one of the most important norms of international politics—that democracies do not fight preventive wars. [The United States] has never attacked to stop a state from gaining military power. Iraq would be the first preventive war for the United States."[5]

Professor Pape may well have been correct descriptively, but it does not follow that his normative conclusion is likewise correct. Had the United States (or Great Britain) attacked German military targets in the 1930s, *before* Germany's aggression against Poland, and had it prevented the German conquest of Europe with its enormous casualties, the historical assessment of preventive war might well have been quite different. Indeed, it is the inaction of Chamberlain that has become a paradigm of immoral and ineffective appeasement. But if Hitler's Germany had been destroyed or disarmed by preventive military action, the world would never have experienced the horrors of Nazi aggression. It would have experienced only British "aggression," which, despite Germany's violation of its treaty obligations, might have seemed disproportionately harsh without actual knowledge of what might have been. This is the paradox of prevention: When it is employed successfully, we rarely can be sure what it prevented. When it is not employed, it is difficult to assess if it could actually have prevented the horrors that did occur. With the benefit of hindsight, it now seems relatively clear that the democracies should have taken preventive action, including, if necessary, the waging of a preventive war against Nazi Germany. It does not follow from that conclusion, of course, that the United States should have fought a preventive war against Iraq, despite the flawed analogies often invoked between Hitler's Germany and Saddam's Iraq. What does follow is that any categorical statement about the impropriety of democracies' *ever* fighting preventive wars is not supported by the verdict of history.

The U.S. Conference of Catholic Bishops also expressed its deep concern about "recent proposals to expand dramatically traditional limits on just cause to include preventive uses of military force to overthrow threatening regimes or to deal with weapons of mass destruction."[6] Yet there were some in the Vatican hierarchy who, during the early years of the Cold War, favored preventive war against the Soviet Union because of the fear that this atheistic regime, which had stifled the practice of Catholicism throughout Eastern Europe and endangered values important to the church, would spread its godlessness throughout Europe and the rest of the world.[7]

Professor Richard Falk of Princeton, who is generally critical of Israeli actions, distinguished the use of preemption by Israel in 1967 from the preventive war threatened by the United States against Iraq: "Preemption . . . validates striking first—not in a crisis as was done by Israel with plausible, if not entirely convincing, justification in the 1967 war, when enemy Arab troops were massing on its borders after dismissing the UN war-preventing presence, but on the basis of shadowy intentions, alleged potential links to terrorist groups, supposed plans and projects to acquire weapons of mass destruction, and anticipations of possible future dangers. It is a doctrine without limits, without accountability to the UN or international law, without any dependence on a collective judgment of responsible governments and, what is worse, without any convincing demonstration of practical necessity."[8]

Professor Falk may have been right about Iraq, but I strongly suspect that he would have taken a somewhat different view with regard to the "shadowy intentions" of Nazi Germany in the mid-

1930s.[9] The "practical necessity" of purely preventive military action was proved by subsequent events and was anticipated by some even at the time. Germany had, after all, armed itself to the teeth in open violation of its treaty obligations. Its designs on neighboring lands were plain, its involvement in the Spanish Civil War was obvious, and Hitler's program for the Jews was set out in detail for all to read in *Mein Kampf.* "By regularly linking acts of aggression with assurances of peaceful intentions . . . [Hitler] continually duped and paralysed his opponents. Before their partly horrified, partly helpless eyes . . . he succeeded in everything he undertook, from the withdrawal from the League of Nations in October 1933 through the introduction of universal military service and the occupation of the Rhineland to Vienna, Munich and Prague."[10] Yet only with the benefit of hindsight could anyone have been certain of the unprecedented extent of Germany's predation between September 1939 and May 1945.

Although the use and threatened use of preventive or preemptive force are associated with the Bush Doctrine, the current debate over these controversial issues began in earnest during the Clinton administration. The focus of that debate was not, however, Iraq; it was Libya, which was believed to be constructing an underground chemical plant at Tarhunah.[11]

As a 1997 report put it, "Preemption—that meaningful and value-packed word that excites journalists and sends politicians scrambling for cover—was a clear policy option, according to the Secretary of Defense."[12] The report, like the Bush Doctrine paper that followed it five years later, did not really distinguish between short-term preemption and longer-term prevention. It generally used the word "preemption" to cover both. Indeed, its primary focus was on the possibility of an attack on a facility that did not seem to pose an imminent danger. Nor was it about to become unattackable (like the Osirak reactor in June 1981). The attack therefore would have been closer to a preventive than preemptive military action.

The 1997 report, written by a group of military officers for the National Security Program at Harvard's Kennedy School, outlined the policy considerations involved in any decision to use preemptive military force against a dangerous adversary. It predicted that "preemption will increasingly face the decision-maker as an option" for two reasons: First, the costs of not acting preemptively are rising, because "the death, destruction and dislocation that [rogue states, terrorist groups, and transnational organized criminals] can bring upon America is likely to be so massive and debilitating that the act cannot be allowed to occur if there is any possibility of preventing it," and second, we are more capable of acting preemptively, because of enhanced information processing, intelligence and "strategic strike capabilities."[13]

The report went on to catalog a series of general criteria that might be relevant in any preemptive military decision:

> Specific, accurate, and timely intelligence is a critical precursor—an enabler and a catalyst—for preemption. Intelligence sharing with non-traditional domestic and international partners may be necessary to achieve the sufficient evidence for justification necessary for timely and feasible preemption. Intelligence assets must focus on capabilities and intentions of potential adversaries, and on their opportunity to carry out those intentions. The convergence in time and space of an adversary's capability, intention, past history, opportunity, and current actions are [sic] key to the decision to preempt. These five critical intelligence insights bear directly and decisively on the key decision variables. Without these, the possibilities for moral and legal justification, as well as political and military feasibility, are tenuous.

The report then concluded: "U.S. leaders must consider preemption as a viable, sometimes necessary option to prevent unacceptable loss of life or damage to essential institutions."[14]

Applying the criteria they had articulated, the authors of this report opposed military preemption against the Libyan chemical factory, favoring instead a combination of diplomatic, political, and economic pressures. Military preemption was not attempted, and in the end Libya seems to have accepted a diplomatic resolution, coerced perhaps by the threat of military force.[15] In that case, the decision not to preempt seems to have worked. In hindsight, the decision seems correct, though we might have a different view if the Libyan military had subsequently used chemical weapons against U.S. targets. It is also difficult to determine what reprisals might have taken place if the chemical factory had been attacked.[16]

The difference, therefore, between the approaches taken by the Clinton and Bush administrations lies not so much in the policies each articulated—they both supported preemption when American security was threatened—but rather in the implementation of the policies. The Clinton administration appears to have been more cautious, demanding a higher level of threat. It was also prepared to try other means first and for a longer period of time. The Bush administration, on the other hand, seemed prepared to employ military preemption earlier in the process. It is not certain, however, that Bush would have come out differently on Lybia or that Clinton would have come out differently on Iraq, based on the available intelligence.[17]

There is another important difference as well. The Kennedy School report posed the question of whether if preemption is included as an option, it should be announced publicly as part of a strategic policy. This is what the report recommended: "A deliberately ambiguous policy that neither rejects nor recommends preemption may be best. To our potential opponents, what we do is

far more important than what we say. For the American public and
the rest of the world, what we say is important."[18]

The Clinton administration seems to have adopted that policy.
The Bush administration, as we shall see, did not.

Whether to Announce a Doctrine of Preemption

The Bush Doctrine with regard to Iraq was twofold: first, to
announce that the United States now had an explicit policy of
stopping "rogue states and their terrorist clients *before* they are
able to threaten or use weapons of mass destruction" and second,
to use that policy and actually to attack Iraq. Most of the discussion surrounding Iraq has naturally focused on the second issue
because guns speak louder than words. But the first issue—the
decision to announce a policy of prevention or preemption—also
warrants consideration.

There seems to be agreement among unbiased observers that
there is a difference between retaining the option of preemptive
attack in certain limited situations, on the one hand, and announcing and implementing a broad policy of preemptive war, on the
other. Following the horrific deaths during the Russian school
shoot-out in Beslan, Russia went out of its way to announce a new
policy of preemption: "Russia warned it could launch preemptive
strikes on terror bases anywhere in the world and put a bounty on
two top Chechen rebels after the broadcast of a chilling video of
the school hostage siege." The Russian chief of staff, General Yury
Baluyevsky, announced that his military "will take steps to liqui-
date terror bases in any region." He also noted that "the doctrine
of preventive military action against terror targets had been spelled
out publicly before and said such steps were only an 'extreme meas-

ure' that did not include use of nuclear force." Despite his reference to prior articulation of the doctrine, his announcement was
understood to reflect "a hardening mood in Moscow a day after
one television network aired video footage of scared children and
parents sitting in the school gym in southern Beslan as masked
militants rigged bombs over their heads." The European Union
reacted negatively to the Baluyevsky announcement, seeking to
"downplay the warning on preemptive action against terror targets
and said statements like those from Baluyevsky 'are not the first
instrument that will bring results' in combatting terrorism."[19]

Several days after the statement by General Baluyevsky,
Vladimir Putin, the president of Russia, confirmed that preemption against terrorism was now the official Russian policy: "Terrorists must be eliminated directly in their lairs, and if the
situation requires it they must be attacked, including abroad."[20]

There are considerable potential downsides to any policy of
military preemption, announced or unannounced, as well as to any
preemptive military actions, threatened or taken. Some of these
downsides, such as the risk of false positives, are obvious. Others
may be more subtle. For example, an announced policy of preemption may drive an enemy who is contemplating the development of nuclear weapons to speed up its program. The *New York
Times*, in an editorial on September 19, 2004, made this observation: "Mr. Bush once lumped Iraq, Iran and North Korea together
as an 'axis of evil.' Bush's decision to invade Iraq limited the diplomatic and military tools left available to influence North Korea and
Iran—which were undoubtedly taught by the Iraq experience that
the best protection against a preemptive strike is a nuclear arsenal." This may or may not be true in any particular case, as the
Libyan experience demonstrates. In that case the threat of a preemptive attack, coupled with diplomatic pressures and the desire
of Colonel Muammar Khadafy to avoid further sanctions and

international ostracism, brought about a nonmilitary resolution to a dangerous threat.

There are probably situations in which a rogue nation has been deterred from developing a nuclear military option by the credible threat of preemption. For example, Syria knew that Israel had the military capacity as well as the announced intention of preempting any Syrian effort to develop a nuclear bomb that could target Israeli population centers or shift the balance of power. As far as can be determined, Syria had made no serious effort to develop a nuclear bomb, though it almost certainly wanted one, and it did develop chemical and perhaps biological weapons.[21]

There is no question, however, that a rogue nation that manages to win the nuclear preemption race, that develops a nuclear arsenal *before* it can be preempted, will be in a better position to deter a preemptive attack from its enemy by threatening a nuclear response to an unsuccessful preemptive attack.[22] North Korea has learned this lesson, and Iran is seeking to emulate its success. In this high-stakes game of threat and counterthreat, timing may be everything.

An announced policy of preemption can also serve as a counterdeterrent by incentivizing a pre-preemptive first strike by an enemy who fears a preemptive attack. "On November 9, 2004, Iran announced it was capable of mass-producing the Shahab-3 missile and reserved the right to use the missile in preemptive strikes should its nuclear facilities be threatened with attack."[23] Iran has thus threatened to preempt any preemptive attack. A system of international law and morality that accepts preemption may encourage a potential target of preemption to strike first. Had Egypt known that Israel was planning to attack its air force on the ground in 1967, it would certainly have taken some action, perhaps even attempted a preemptive strike itself against the Israeli Air Force.[24]

The same might have been true of the United States had it known of the Japanese intention to attack its naval base at Pearl Harbor. This potential downside is more theoretical than practical, since nations generally take actions based on actual intelligence about enemy intentions rather than on announcements of policy or concerns about vague principles of international law and morality. But an announced policy of preemption can serve as post facto justification, if not an actual reason, for a preemptive first strike.

These observations may be more relevant to the decision whether to announce a policy of preemption, as the United States, Russia, Israel, and Australia have now done,[25] than to the decision to take an unannounced, surprise preemptive action, such as the attack on the Iraqi nuclear reactor by Israel in 1981. But a singular preemptive military action without an announced policy can also have significant downsides, even when it succeeds in the short term. In the first place, any preemptive military action that is taken necessarily serves as a signal that preemption has become part of that nation's policy options. Thus all the disadvantages (as well as advantages) of an announced policy of preemption follow from a preemptive attack. To put it another way, a nation can secure the advantages of a surprise preemptive action only once before also being burdened by its possible disadvantages.

As the authors of the 1997 Kennedy School report on military preemption concluded:

Preemption may have significant deterrence value, especially after a rogue state or terrorist has once been preempted. It may, however, drive a determined adversary to extreme measures of retaliation and reprisal. These consequences could be worse than the original threat that was preempted.

Paradoxically, although preemptive actions may eliminate immediate threats, they may also cause the adversary to go underground, figuratively and literally, thereby masking future activities from detection and making future interdictive efforts much more difficult. The impact of this "preemption paradox" is that decision-makers must have a clear understanding of their objectives and of what constitutes success: in some cases, preemption serves only to delay or prolong crisis in favor of "buying time" to seek alternative solutions.

The Bush administration, in contrast with prior administrations, decided to announce a distinct policy of military preemption under specified circumstances. If this announcement was intended to deter Iraq from continuing its refusal to cooperate more fully with weapons inspectors, it failed. The administration then carried out its threat to act preemptively and invaded Iraq.

The Postattack Debate

Following the invasion of Iraq and the subsequent developments—no WMDs found, a difficult occupation with many casualties on both sides, much international condemnation—the nature of the debate over preemption became even more charged. Criticism of the attack on Iraq often turned into condemnation of the doctrines of preemption and preventive war.

An article in the *Financial Times* declared that "for all Bush's bravado, the preemption doctrine is dead" and the president's assertion of "America's right to preemptive action 'before threats materialize' had a hollow as well as a hubristic ring." The Bush Doctrine of preemption, "unveiled in the wake of September 11, 2001 survives only in name."[26]

The *Los Angeles Times* headlined an article SHOOTING FIRST:

THE PREEMPTIVE WAR DOCTRINE HAS MET AN EARLY DEATH IN IRAQ.[27] Its text concluded that the problems that have plagued the occupation "make it highly unlikely that preemption is a tactic that he will employ elsewhere anytime soon." It too declared that "Bush's doctrine of preemption is, for all intents and purposes, dead."

A lead editorial in the *New York Times* of September 12, 2004, was headlined PREVENTIVE WAR: A FAILED DOCTRINE. It observed that the preventive war doctrine had had only "one real test" and that the failure to find any weapons of mass destruction or any link between the Iraqi regime and al-Qaida had shown it to be a failure: "The real lesson is that America dangerously erodes its military and diplomatic defenses when it charges off unwisely after hypothetical enemies."[28] The editorial sought to draw precisely the distinction between "preventive war" and "preemptive attacks" that the Bush Doctrine had elided.[29] It noted that American policy had always "left room for pre-emptive attacks" when the "nation's vital interests were actively threatened" and all reasonable diplomatic efforts had been tried and failed:

> America is under no obligation to sit and wait, if it is clear that some enemy is actually preparing to strike first. But it correctly drew the line at preventive wars against potential foes who might, or might not, be thinking about doing something dangerous. As the administration's disastrous experience in Iraq amply demonstrates, that is still the wisest course and the one that keeps America most secure in an increasingly dangerous era.
>
> The terrorist attacks of Sept. 11, 2001, plainly ushered in a new era of catastrophic threats to the American homeland. If these are to be met effectively, major changes in national security policy will be required. But a shift toward preventive wars is not one of them.[30]

Some writers continued to favor preemption, despite (or because of) the Iraqi experience. Another article in the *Los Angeles Times* predicted that preemption as an option "will not go away" and that even Kofi Annan was now suggesting that discussions begin about "the criteria for an early authorization of coercive measures to address certain types of threats."[31] Professor Ruth Wedgwood observed that the "question remains whether a state can ever resort to the use of preventive force in unique cases—when intelligence is reliable and timing is sensitive, multilateral authorization is not practically available, and a state is sponsoring or hosting a network acquiring weapons of mass destruction. . . . [T]he abstract answer to many strategists is yes—a given regime might have a record of conduct so irresponsible and links to terrorist groups so troubling that the acquisition of WMD capability amounts to an unreasonable danger that cannot be abided."[32]

Miriam Sapiro, in an article in the *American Journal of International Law*, suggested: "Perhaps Iraq will be the case that highlights the risks of adopting a new doctrine of preventive war, while persuading skeptics that the constraints governing the more traditional justification of anticipatory self-defense make sense."[33]

Whether or not Iraq will persuade policy makers that the risks associated with preventive war outweigh its benefits—at least as a general matter—there is little doubt that our first full-scale preventive war will have considerable impact on how we think about preventive and preemptive warfare. It may, however, require some distance from the passions generated by that controversial and divisive war, and some historical perspective, before the lessons of Iraq can be fully understood and incorporated into a general jurisprudence. In the meantime, the process of evaluating an ongoing war will continue even if it provides only a first draft of the ultimate historical conclusions.

Evaluating Decisions Relating to Iraq

Applying the criteria outlined in this book to the United States' Iraq policy requires that we examine a number of factors that were involved, or should reasonably have been known, at the time that critical decisions were made and implemented. Subsumed within this broad framework are issues relating to intelligence gathering, evaluation, and determination, both within the government and to the public.

We should begin by first asking whether, if had all the allegations claimed to be true and relied on by the government turned out to be accurate, the action would have been justified. We know, in retrospect, that many, perhaps most, of these allegations could not be confirmed: No weapons of mass destruction were found; no hard links between the specific al-Qaida attacks of 9/11 and the Saddam Hussein administration could be established; no proof exists that more innocent lives were saved by toppling the Hussein dictatorship than by allowing him to continue in his murderous ways; and there was no evidence of American "liberators" being widely greeted with appreciative gestures rather than with a determined resistance. On a more general level, it is difficult to prove or disprove the claim that in the long run, democracy will be promoted, terrorism reduced, and other broad values served by our actions.

But what if all these allegations had proved to be valid? It is nearly impossible now to conjure the image of Iraqi citizens lining up to shower our troops with flowers, as captured nuclear weapons are paraded through the streets, victorious Americans produce hard evidence of direct links between the toppled dictator and Osama bin Laden, and the American military ends its brief occupation while Iraq quickly moves on the road to democracy, followed by

Syria, Iran, and Saudi Arabia. However, let us suspend the bitter reality for a moment and imagine a utopian result. Even then the case for a full-scale preventive invasion is subject to debate.

In the run-up to the attack I personally believed most of the administration's claims: the presence of weapons of mass destruction, including nuclear weapons; possible links to terrorists sufficient to cause at least some concern about Iraqi weapons of mass destruction getting into the hands of some terrorists; a more welcoming reception by most Iraqis to the ending of a brutal dictatorship; and a possible warning to other Islamic and Arab dictatorships that their days were numbered. I did oppose a full-scale invasion of Iraq, but my conclusion was not open-and-shut. I publicly stated that my opposition was "a 51–49 percent" matter, with the deciding 2 percent based on the law of unintended consequences.* I made references to the transition from the dictatorship of the relatively secular shah of Iran to the far worse dictatorship of the religiously extremist cabal that succeeded him, and I pointed out that in general it is better to deal with secular dictators who fear death than with religious zealots who welcome it. I worried about a long occupation, with many casualties on both sides and with the strengthening of Islamic fundamentalism (such as occurred in Israel, following the long-term occupation of the Gaza and West Bank).

I claim no special prescience, only the general pessimism that results from long experience watching the best-laid (and best-intentioned) plans of men and women go awry. The law of unintended consequences is more powerful, more certain, and more enduring than most other human laws. It must be factored into

---

* I also said that I did not regard the decision to invade, despite my opposition to it, as a "marchable" event, warranting shrill public protest, because I believed that reasonable people could disagree about its wisdom and morality.

any predictive equation regarding the consequences of complex human actions. But there are unintended consequences to inaction as well, as the tragic events of World War II demonstrate.

There are always lessons to be learned from a military action that has gone wrong, as the invasion and occupation of Iraq seem to demonstrate. These lessons must become part of our collective thinking as we move toward constructing a jurisprudence and morality of preventive and preemptive war. The lessons of Iraq will also have an influence on any decision regarding preemptive or preventive military action against Iran. But it would be a mistake to build an entire jurisprudence on one experience that has divided reasonable people and entire nations. The lessons of Iraq are ongoing and incomplete. The end of the story has not yet been written in the blood of the many who will yet suffer. Elections, suicide bombings, trials, the establishment of a stable government, assassinations, progress toward a constitution, victories, defeats— all these occur on a daily basis. The one lesson that is clear is that wars of this kind—unlike singular preemptive attacks, rarely go smoothly or are without very high costs. There are other lessons as well, ones that mandate extreme caution before embarking on full-scale preventive wars, invasions, and occupations but that also mandate that no option, not even full-scale preventive war, should be taken off the table if the dangers are grave enough, if the certainty is high enough, and if other options are unrealistic enough.

One vexing question—and perhaps another testing case—is how to apply these lessons and cautionary principles to the far more difficult case of the multiple nuclear facilities in Iran, which are protected, spread out, and deliberately located near population centers. The case is also more complex because of the different internal dynamics within Iran. It is this issue to which we now turn, before we try to articulate a general jurisprudence capable of informing preemptive and preventive decisions.

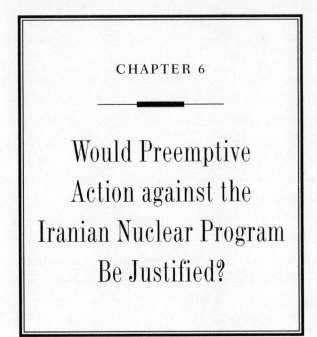

CHAPTER 6

Would Preemptive Action against the Iranian Nuclear Program Be Justified?

T his chapter consists of a case study of the options regarding Iran's nuclear program. It seeks to apply the experiences outlined above to an ongoing situation, a potential crisis, now faced by the international community. It is an ever-changing crisis, as most are. The experiences that form the basis for meaningful guidance—especially those growing out of the Iraq War—are also ongoing. Even more historically grounded experiences, such as the Israeli attack on the Iraqi reactor back in 1981, still have ramifications today, as we shall soon see. It is challenging, to say the least, to try to draw static conclusions from dynamic events, but all jurisprudence—especially common law jurisprudence—is dynamic and adaptive to changing circumstances and understandings.

No reasonable person can doubt that the Iranian government wants to develop a nuclear weapons capacity. Despite its claim that it is seeking only to expand its energy sources, the evidence to the contrary is significant, if not overwhelming. First, Iran has enormous oil reserves and access to other nonnuclear sources of energy. Second, the material it is trying to import is of the type necessary for the construction of nuclear weapons, not merely for nuclear energy. Third, several prominent Iranian politicians have acknowledged the military goals of the nuclear program. Hashemi Rafsanjani, the former president of Iran, has threatened Israel with nuclear destruction, boasting that an Iranian attack would kill as many as five million Jews. Rafsanjani estimated that even if Israel retaliated by dropping its own nuclear bombs, Iran would probably lose only fifteen million people, which he said would be a small "sacrifice" from among the billion Muslims in the world.[1] "He seemed pleased with his formulations."[2] President Mohammad Khatami has threatened to use Iran's missiles to destroy Jewish and Christian civilization: "Our missiles are now ready to strike at their civilization, and as soon as the instructions arrive from the leader 'Ali Khamenei, we will launch our missiles at their cities and installations."[3]

Khamenei has in turn urged his military to "have two [nuclear] bombs ready to go in January [2005] or you are not Muslims."[4] On September 21, 2004, the Iranian military paraded its Shahab-3 missiles through the streets of Teheran. These missiles, which can reach Israeli and Iraqi cities, were draped with banners that read CRUSH AMERICA and WIPE ISRAEL OFF THE MAP.[5] In late October 2004, the Iranian legislature rejected a proposal to assure peaceful use of nuclear technology, after which some lawmakers shouted, "Death to America!"[6] In May 2005 it was disclosed that Iran had converted thirty-seven tons of uranium into gas, which "could theoretically yield more than 200 pounds of weapons-grade uranium, enough to make five crude nuclear weapons."[7]

Several days later Prime Minister Tony Blair of Britain warned that he was prepared to seek sanctions from the UN Security Council if Iran proceeded with plans to resume uranium reprocessing. The foreign ministers of Britain, France, and Germany wrote a sharply worded letter warning that any attempt to restart Iran's nuclear program "would bring the negotiating process to an end." Iran responded defiantly that it "will definitely resume a part of its enrichment activities in the near future."[8]

France, Germany, and Britain submitted a resolution to the board of the International Atomic Energy Agency (IAEA), the nuclear watchdog agency, referring Iran to the United Nations Security Council. At the end of September 2005, the IAEA passed the resolution, citing Iran for breaches of the Nuclear Non-Proliferation Treaty. The resolution does not specify when Iran would be referred to the Security Council, leaving some time for Iran to negotiate, though Iranian leaders have angrily denounced the resolution.[9] About three hundred protestors, angry about the resolution, "hurled stones and smoke bombs at the British embassy" in Tehran.[10]

At a conference entitled "The World Without Zionism" in October 2005, Rafsanjani's successor, Ahmadinejad, declared that Israel "must be wiped off the map." He proclaimed that

> [t]he establishment of a Zionist regime was a move by the world oppressor against the Islamic world. . . . The skirmishes in the occupied land are part of the war of destiny. The outcome of hundreds of years will be defined in Palestinian land.[11]

Furthermore, Ahmadinejad warned that "[a]nybody who recognizes Israel will burn in the fire of Islamic nation's fury," and that any Islamic leader "who recognizes the Zionist regime means he is acknowledging the surrender and defeat of the Islamic world."[12]

Steven R. Weisman of the *New York Times* reported that following Ahmadinejad's remarks, thousands of Iranians marched through the streets of Tehran chanting "Death to Israel" and "Death to America."[13] The same article quoted a member of the Basiji militia as having said: "Ahmadinejad talks on behalf of all Iranians. We are ready to die for Palestine." Weisman concluded that

> [a]lthough Mr. Ahmadinejad's comments about Israel were extreme, many diplomats point out that they reflected long-standing Iranian policy. "He said it more loudly, more directly, more forcefully and more offensively than anyone has said for a long time," said one Western diplomat. "But he is essentially stating what is known to be Iranian policy."[14]

Nor is it certain that Israel could eliminate the Iranian nuclear threat by making peace with the Palestinians or by any other actions it may take or refrain from taking. In the world of Islamic extremism, Israel gets blamed for every Muslim death, and virtually every Muslim problem, regardless of whether it had anything to do with causing it. On November 12, 2005, after the suicide bombings on three hotels in Jordan, the *New York Times* reported that many Muslims blamed Israel for the attacks, despite the fact that al-Quaida assumed responsibility for them: "While most Arabs have long viewed Israel as their enemy, the extent to which Israel weighs on the regional psyche and diverts attention away from social, political, religious and economic issues . . . cannot be ignored, many social and political analysts say. Blaming Israel is not just a knee jerk, they say; for many Arabs, it is their reality." The article quoted a Jordanian political commentator as having said: "[T]his [scapegoating] became an easy way not to deal with our problems that are based in our own society."[15] Similarly, in many parts of the Muslim world, Israel was blamed for the suicide

bombings in Egypt in 2004, for the assassination of the former
Lebanese prime minister Rafik Hariri, and even for the terrorist
attacks of 9/11.[16] An Egyptian weekly magazine went so far to
blame Israel for causing the tsunami in December 2004.[17]

For many Islamic extremists, the only solution to these problems is to wipe Israel off the face of the earth, and any Muslim
leader who accomplished this would be regarded as a hero,
regardless of the cost in Muslim lives.

This apocalyptic attitude, combined with an expectation of
heavenly reward for killing millions of Jews and Americans, makes
the effectiveness of the usual deterrent approach to nuclear
threat somewhat less promising than if it were directed against a
more secular regime. Some Muslim extremists, whether conventional suicide bombers or nuclear suicide bombers, will not be
deterred by the threat of mere death and certainly not by sanctions. They welcome martyrdom as a necessary prelude to a paradise in which they will be rewarded for their martyrdom. This
does not mean of course that a credible threat of material or economic damage will necessarily be ignored by all those in power.
There are pragmatists and materialists even among the most fundamentalist zealots. Moreover, there are genuine moderates and
reformers inside and outside the Iranian government, and their
potential impact on Iranian nuclear policy cannot be overlooked.
But in any worst-case scenario, which cannot be ignored especially by the potentially targeted state, the threatening statements
made by those in power must be given considerable weight.

Estimates vary on the timing of Iran's independent development of deliverable nuclear weapons. Some believe it is as far as
three to five years away—if it does not receive outside help. As
one retired CIA official has put it, "The big wild card for us is that
you don't know who is capable of filling in the missing parts for them
. . . North Korea? Pakistan? We don't know what parts are missing."[18]

What is clear is that "its [Iran's] work on a missile-delivery system is far more advanced" than its development of nuclear weapons and that it has plans to arm its missiles with nuclear, chemical, and/or biological warheads capable of mass destruction and the murder of millions of civilians. Whether there are people in positions of authority who are actually contemplating the suicidal deployment of such weapons is of course far less clear, though the events of 9/11 have made nothing unthinkable.

No democracy can afford to wait until such a threat against its civilian population is imminent. Both Israel and the United States should have the right under international law to protect their civilians and soldiers from a threatened nuclear holocaust, and that right must include—if that is the only realistic option—preemptive military action of the sort taken by Israel against the Iraqi nuclear reactor at Osirak in 1981, especially if such action can again be taken without an unreasonable number of civilian casualties.

Although the UN Security Council unanimously voted to condemn Israel's attack on the Iraqi reactor, Secretary of State Condoleezza Rice has said that history vindicated the Israeli strike by preventing Saddam Hussein from gaining access to nuclear weapons, but she has declined to say whether the United States would support an Osirak type of attack by Israel against Iranian nuclear facilities. No two situations are ever exactly the same, and the considerations that must go into any military decision depend on many subtle factors. Secretary Rice did say, however, that the United States and its allies "cannot allow the Iranians to develop a nuclear weapon."[19] That appears to be the constant in the equation, with the variable being the means that might appropriately be employed to assure that neither the United States nor its allies will have to confront an Iran with a nuclear weapons capability (as we are already apparently facing a North Korea with such a capability).

Recent reports suggest that the United States may be selling bunker-busting bombs to Israel, weapons that could be used to destroy the underground nuclear facilities being used by Iran to protect its nuclear weapons work in progress.[20] Whether this information was leaked in order to bolster the deterrence threat as well as to enhance Israel's actual capacity to destroy the Iranian nuclear facilities is unknown.

Despite recent statements about the propriety of Israel's attack against the Iraqi nuclear reactor and the unacceptability of Iran's developing a nuclear bomb, the American policy with regard to the Iranian nuclear program remains unclear. The undersecretary of defense for policy has said that "I don't think that anyone should be ruling in or out anything while we are conducting diplomacy,"[21] but the president has not spoken directly about the military issue. To the contrary, he has said that "diplomacy must be the first choice, and always the first choice of an administration trying to solve an issue of . . . nuclear armament. And we'll continue to press on diplomacy."[22] That is certainly the correct view in any situation in which there is a heavy burden on those contemplating a military option. Former President Bill Clinton has commended President Bush for keeping "the military option on the table, but not pushing it too far."[23] But the question remains: If all diplomatic options fail, as they did with regard to Iraq in 1981, must a democratic nation committed to the rule of law as well as to its own survival and the protection of its citizens wait for help from an unfriendly Security Council (some of whose members have supplied Iran with the materials it may now be using to build nuclear weapons), or may it—as a last resort—take preventive military action, as Israel did in 1981?

Today most reasonable people look to Israel's surgical attack against the Osirak nuclear reactor as the paradigm of proportional preemption, despite the Security Council's condemnation. (Many forget that Iran actually attacked the Iraqi reactor before Israel did but failed to destroy it; there was no UN condemnation of *that* attack.) If all the Iranian nuclear facilities were in one place and away from any civilian population center, it would be moral (and, under any reasonable regime of international law, legal) for Israel or the United States to destroy it if all nonmilitary options failed. But the Iranian militants have learned from the Iraqi experience and, according to recent intelligence reports, have deliberately spread Iraq's nuclear facilities around the country, including in or near heavily populated areas. This could force Israel and the United States into a terrible choice: either allow Iran to complete its production of nuclear bombs aimed at their civilian population centers and other targets, or destroy the facilities despite the inevitability of Iranian civilian casualties. The longer they wait, the greater the risks to civilians, especially if they wait until an attack on the reactors might spread radiation.

The laws of war prohibit the bombing of civilian population centers (even, apparently, in retaliation for or deterrence of attacks on cities),[24] but they permit the bombing of military targets, including nuclear facilities during wartime. By deliberately placing nuclear facilities in the midst of civilian population centers, the Iranian government has made the decision to expose its civilians to attacks, and it must assume all responsibility for any casualties caused by such attacks. In the context of domestic law, when a criminal uses an innocent bystander as a shield against the police, and the police, in a reasonable effort to apprehend the criminal, unintentionally shoot and kill the innocent shield, it is the criminal who is guilty of murder, even though the police fired the fatal shot.[25] The same rule of culpability should apply in the military context. Israel, the United States, and other democracies place their military facilities away from population centers precisely in order to minimize danger to its civilians. Iran does exactly the opposite because its leaders realize that decent democracies would hesitate to bomb a nuclear facility located in an urban center.[26] Iran uses its own civilians as a deterrent against a preventive attack.

Israel (with the help of the United States) should first try everything short of military action—diplomacy, threats, bribery, sabotage, targeted killings of individuals essential to the Iranian nuclear program, and other covert actions—but if all else fails, it (or the United States) must have the option of taking out the Iranian nuclear threat before it is capable of the genocide for which its leaders assert it is being built. The chief of staff of the Israel Defense Forces put it this way: "We believe there is a chance of success when talking about the elimination of the Iranian capabilities of weapons of mass destruction, first of all using political and economic resolutions. From my point of view and my recommendation, this has to be used first of all. If not we have to be prepared, and I am talking about the Western community, to use other options in order to eliminate the Iranian capabilities."[27]

In June 2004 it was reported that "Israel already had rehearsed a military first strike on Iran. 'Israel will on no account permit Iranian reactors—especially the one being built in Bushehr with Russian help—to go critical,' an Israeli defense source told reporters. Prime Minister Ariel Sharon went on the record that Iran was the 'biggest danger to the existence of Israel.' Sharon left no doubt as to his meaning: 'Israel will not allow Iran to be equipped with a nuclear weapon.'"[28]

In early 2005 Israel's foreign minister, Silvan Shalom, reiterated the point that if European diplomatic efforts fail, "Israel cannot live with Iran having a nuclear bomb."[29] Again, that appears to be the constant, with the variables dependent on the success of international diplomacy, sanctions, or other forms of intervention. It is possible of course that neither Israel nor the United

States has any current fixed intention to attack preventively Iran's nuclear facilities but that both are issuing tough statements as part of an overall deterrent strategy.

According to an article in the January 24, 2005, issue of *The New Yorker* by Seymour Hersh, the United States is preparing for the possibility of a preemptive military attack against Iran's nuclear weapon program: "The Administration has been conducting secret reconnaissance missions inside Iran at least since last summer. Much of the focus is on the accumulation of intelligence and targeting information on Iranian nuclear, chemical, and missile sites, both declared and suspected. The goal is to identify and isolate three dozen, and perhaps more, such targets that could be destroyed by precision strikes and short-term commando raids. 'The civilians in the Pentagon want to go into Iran and destroy as much of the military infrastructure as possible,' the government consultant with close ties to the Pentagon told me."

According to this report, the United States has been conferring with Israel about a possible military preemption: "There has also been close, and largely unacknowledged, cooperation with Israel. . . . (After Osirak, Iran situated many of its nuclear sites in remote areas of the east, in an attempt to keep them out of striking range of other countries, especially Israel. Distance no longer lends such protection, however: Israel has acquired three submarines capable of launching cruise missiles and has equipped some of its aircraft with additional fuel tanks, putting Israeli F-16I fighters within the range of most Iranian targets.) They believe that about three-quarters of the potential targets can be destroyed from the air, and a quarter are too close to population centers, or buried too deep, to be targeted. . . ."

But there are some who doubt the benefits of a military approach:

. . . Shahram Chubin, an Iranian scholar who is the director of research at the Geneva Centre for Security Policy, told me [Hersch], "It's a fantasy to think that there's a good American or Israeli military option in Iran." He went on: "The Israeli view is that this is an international problem. 'You do it,' they say to the West. 'Otherwise, our Air Force will take care of it.'" . . . But the situation now is both more complex and more dangerous [than it was in Iraq in 1981], Chubin said. The Osirak bombing "drove the Iranian nuclear-weapons program underground, to hardened, dispersed sites," he said. ". . . The U.S. and Israel would not be certain whether all the sites had been hit, or how quickly they'd be rebuilt. Meanwhile, they'd be waiting for an Iranian counter-attack that could be military or terrorist or diplomatic. Iran has long-range missiles and ties to Hezbollah, which has drones—you can't begin to think of what they'd do in response.[30]

In January 2005 I asked a former very high-ranking Israeli intelligence official if an Osirak type of preemptive attack was feasible against the Iranian nuclear program. He told me that any such attack would have to be very different from the surgical air attack of 1981. "It would be more difficult, because it would have to be multifaceted. If it were to be carried out, it would be something unprecedented in military history." He also told me that "Israel should not bear the burden alone because the development of an Iranian nuclear rocket would endanger many other countries as well." He said that the United States would be particularly vulnerable to nuclear terrorism if an Iranian nuclear bomb found its way into the hands of Islamic terrorists.

The issue is made even more complex by the internal dynamics of Iranian society, which is deeply divided between the religious zealots now in control and a secular (or at least somewhat more secular) minority (or majority, no one really knows). *New York*

Times columnist Thomas Friedman reports that if a free and fair election were held in Iran, it might go against what many Iranians regard as the current despotic leadership. But in June 2005 Mahmoud Ahmadinejad, "the ultraconservative mayor of Tehran,"[31] was elected president of the country. In an upset, he defeated Ali Akbar Hashemi Rafsanjani, the former president of Iran, who was regarded as the "more moderate" candidate[32] despite his immoderate views on nuclear war with Israel. Ahmadinejad is the man who threatened to wipe Israel off the map. The problem is that, according to some experts, there is no division within Iran on its right to develop nuclear weapons: "[T]he nuclear ambition in Iran is supported across the political spectrum, and Iranians will perceive attacks on these sites as attacks on their ambitions to be a major regional player and a modern nation that's technologically sophisticated."[33]

Two Iranian human rights activists have argued that "for human rights defenders in Iran, the possibility of a foreign military attack on that country [by the United States or Israel] represents an utter disaster for their cause." They worry that "the threat of foreign military intervention will provide a powerful excuse for authoritarian elements to uproot these [nascent human rights groups] and put an end to their growth."[34] But they neglect entirely the threat posed by a nuclear Iran. Demanding that Israel and the United States put the human rights of Iranians ahead of the lives of their own citizens and soldiers is both naive and selfish—unless the unexpressed assumption is that if human rights were to become strengthened in Iran, the threat of nuclear weapons would diminish, as it almost certainly would. Still, the likelihood that the human rights movement would become strong enough soon enough to eliminate the nuclear threat is very slight. I put this question to Israeli Knesset member Natan Sharansky when he spoke at the Harvard Kennedy School in February 2005. Sharansky had made a strong case that democracies do not attack other democracies and that the best long-term approach to Iran is to help strengthen its human rights movement. He also believes that the current leadership of Iran is determined to develop and use nuclear weapons against Israel, and he seems to agree with the Iranian human rights activists that a foreign attack might weaken the human rights movement. Much will depend on timing. How quickly will the mullahs get their nuclear bomb? How quickly will the dissidents increase their influence?

Moreover, an Israeli planner has told me that in light of the endemic instability in Iran, Israel would not tolerate nuclear weapons in that country even if moderates, with no intention of using them aggressively, were to assume control. "Moderate control is temporary, but nuclear weapons in Iran would be permanent," the Israeli said. In addition, there is always the risk that Iranian nuclear weapons could fall into the hands of Hezbollah or other terrorists who work closely with Iranians. The Israeli position, as well as the American view, still seems to be that regardless of the internal dynamics of Iranian politics, the constant remains that no nuclear weapons will be tolerated regardless of who is in charge.

Thus the likelihood that this issue will be resolved internally is slim at best, but internal dynamics should not be ignored. If there were to be an internally generated (or mostly internally generated) regime change within Iran, that might not diminish the government's desire to become a nuclear power, but it could diminish the dangers posed by its access to nuclear weapons. A more secular, democratic regime—or one less belligerent toward the United States (and thus possibly toward Israel)—might be more tolerable to the United States and Israel than the suicidal religious extremists who would currently control any nuclear weapons developed or obtained by Iran. A new regime might also pose a smaller risk of having such weapons fall into the hands of terrorists, but it would not eliminate all the risks.[35]

There are of course no guarantees, and all this is a matter of degree and probability. But the risks of a preemptive attack are so considerable that these probabilities and subtle matters of degree must be factored into any calculation of the costs and benefits of every available option. Even if the United States and/or Israel have the legal and moral right to act preemptively against the development of an Iranian nuclear weapon, it does not necessarily follow that they should exercise that right by means of a difficult and risky military strike that might set back any nascent reform movement by uniting all (or most) Iranians against the external threats posed by the United States and Israel.

There are some, however, who argue the opposite: that the destruction of the Iranian nuclear capacity would weaken the mullahs and strengthen the hands of dissidents. No one can be certain what the effects of a successful or failed preemptive attack would be, except that the law of unintended consequences would rear its always unpredictable and often ugly head.

As of now, it is unclear whether the United Nations, the International Atomic Energy Agency, the European Community, or anyone else is making significant progress in stopping the Iranian nuclear weapons program, which has been assisted by several nations, including France, Germany, Russia, and Pakistan. Several of these countries, which have profited enormously from doing dirty business with Iran, seem less than anxious for a confrontation with their trading partner. Diplomacy appears to be delaying certain aspects of the program, but for how long no one can be certain. American indecision—a *New York Times* headline of September 21, 2004, read BUSH AIDES DIVIDED ON CONFRONTING IRAN OVER A-BOMB—seems to be encouraging the Iranians to speed up their program, so as to be able to deter a preemptive strike by threatening a counterstrike with nuclear weapons. During the U.S. presidential election campaign of 2004, Hasan Rowhani, the head of the Iranian Supreme National Security Council, said he was hoping that President Bush would be reelected because his administration was doing little to prevent Iran from developing its nuclear program. He said that despite President Bush's "hard-line and baseless rhetoric," he had not taken "in practical terms" any "dangerous actions" against the mullahs or their nuclear program.[36] Perhaps the disclosures regarding Pentagon planning for a possible attack were intended to counter this perception and to increase the pressure on Iran. The situation may soon reach crisis proportions. Yet there is certainly no consensus among international law scholars about the legality, propriety, morality, or wisdom of a preventive attack on Iran's nuclear facilities.

There is not even consensus on the factors that should be considered in making such a decision, as we shall see in the next chapter.[37]

Were the nightmare scenarios of a nuclear mass casualty attack by Iran (or by a terrorist surrogate like Hezbollah) to occur because of the failure to act by nations capable of preventively destroying Iran's nuclear capacity, we may someday hear an Iranian mass murderer echo Goebbels's bewilderment about why the World War I victors had not prevented Nazi Germany from arming. In retrospect, the bewilderment Goebbels expressed sounds like an apt warning, but in prospect—without any certain knowledge of how the Iranian situation will play out—it is only one of many historical lessons from which to learn.

In the end, any decision with regard to the Iranian nuclear program will probably be based less on international law than on the practical, military capacity of those nations most at risk—the United States and Israel—to destroy the Iranian reactors without undue civilian casualties and other costs.* It will also depend on whether the international community demonstrates a capacity to confront threats of this kind by collective action. It will not depend on any widely accepted jurisprudence of preemptive or preventive action, because as we shall see in the next chapter, no such jurisprudence as yet exists. Among the questions posed in the coming chapter is whether any jurisprudence—no matter how well conceived or widely accepted—can really be expected to influence the actions of nations that believe themselves to be under the gun, especially the nuclear gun. The answer to this question as well as the outcome of the Iranian situation remains unresolved at the time of this writing and is likely to remain uncertain in the foreseeable future.

---

* On November 13, 2005, the *New York Times* reported that a stolen Iranian computer "showed a long effort to design a nuclear warhead," and is the "strongest evidence yet that . . . the country is trying to develop a compact warhead to fit atop its Shahab missile, which can reach Israel and other countries in the Middle East." William J. Broad and David E. Sanger, "Relying on Computer, U.S. Seeks to Prove Iran's Nuclear Aims," *New York Times*, November 13, 2005, p. 1. On December 3, 2005, the *New York Times* reported that Russia was selling Iran an antiaircraft missile system that "would complicate a potential airstrike by the United States or Israel on Iran's Bushehr nuclear power plant, which Russia is helping to build." Andrew E. Kramer, "Russia to Sell Antiaircraft Missiles to Iran in Billion-Dollar Deal," *New York Times*, December 3, 2005, p. A10.

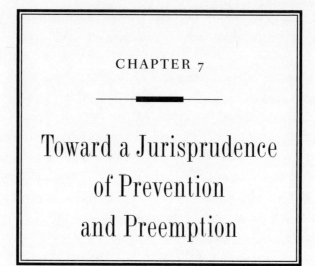

CHAPTER 7

Toward a Jurisprudence of Prevention and Preemption

Some Preliminary Observations about Jurisprudence

Constructing a jurisprudence for a democracy is a daunting task. It requires the framing of issues so that citizens can make the substantive choices and weigh the competing values. Efforts are now under way in many newly free (or freer) nations— from the former Soviet Union and its satellites to Iraq to the Palestinian Authority to China—to draft constitutions, codify laws, and create processes for resolving disputes. There are also efforts all around the world to devise rules governing new and changing phenomena, such as the Internet, DNA and cloning, outer space, artificial intelligence, and other technological innovations. Though no jurisprudence is ever without roots in existing or prior law, and therefore no jurisprudence is ever built from scratch, each of these efforts at building a jurisprudence on the foundations of existing law involves something new, something that has changed, something that could not easily have been anticipated.

What is remarkable about the absence of a jurisprudence governing preemptive or preventive governmental action is that these phenomena are as old as recorded history. We have been practicing preemption and prevention for millennia. The philosophers, legal scholars, religious leaders, and politicians have seen these phenomena in action. Yet no systematic jurisprudence in any way comparable to the jurisprudence governing responses to past harms has emerged. Nor can this absence be fully attributed to the sage observations by Roscoe Pound quoted near the beginning of the book, that juristic theories come after lawyers and judges have dealt with concrete cases and learned how to dispose of them. It is certainly true that laws tend to grow out of experience and are not a priori postulates. Oliver Wendell Holmes, Jr., was correct in his observation that "the life of the law has not been logic; it has been experience."[1] But the world has had considerable experience, both positive and negative, with preemptive and preventive governmental actions of many types. Legal systems have long "dealt with" and "disposed of" claims growing out of such actions.

The results have not always been satisfactory, but that is in the nature of the development of law. Jurisprudence grows largely out of mistakes. The proverb that "Good laws come from bad lives" may overstate the case somewhat, but there is certainly some truth to the observation that good deeds done by good people do not generate the kinds of legal controversies on which the law is built. The common law is a never-ending history of errors and anachronisms corrected over time. Precedent has a vote but not a veto. As Holmes once quipped, "It is revolting to have no better reason for a rule of law than that so it was laid down in the time of Henry IV.

It is still more revolting if the grounds upon which it was laid down have vanished long since, and the rule simply persists from blind imitation of the past."[2] Human beings learn from their mistakes. To paraphrase George Santayana, those who cannot learn from the past are condemned to repeat it.[3]

I have argued elsewhere, in detail, that "rights come from wrongs"—"from human experience, particularly experience with injustice."[4] This point can be generalized beyond rights: Jurisprudence comes from experience, particularly negative experience. We build jurisprudence on the tragedies of the past in order to avoid their recurrence. Even in the Bible, the Ten Commandments of Exodus are preceded by the narratives of Genesis, narratives that described lawless human beings struggling to be just in the absence of rules or even role models. The jurisprudence of Exodus is built on the mistakes made by Cain, Lot, Abraham, Jacob, Joseph, even God in the narratives of Genesis.[5]

That is why I have waited until the final chapter to try to construct even a preliminary and tentative jurisprudence of preemption and prevention because it is essential first to narrate and critically to assess the history of these concepts, both ancient and modern. Nor is it possible to construct a full-blown and enduring jurisprudence even after a thoughtful review of the past. Jurisprudence is always a work in progress, based on assessments and reassessments of past experiences coupled with adaptations to ongoing experiences. Roscoe Pound put it well: "Law is experience developed by reason and applied continually to further experience."[6] Gods may be capable of revealing an enduring set of eternal laws from mountaintops, but humans can only struggle to cobble together ever-changing best efforts at regulating conduct through imperfect legislation and judicial interpretation.[7] Such efforts rarely produce perfect rules that are cost-free, but rather compromises that seek to balance costs, benefits, and other moral considerations. A Midrash has Abraham telling God, "If you want the world to exist, you cannot insist upon complete justice; if it is complete justice you want, the world cannot endure."[8] Jurisprudence is an imperfect and dynamic process, not a static result. The struggle to balance liberty and security never stays won.

Among the components of any jurisprudence are the mechanisms for making the kinds of balancing decisions that will inevitably be required; the checks and balances on any such mechanisms; a recognition that errors will inevitably be made; principles for weighing the costs of different types of errors in different contexts (false positives, false negatives); methods for allocating burdens of going forward and burdens of proof; default rules in situations of equipoise; consideration of absolute (or relatively absolute) prohibitions on, or requirements of, certain actions; efforts to integrate new jurisprudential rules into the traditional jurisprudence; processes for evaluation, reevaluation, and change of rules; theories of human action, of sanctions and of the values of life, security, and liberty; the inevitability of unintended consequences, unanticipated events, and unknown elements.

What is *not* needed to construct a jurisprudence in a diverse democracy is a *singular* philosophy. Nations or groups that have rested their jurisprudence on a single philosophical, religious, political, or social "truth" have tended toward tyranny. We should not strive for the uniformity of one absolutely correct morality, truth, or justice. I am speaking not of scientific or empirical truth, which may well be singular and uniform (though always subject to challenge and reformulation), but rather of moral truth, which is not nearly as objective. It does not follow from the absoluteness of empirical truths that there are absolute moral truths. The confusion grows, at least in part, out of traditional religions, which are based on assumed empirical truths—Moses received the commandments at Sinai, Jesus was resurrected, Muhammad ascended to heaven on his horse—and seek to derive from these alleged empirical truths such absolute moral truths as "Thou shalt not kill." But the absoluteness of moral truths is generally in the mind of the beholder. There are few, if any, moral truths (beyond meaningless platitudes) that have been accepted in all times and places. The active and never-ending processes of moralizing, truth searching, and justice seeking are far superior to the passive acceptance of one truth. The jurisprudencing process, like the truthing process, is ongoing. Indeed, there are dangers implicit in accepting, and acting upon, any one philosophy or morality. Conflicting moralities serve as checks against the tyranny of singular truth. I should not want to live in a world in which Jeremy Bentham's or even John Stuart Mill's utilitarianism reigned supreme to the exclusion of all Kantian and neo-Kantian approaches, nor would I want to live in an entirely Kantian world in which categorical imperatives were always slavishly followed. Bentham serves as a check on Kant and vice versa, just as religion serves as a check on science, science on religion, socialism on capitalism, capitalism on socialism. Rights serve as a check on democracy, democracy as a check on rights, jurisprudence serves as a check on realpolitik, and realpolitik as a check on jurisprudence.

Our constitutional system of checks and balances has an analogue in the marketplace of ideas. We have experienced the disasters produced by singular truths, whether religious, political, ideological, or economic. Those who believe they have discovered the ultimate truth tend to be less tolerant of dissent. As Thomas Hobbes put it, "nothing ought to be regarded but the truth," and it "belongeth therefore to [the sovereign] to be judge" as to that truth.[9] To put it more colloquially, who needs differing—false— views when you have the one true view? Experience demonstrates we all do! The physicist Richard Feynman understood the lessons of human experience as well as the limitations of human knowledge far better than the philosopher Hobbes when he emphasized the basic freedom to doubt, a freedom that was born out of the "struggle against authority in the early days of science."[10] That struggle persists, as we seek to construct a new jurisprudence to regulate an old phenomenon that has operated for centuries with few constraints.

Acknowledging the Phenomenon

The first step in constructing a jurisprudence to govern the use of a given governmental activity, such as preemptive or preventive self-defense, is to acknowledge the existence and possible legitimacy of that activity.

So long as nations are threatened by other nations or terrorist groups, preemptive or preventive military action will remain an option and will on occasion be employed. When international organizations are incapable of, or refuse to, intervene in situations where intervention is deemed necessary, nations will act unilaterally or with selected allies. That is the reality, and no jurisprudence will ever change that because a nation's survival is not, and never will be, purely a matter of law. No nation will ever commit "politicide" simply to avoid violating unrealistic and hypocritical laws. If a jurisprudence has any prospect of influencing the behavior of nations, it must reflect the reality that all nations will place their own survival and that of their citizens above any obligations to comply with international law, especially if other nations routinely ignore such law, treating it as merely hortatory or hypocritical. It is not particularly useful therefore to debate preemption or prevention as a yes or no, black or white, legal or illegal policy. Far more useful is the consideration of which factors should inform any decision on whether to act in anticipation of inchoate dangers and whether, and under what circumstances, such actions may properly include, for example, full-scale preemptive war of the kind initiated by the United States against Iraq in 2003, the kind of targeted killings of ticking bomb terrorists that Israel and the United States have employed, the multifaceted in-and-out type of strike currently being considered against Iranian nuclear facilities, or any other of the controversial mechanisms currently in use or contemplated for the future.

The Limited but Important Role of Jurisprudence in International Relations

Before we consider the factors that should become part of any jurisprudence of international preemption or prevention, it is important to answer the question earlier posed: In light of the reality that no nation will place its obligations to comply with international law above its obligations to protect its citizens and assure its own survival, is there any realistic prospect that a jurisprudence can be constructed that can actually influence the actions of nations that believe they are under the gun?

My answer is a "qualified yes," with equal emphasis on both words. I agree generally with the pithy assessment of Professor Louis Henkin: "It is probably the case that almost all nations observe almost all principles of international law and almost all of their obligations almost all of the time."[11] (I would disagree only with his inclusion of "almost all nations," since there are a considerable number of nations that simply disregard international law nearly all the time. I prefer to state the proposition in its more negative form: Almost no nations observe all the principles and all their obligations all the time. Our points are similar but differ in nuance.)

The likelihood that a nation will comply with international law increases as the law comes closer to reflecting reasonable reality. The law should not merely *follow* what nations would actually do in the absence of any legal constraints. Such a law would not influence behavior; it would merely mirror and legitimize existing behavior, whether it was reasonable or not. The Talmud says, "See how people act, and that is the law."[12] But such a law would merely be descriptive rather than prescriptive. The goal of international law should be to influence the behavior of nations at least near the margins, to nudge them in the right direction in close cases, to become one of the primary considerations in the decision on whether to act in certain ways under pressure. That is a modest but important goal. It is modest because it recognizes that law alone will never become the only factor in a nation's decision on when and how to defend itself in the face of a serious threat or in anticipation of a serious harm. It is important because if international law is to be taken seriously in *any* context, it must have some influence in *every* context, even the most extreme. It should never be ignored completely, as it often is today because of its merely hortatory and thus unrealistic nature.

An analogy to the law of domestic self-defense might prove instructive. Justice Holmes wisely observed that "detached reflection cannot be demanded in the presence of an uplifted knife."[13] In other words, when an assailant is threatening to kill an innocent person, that person will not necessarily focus on the intricacies of the law of self-defense in deciding how to respond. He will act immediately to save his own life. If the law required the person to try to reason with his assailant before drawing his gun and killing him, even if the delay caused by this requirement would increase his own chances of being killed, that law would be ignored because it does not reflect reality in imposing an unreasonable risk on the potential victim of an unlawful assault. But it does not follow from this extreme example that *all* laws regulating and even restricting the use of self-defense will always be ignored. Consider, for example, the current debate, stimulated by the National Rifle Association, over whether a person who is being threatened (say, by a slow man with a knife) should be obliged to retreat if he can do so with safety or is entitled to stand his ground and kill his assailant. The traditional rule has been that a threatened person need not retreat *from his own home* (presumably because of the protection afforded by familiar surroundings), but that if he can safely retreat *in a public place* (say, by getting into his car and driving away from an assailant on foot), he must do so before resorting to lethal force. The NRA is lobbying to allow anyone threatened to stand his ground and kill even on a public street and even if he can do so with safety.[14] "Law-abiding people should not be told that if they are attacked, they should turn around and run," an NRA lobbyist told Florida legislators, who approved a bill that would eliminate the duty to retreat. "This bill gives back rights that have been eroded and taken away by a judicial system that at times appears to give preferential treatment to criminals."[15]

The object of the law of self-defense is to influence conduct at the margins, to nudge individuals who are under immediate threat to act reasonably in close cases. States that insist on the obligation to retreat when retreat would not raise the risk of death do so for a reason: They wish to reduce the frequencies of deaths in such situations because they value life—even the life of the guilty assailant—over values such as machismo and even dignity. It may well be demeaning for a person to have to run away from an assault rather than stand his ground and confront his assailant by force, but being demeaned is less bad than killing if there is a realistic option. A person is allowed to take the law into his own hands only if there is no other alternative consistent with society's preference for the life of the innocent victim over the life of the guilty assailant, only if he finds himself essentially in "a state of nature," with no realistic recourse to the police or to self-help short of killing. If there is an alternative—even if it involves running away in a demeaning manner—that is to be preferred. At least that is the judgment of those who favor laws requiring retreat. Those who oppose such laws believe either that as an empirical matter more lives (or more innocent lives) will be saved by not requiring retreat or that as a normative matter it is wrong to require someone to retreat from an unlawful assailant. Both will agree, however, with the point most relevant to this discussion—namely, that even in the context of an uplifted knife the law is capable of influencing behavior at the margins, that at least *some* people may be influenced in *some* of their actions *some* of the time by whether the law does or does not require retreat.

If individuals can sometimes be influenced even in the presence of an uplifted knife, then it seems likely that nations, whose actions tend to be more deliberative, more calculated, and more communal, can also be influenced in situations of danger, even imminent danger, if laws that seek to influence them do not ask too much of them and are realistic and reasonable.

The analogy between the domestic law of individual self-defense and the international law of national self-defense is of course incomplete because there are so many crucial differences in context. One of the most challenging tasks in the construction of a jurisprudence for a discrete subject area, such as preemption and prevention, is to integrate it into the existing general jurisprudence. Analogy is a powerful tool in accomplishing such integration. The key to employing analogy fruitfully is to understand both the similarities and the differences between the areas to be analogized. It is to this question that we now turn, comparing and contrasting the law (to the extent it can be characterized as law) of anticipatory self-defense in the international sphere to the (fairly well-established) law in the domestic context.

The Analogy between International Self-defense and Domestic Self-defense

Just as there are differences between individual "retail" crime and group "wholesale" terrorism, so too there are differences between domestic and international law with regard to preemption and prevention. There seems to be an implicit recognition that the rules authorizing preventive self-defense among nations in the international arena is, and should be, different from the rules governing self-defense among individuals within a domestic legal system. International law recognizes anticipatory military actions under narrow but meaningful circumstances, whereas domestic law generally forbids any anticipatory self-defense, even if death is highly unlikely. For example, if a nation declares war on its enemy and masses troops at its border in anticipation of an imminent attack, the enemy has the right to strike first, as Israel did in 1967. Even reasonable advocates of the most restrictive views of anticipatory national self-defense would agree with Professor Myres McDougal's reading of the United Nations Charter:

> [U]nder the hard conditions of the contemporary technology of destruction, which makes possible the complete obliteration of

states with still incredible speed from still incredible distances, the principle of effectiveness, requiring that agreements be interpreted in accordance with the major purposes and demand projected by the parties, could scarcely be served by requiring states confronted with necessity for defense to assume the posture of "sitting ducks." Any such interpretation could only make a mockery, both in its acceptability to states and in its potential application, of the Charter's major purpose of minimizing unauthorized coercion and violence across state lines.[16]

On the other hand, if a Mafia capo puts out a contract on an enemy and hires a hit man to kill him, the enemy may not lawfully kill the hit man unless he is in the process of actually carrying out the contract. The difference is that in the Mafia case, the potential victim is required by the law to call the police, whose job it is to protect him and arrest his prospective killer. In the context of war, the potential victim state is also supposed to call upon the UN, and especially the Security Council, to protect it from attack. That at least is the theory. But the reality is that in many situations there is no police force capable of preventing the attack upon the victim nation. Self-help is often the only remedy, and it must include a reasonable opportunity to strike before being struck.[17] An analogy in the domestic context may be helpful. A battered woman is not authorized to engage in anticipatory self-defense by killing her batterer while he is asleep. She is supposed to leave and call the police. But until recently (and even now in some parts of the world) a battered woman could not realistically count on the police to prevent a recurrence of the battery or even an escalation that will place her life in jeopardy. Some jurors therefore have ruled in favor of battered women who took the law into their own hands and killed their sleeping batterers.[18]

The United Nations' Charter provides little guidance to the circumstances, if any, under which preemptive military action is lawful. Article 51 confirms "the inherent right of individual or collective self-defense if an armed attack occurs against a member." The use of the word "occurs" suggests that preventive self-defense against an imminent and certain attack is never lawful and that a member state must wait until an armed attack is actually initiated by an enemy. If this is the intended meaning of Article 51, then it is not only unrealistic, but also morally unacceptable, especially in an age of weapons of mass destruction, when a first strike can be catastrophic and make reactive self-defense more difficult or even impossible. Not surprisingly, Article 51, in its most restrictive interpretation, has been widely ignored. It is not law at all. It is merely hortatory, and it is bad hortatory to boot!

Under the literal meaning of Article 51, Israel's preemptive attack against the Egyptian and Syrian air forces in June 1967 would have been unlawful since Israel was not defending itself against an armed attack that had already occurred. The closing of an international waterway to Israeli shipping (which is a casus beli under customary international law but is not an "armed attack" under Article 51) would not have been enough. Nor would have the expulsion of UN peacekeepers, the massing of Egyptian troops along the Israeli border, or the specific threats of genocidal war that required Israel to call up its civilian reserves. An actual armed attack—an illegal first strike by Egypt that could have put Israel at a significant military disadvantage—was a necessary prerequisite for Israeli military action.

Israel did not wait for an actual armed attack to strike. It acted preemptively and was not condemned by the Security Council.[19] This inaction in the face of a preemptive attack may be seen as a confirmation of the lawfulness of the Israeli action, though it is always speculative to ascribe too much meaning to institutional inaction, especially by the Security Council with the potential veto power of all its permanent members.

One reason why Israel's preemptive attack may have escaped condemnation is that it may fall within the narrow criteria that had been articulated in the famous *Carolina* case in which U.S. Secretary of State Daniel Webster considered the legal status of a British attack on a ship, then moored in the United States, that was being prepared for use against the British forces in Canada. Webster justified the use of cross-border anticipatory force only when the "necessity of . . . self-defense is instant, overwhelming and leaving no choice of means, and no moment of delibera-tion."[20] This sounds very much like the domestic law of self-defense, but it has been interpreted more broadly because of the reality that most nations live in a state of nature when it comes to defending themselves from potential aggression. Though there is nearly always time for a "moment of deliberation," Israel was forced by the Egyptian actions to preempt what it reasonably believed, and what Egypt wanted it to believe, was an imminent and potentially catastrophic attack.

In December 2004 a report was issued by the United Nation's High-level Panel on Threats, Challenges and Change. This long-awaited and highly publicized report, by a group of distinguished international lawyers and diplomats, recommended significant changes in the Security Council's approach to the prevention of nuclear terrorism. It acknowledged that despite the "restrictive" language of Article 51, "a threatened state, according to long established international law, can take military action as long as the threatened attack is *imminent*, no other means would deflect it and the action is proportionate."[21] The former foreign minister of Australia Gareth Evans, who served on the panel that issued the report, argued against a restrictive, literal interpretation of the narrow words of Article 51:

It has long been accepted, both as a matter of customary international law predating Article 51 and international practice
since, that notwithstanding the language of the article referring
only to the right arising "if an armed attack occurs," the right of
self-defence extends beyond an actual attack to an imminently
threatened one. Provided there is credible evidence of such an
imminent threat, and the threatened state has no obvious alternative recourse available, there is no problem—and never has
been—with that state, without first seeking Security Council
approval, using military force "preemptively." If an army is mobil-
ising, its capability to cause damage clear and its hostile intentions unequivocal, nobody has ever seriously suggested that you
have to wait to be fired upon. In this sense, what has been
described generically as "anticipatory self-defence" has always
been legal.[22]

According to this view, Israel's preemptive attack of 1967 was
entirely legal, as would have been an Israeli preemptive attack in
the hours before the Yom Kippur War. The "problem," according
to the report, "arises where the threat in question is not imminent
but still claimed to be real: for example, the acquisition, with
allegedly hostile intent, of nuclear weapons-making capacity": the
Iraqi situation in 1981 or the current Iranian and North Korean
situation. Evans elaborated on this issue:

The problem arises with another kind of anticipatory self-
defence: when the threat of attack is claimed to be real, but there
is no credible reason to believe it is imminent, and where—as
linguistic purists insist—the issue accordingly is not preemption
but *prevention*. (The English language seems to be unique in
having two words here—"preemption" to describe responses to
imminent threats, and "prevention" for non-imminent ones:

that luxury, however, cherished though it may be by policy afi-
cionados who happen to be native English speakers, seems to
have done far more to confuse than clarify the debate for every-
one else, who tend to use the words, if at all, interchangeably.)
The classic non-imminent threat situation is early stage acquisition of weapons of mass destruction by a state presumed to be
hostile—the case that was made against Iraq by Israel in justifying its strike on the half-built Osirak reactor in 1981. . . .[23]

As we have seen, the Security Council condemned Israel for
its preemptive attack against the Iraqi nuclear reactor in 1981.
The condemnation was unanimous, with even the United States
joining. This would seem to suggest that all preventive attacks
against nonimminent threats, even of mass destruction, are
unlawful. Yet the United States threatened to attack the Soviet
missiles that had been placed in Cuba in 1962 and did attack Iraq
in 2003, at least in part to prevent the possible use of alleged
weapons of mass destruction in the uncertain future. Secretary-
general Kofi Annan declared the American attack "illegal" and in
violation of the UN Charter: "[F]rom our point of view and from
the Charter point of view it was illegal."[24] He did not issue that
declaration until eighteen months after the attack, and the
United States rejected his conclusion.

The United States has changed its view of the legality and propriety of the Israeli attack on the Iraqi nuclear reactor in the years
following the attack. In December 1991 Secretary of Defense
Dick Cheney gave the Israeli general who had organized the
attack on Osirak a satellite photograph of the destroyed reactor
with the following inscription: "With thanks and appreciation for
the outstanding job . . . on the Iraqi nuclear program in 1981,
which made our job much easier in Desert Storm."[25]

Although one of the chief authors of the UN report cited the

Israeli attack on the Osirak reactor as an example of a "classic non-imminent threat" by a hostile state, he would still deem such an attack unlawful under the criteria actually promulgated by the UN report. The same would be the case if Israel—or the United States—were to attack Iranian nuclear facilities, even as a last resort. Such preventive—as distinguished from preemptive, attacks would still be unlawful because even if the threat were certain and catastrophic, they were not imminent, and because they were not imminent, they could not lawfully be done *unilaterally*, without prior approval of the Security Council. This is how the report frames the question:

> Can a State, without going to the Security Council, claim in these circumstances the right to act, in anticipatory self-defence, not just pre-emptively (against an imminent or proximate threat) but preventively (against a non-imminent or non-proximate one)? Those who say "yes" argue that the potential harm from some threats (e.g., terrorists armed with a nuclear weapon) is so great that one simply cannot risk waiting until they become imminent, and that less harm may be done (e.g., avoiding a nuclear exchange or radioactive fallout from a reactor destruction) by acting earlier.[26]

The answer provided by the UN report is clear, if not entirely persuasive in all circumstances: "The short answer is that if there are good arguments for preventive military action, with good evidence to support them, they should be put to the Security Council, which can authorize such action if it chooses to. If it does not so choose, there will be, by definition, time to pursue other strategies, including persuasion, negotiation, deterrence and containment—and to visit again the military option."[27]

The report does not suggest what a country should do if all nonmilitary options fail and the Security Council refuses to authorize military action. Nor does it tell a country what to do if the *threat* itself is not imminent but the *opportunity* to prevent the threat will soon pass, as was claimed by Israel with regard to the soon-to-be-hot Iraqi nuclear reactor. The implication is that it should do nothing, at least not without Security Council authorization, until and unless it is attacked first or an attack becomes imminent.

The reason given for this answer is in the form of a "slippery slope" argument: "For those impatient with such a response, the answer must be that, in a world full of perceived potential threats, the risk to the global order and the norm of non-intervention on which it continues to be based is simply too great for the legality of unilateral preventive action, as distinct from collectively endorsed action, to be accepted. Allowing one to act is to allow all."[28]

Once again Evans elaborates:

The problem here is not with the principle of military action against non-imminent threats as such. It is perfectly possible to imagine real threats which are non-imminent—including the nightmare scenario combining rogue states, WMD and terrorists. The problem boils down to whether or not there is credible evidence of the reality of the threat in question (taking into account, as always, both capability and specific intent); whether the military attack response is the only reasonable one in all the circumstances; and—crucially—who makes the decision. The question is not whether preventive military action can ever be taken: it is entirely within the scope of the Security Council's powers under Chapter VII to authorise force if it is satisfied a case has been made (and the Council and others these days are quite properly giving increased attention, in relation to both WMD proliferation and terrorism, to circumstances in which such cases might be made). The question is whether military action in response to non-imminent threats can ever be taken *unilaterally*.[29]

The "biggest problem" with unilateral anticipatory self-defense in situations in which the threat is not imminent is that "it utterly fails to acknowledge that what is sauce for the goose is sauce for the gander, legitimising the prospect of preventive strikes in any number of volatile regions, starting with the Middle East, South and East Asia. To undermine so comprehensively the norm of non-intervention on which any system of global order must be painstakingly built is to invite a slide into anarchy. We would be living in a world where the unilateral use of force would be the rule, not the exception."[30]

The point is an important one that raises questions about the possibility of constructing a singular jurisprudence capable of governing all situations. We should heed the wise counsel of Giordano Bruno, a sixteenth-century philosopher, who cautioned that there is "no one law governing all things,"[31] certainly no one moral or jurisprudential law or even principle. There may be very general guidelines for conduct, such as those reflected in the story of the skeptic who asked Rabbi Hillel, who lived just before Jesus, to summarize the Torah while standing on one foot. Hillel provided the following translation: "What is hateful to you, do not to your neighbor. That is the whole Torah, while the rest is the commentary thereof . . ."[32] Nor should we simply accept self-serving conduct as an alternative to jurisprudence. A rule that authorizes any country to act unilaterally in cases of nonimminent danger, even nuclear danger, would indeed invite self-serving decisions, if not "anarchy." But a rule that requires nations to put their own survival in the hands of a potentially hostile international organization will simply not be followed. The concern is not so much with the rule in theory as with the failure to take into account the reality of how the Security Council is constituted and how it makes its decisions. The problem is more with the mechanism of applying and enforcing the jurisprudence than with the content of the jurisprudence itself.

The premise underlying the report's argument—that any government in reasonable fear of a relatively certain but not imminent nuclear attack can rely on the Security Council to prevent a catastrophe—is demonstrably false. That premise is that the members of the Security Council, particularly its members with the power to veto, would vote in accord with the *principles* governing preventive and preemptive self-defense. These principles, this attempt to articulate a jurisprudence, are set out in the report as follows:

> In considering whether to authorize or endorse the use of military force, the Security Council should always address—whatever other considerations it may take into account—at least the following five basic criteria of legitimacy:
>
> a) *Seriousness of threat.* Is the threatened harm to State or human security of a kind, and sufficiently clear and serious, to justify *prima facie* the use of military force? In the case of internal threats, does it involve genocide and other large-scale killing, ethnic cleansing or serious violations of international humanitarian law, actual or imminently apprehended?
>
> b) *Proper purpose.* Is it clear that the primary purpose of the proposed military action is to halt or avert the threat in question, whatever other purposes or motives may be involved?
>
> c) *Last resort.* Has every non-military option for meeting the threat in question been explored, with reasonable grounds for believing that other measures will not succeed?

   d) *Proportional means.* Are the scale, duration and inten-
      sity of the proposed military action the minimum nec-
      essary to meet the threat in question?

   e) *Balance of consequences.* Is there a reasonable chance
      of the military action being successful in meeting the
      threat in question, with the consequences of action not
      likely to be worse than the consequences of inaction?[33]

Whatever one may think of these principles in the abstract—
and they are quite abstract and subject to varying interpretations
in concrete cases—there is absolutely no evidence to support the
premise that Security Council members vote in accord with *any
principle* other than that of self-serving advantage and realpolitik
bias. The historical evidence is all to the effect that the Security
Council is not a principled institution, with constituent members
who vote on the basis of neutral or objective criteria of justice or
law. Professor Michael Glennon has realistically described existing international law: "[T]here is, today, no coherent international
law concerning intervention by states. . . . The received rules of
international law neither describe accurately what nations do, nor
predict reliably what they will do, nor describe intelligently what
they should do when considering intervention."[34]

    The decisions of the Security Council are in fact predictable,
but not on the basis of any legal or moral criteria. Instead they are
predictable on the basis of whose ox is being gored and which
entity is accused of goring it. There is an old story about a young
lawyer who finds two cases with exactly the same facts that were
decided differently. He asks his senior partner how this disparity
in results can be explained in light of the facts. "You've ignored the
most important facts," the more experienced lawyer quips. "The
names of the parties." Whether or not this is sometimes an exception to the rule of equal justice before courts of law—and it surely

is of at least some[35]—it is the *rule* in the Security Council. The names of the countries matter far more than their actions. Votes are traded, extorted, bought, and sold. That is the reality, as anyone who has studied the institution in operation will attest.

Despite having been a member of the United Nations since 1949, Israel has never been given the opportunity to sit on the Security Council.[36] Nor can it obtain protection from that body because of who does serve on it.[37] There was no realistic possibility that Israel could have ended the Iraqi nuclear program in 1981 through the Security Council. Nor could it have prevented it through diplomacy, which it tried for months without any prospect of success. The French, who were the primary suppliers of nuclear material to Iraq, simply refused to take any action that would have eliminated the dangers to Israel. Accordingly, Israel had only two options: allowing the Iraqis to develop an offensive nuclear capacity or destroying it unilaterally when they did. It made the right choice, the choice any other nation facing such options would have made. I am certain that Gareth Evans, when he was foreign minister of Australia, would have made the same choice in the absence of realistic alternatives. Indeed, Prime Minister John Howard of Australia told me during a meeting in his office in the spring of 2004 that if his nation could have prevented the devastating terrorist attack on Australian tourists in Bali in 2002, he would have authorized any reasonable military action, even if it had had to be taken unilaterally. He has announced that he would support launching preemptive military strikes against terrorists based in neighboring countries if they posed a threat to Australia, saying that "any Australian prime minister" would do the same. He has also called for a change in the UN Charter to allow a country to launch a preemptive strike against terrorists in other countries.[38]

The UN report fails to address the situation confronting a democracy with a just claim that is unable to secure protection

from the Security Council and that reasonably concludes that failing to act unilaterally will pose existential dangers to its citizens.
The report's deliberate refusal to consider this pressing issue rel-
egates its conclusions to the realm of academic debate—and not
very realistic academic debate at that. It also reveals an unwillingness by the United Nations to face up to its own shortcomings
and failures. Perhaps the best evidence of the current inability of
the UN to deal with dangers that may require preventive intervention lies in the tragic history of its impotence—as well as that
of the rest of the world—in the face of humanitarian threats to
millions of innocent people, especially in third world countries.

The Analogy between Humanitarian Preemption and Anticipatory Self-defense

We have seen that there are both similarities and differences
between anticipatory self-defense in the international and domestic contexts. The most significant difference is the absence of an
objective and effective mechanism for implementing any fair
jurisprudence. The absence of a jurismechanism necessarily influ-
ences the content of a jurisprudence, since no nation can fairly
be asked to put its survival, or the lives of its citizens, in the hands
of an institution that discriminates against it. We now move to the
analogy between humanitarian intervention and anticipatory self-
defense. Here too we shall see similarities and differences.

One of the most complex issues faced by a world power such
as the United States is whether and when to intervene militarily
to protect the lives of strangers, who live in faraway places and are
being threatened by their own governments. Genocides based on

ethnicity, religion, tribalism, and other factors have been all too common throughout history. In the twentieth century alone, genocide was committed against the Jews, Roma, Armenians, Cambodians, Sudanese, Rwandans, Bosnians, and Bangladeshis. All these could have been prevented, or at least reduced in scope, by preventive military intervention or other measures. Yet the world stood by silently and impotently as millions of people—children, the elderly, women, and men—were slaughtered. One important justification for the creation of the United Nations—and more recently of the International Criminal Court—was to prevent such genocides. But waiting for UN action has been a prescription for disaster. Sometimes the only effective preventive action that can be taken must be taken by individual world powers acting alone or acting in concert outside the official mechanisms of the UN.

What should the criteria be for such unilateral or multilateral "interference" with the "sovereignty" of a nation that is killing its own people? Recently much attention has been devoted to trying to answer this daunting question. The considerations are somewhat similar to those that should govern anticipatory self-defense, though they sometimes differ, because the self-interest of the intervening state is not as directly involved.

Many of those who are most adamantly opposed to military preemption or prevention based on anticipatory *self*-defense strongly favor humanitarian military preemption or prevention based on the need to defend *others*. The opposite is also true: Many who favor anticipatory self-defense oppose anticipatory defense of others. The issue has taken on a somewhat ideological or political coloration. Self-defense is seen as hawkish or conservative, while defense of others is seen as dovish or liberal.[39]

Samantha Power has summarized the dismal history, with a particular focus on the United States:

[T]he United States has consistently refused to take risks in order to suppress genocide. The United States is not alone. The states bordering genocidal societies and the European powers have looked away as well. Despite broad public consensus that genocide should "never again" be allowed, and a good deal of triumphalism about the ascent of liberal values, the last decade of the twentieth century was one of the most deadly in the grimmest century on record. Rwandan Hutus in 1994 could freely, joyfully, and systematically slaughter 8,000 Tutsi a day for 100 days without any foreign interference. Genocide occurred *after* the Cold War; *after* the growth of human rights groups; *after* the advent of technology that allowed for instant communication; *after* the erection of the Holocaust Museum on the Mall in Washington, D.C. . . .

What is most shocking is that U.S. policymakers did almost nothing to deter the crime. Because America's "vital national interests" were not considered imperiled by mere genocide, senior U.S. officials did not give genocide the moral attention it warranted. Instead of undertaking steps along a continuum—from condemning the perpetrators or cutting off U.S. aid to bombing or rallying a multinational invasion force—U.S. officials tended to trust in negotiation, cling to diplomatic niceties and "neutrality," and ship humanitarian aid. . . .

Simply put, American leaders did not act because they did not want to. They believed that genocide was wrong, but they were not prepared to invest the military, financial, diplomatic, or domestic political capital needed to stop it. The U.S. policies [were] not the accidental products of neglect. They were concrete choices made by this country's most influential decision-makers after unspoken *and* explicit weighting of costs and benefits.[40]

The issue of humanitarian intervention is complicated by many factors, among them the reality that a certain threshold of killings must be first reached before a conflict is deemed to be producing "genocide." In that respect humanitarian intervention is rarely pure preemption or prevention. The goal is to prevent *further* killings, but that should make intervention easier to justify since there is already a predicate of past crimes. Another complicating factor, one that cuts against intervention, is that the conflict is often internal, and the legal basis for intervening in internal disputes is more questionable than in international disputes. But analogies to domestic law do provide some basis for some intervention, and developing legal doctrines are strengthening it.

Domestic criminal law authorizes the use of force, even lethal force both for defense of self and for the defense of others. International law is less clear—at least with regard to the unilateral use of force. The United Nations claims a monopoly on the use of military force to prevent humanitarian disasters, such as genocide. In theory, there is no good reason why the UN could not act collectively to prevent such genocides as those committed in Rwanda and Darfur. But the UN has failed miserably in practice, and so have most world powers. A nation will more readily act preemptively or preventively to protect its own citizens and its own interests than to protect the citizens of other nations or to defend abstract principles of humanitarianism. This is especially so when the contemplated action places the lives of its own military personnel at risk. A president who sends American troops into harm's way had better be able to justify his decision by reference to some principle that is acceptable to the public.[41] In a democracy, military actions must be approved—if not initially, then certainly over time—by the citizenry. Self-interest is a pri-

mary motivator, though altruism can also stimulate action. Sometimes, of course, altruism can serve the national interests of a
world power, as the United States learned following the tragic
tsunami in December 2004. Aid to Muslim areas became part of
our war against terrorism.[42] Moreover, preventive self-defense
can be broadly defined so as to include military interventions
that seem at best quite distant from conventional self-defense.
The various domino theories that have been cited to justify wars
far from home illustrate this phenomenon. Thus the difference
between a preventive war of self-defense and a humanitarian war
in defense of others may often be a matter of degree or of articulated justification. Indeed, the invasion of Iraq was justified both
on grounds of self-defense against weapons of mass destruction
and on grounds of humanitarian intervention to prevent a tyrant
from continuing to kill and torture his own people. Neither justification turned out to be compelling, since no WMDs were
found and the invasion almost certainly caused more deaths
among Iraqi civilians than Saddam Hussein was likely to have
caused had he remained in power.

As we shall see in the pages to come, a new doctrine called
"the responsibility to protect" is in the process of being developed,
particularly in the context of humanitarian intervention. This doctrine challenges traditional notions of state sovereignty in situations in which a state is incapable of or unwilling to protect its
own citizens from such humanitarian threats as genocide, famine,
and ethnic cleansing. It has also been suggested that the jurisprudence that underlies this doctrine may provide analogous support
for a doctrine of anticipatory self-defense, particularly in the context of weapons of mass destruction.

An article in *Foreign Affairs* by two distinguished international
scholars, Lee Feinstein and Ann-Marie Slaughter, suggests a
framework for analyzing this issue as well as other preventive

actions. It begins by critically assessing the traditional concept of state sovereignty in the context of humanitarian intervention:

> In the name of protecting state sovereignty, international law traditionally prohibited states from intervening in one another's affairs, with military force or otherwise. But members of the human rights and humanitarian protection communities came to realize that, in light of the humanitarian catastrophes of the 1990s, from famine to genocide to ethnic cleansing, those principles will not do. The world could no longer sit and wait, reacting only when a crisis caused massive human suffering or spilled across borders. . . . As a result, in late 2001, an international commission of legal practitioners and scholars, responding to a challenge from the United Nations secretary-general, proposed a new doctrine, which they called "The Responsibility to Protect." This far-reaching principle holds that today UN member states have a responsibility to protect the lives, liberty, and basic human rights of their citizens, and that if they fail or are unable to carry it out, the international community has a responsibility to step in.[43]

This doctrine, they correctly observe, "took on nothing less than the redefinition of sovereignty itself" and requires "states to intervene in the affairs of other states to avert or stop humanitarian crises." The criteria or threshold for such preventive intervention will, of course, depend on the nature and degree of harm feared and the nature and degree of intervention required to stop or diminish the harm. But it is difficult to disagree with the concept itself—namely, that claims of sovereignty should not always trump humanitarian concerns when a nation inflicts grievous harm on its own citizens or residents.

The authors then proposed a "corollary principle" in the area of global security or self-defense:

. . . a collective "duty to prevent" nations run by rulers without internal checks on their power from acquiring or using WMD. For many years, a small but determined group of regimes has pursued proliferation in spite of—and, to a certain extent, without breaking—the international rules barring such activity. Some of these nations cooperate with one another, trading missile technology for uranium-enrichment know-how, for example. . . . These regimes can also provide a ready source of weapons and technology to individuals and terrorists. The threat is gravest when the states pursuing WMD are closed societies headed by rulers who menace their own citizens as much as they do their neighbors and potential adversaries. Such threats demand a global response. Like the responsibility to protect, the duty to prevent begins from the premise that the rules now governing the use of force, devised in 1945 and embedded in the UN Charter, are inadequate.[44]

This principle too challenges conventional notions of sovereignty:

The commission's effort[s] to redefine basic concepts of sovereignty and international community in the context of humanitarian law are highly relevant to international security, in particular to efforts to counter governments that both possess WMD and systematically abuse their own citizens. . . . We argue, therefore, that a new international obligation arises to address the unique dangers of proliferation that have grown in parallel with the humanitarian catastrophes of the 1990s. The duty to prevent is the responsibility of states to work in concert to prevent governments that lack internal checks on their power from acquiring WMD or the means to deliver them. In cases where such regimes already possess such weapons, the first responsibility is to halt these programs and prevent the regimes from transferring WMD capabilities or actual weapons. The duty to prevent would also apply to states that sponsor terrorism and are seeking to obtain WMD.[45]

As with regard to humanitarian intervention, so too with regard to preventing the spread of WMDs to nations likely to use them aggressively, the principle itself is not controversial: "The utility of force in dealing with the most serious proliferation dangers is not a controversial proposition."[46] Both the United States and European Union have asserted the power to act preventively against proliferation of WMDs. The controversial aspects of this policy revolve around several practical problems, primary among which is the propriety of a single nation's acting alone (or with an ersatz "coalition of the willing") rather than through the United Nations. The authors considered this issue and concluded: "Given the Security Council's propensity for paralysis, alternative means of enforcement must be considered. The second most legitimate enforcer is the regional organization[s]. . . . It is only after these options are tried in good faith that unilateral action or coalitions of the willing should be considered."[47]

This presumption in favor of collective action may seem reasonable when the United States is the nation at risk because we have power and influence, limited as they sometimes are, within the UN and other regional organizations. But it has little practical application to a nation such as Israel, which can never count on UN or regional support and must either go it alone—as it did in its 1981 attack on the Iraqi reactor—or with the support, often covert, of the United States. The United States too may, on occasion, have to go it alone (or relatively alone) when it alone is the target of the WMDs. It is important therefore to consider the appropriate criteria for preventive military self-help against the likely, though not imminent, development and deployment of WMDs. Feinstein and Slaughter suggested the following guidelines:

. . . the resort to force is subject to certain "precautionary principles." All nonmilitary alternatives that could achieve the same
ends must be tried before force may be used, unless they can
reasonably be said to be futile. Force must be exerted on the
smallest scale, for the shortest time, and at the lowest intensity
necessary to achieve its objective; the objective itself must be
reasonably attainable when measured against the likelihood of
making matters worse. Finally, force should be governed by fundamental principles of the laws of war: it must be a measure of
last resort, used in proportion to the harm or the threat of the
harm it targets, and with due care to spare civilians.[48]

These criteria would certainly seem to have justified Israel's
bombing of the Osirak reactor. Indeed, they seem to be based on
the specific facts of that case. In less than a quarter of a century,
therefore, a preventive military action that was unanimously condemned by the Security Council as in clear violation of the UN
Charter and customary international law has become the paradigm for proportional, reasonable, and lawful preventive action.[49]
It has become part of the emerging jurisprudence of preventive
military actions. Whether this jurisprudence would also justify, as
"a measure of last resort," a unilateral or bilateral surgical strike
against Iranian nuclear facilities is a more daunting question.

Absolute Prohibitions on Preemptive or Preventive Actions

One substantive choice that must be addressed by any jurisprudence is whether there are any preemptive or preventive actions
that should always be prohibited under all circumstances. Again,
an analogy might be instructive. In the debate over torture, it has

been plausibly argued that there should be no substantive jurisprudence of torture and no mechanism for ever authorizing it, even to gather intelligence believed necessary to prevent an imminent terrorist attack. Instead, a simple rule—namely, that all forms of torture must fall into one of those categories of conduct absolutely prohibited by moral principles and not subject to cost-benefit analysis—should be universally recognized. That would be the strictly Kantian position, as contrasted with the Benthamite view which justified the torture of convicted criminals to prevent harms worse than torture. (I have participated in this debate, and my views on it can be easily found.)[50] In addition to torture, there are other actions widely believed to be categorically unacceptable—for example, the deliberate targeting of innocent people. It is very likely that the killing of innocent people could be an effective means—perhaps even the most effective means—of preventing or deterring suicide terrorists who do not care about their own lives but might well be influenced by the threat of having loved ones killed. A former high-ranking government official told me that he heard the following account (which he could not independently confirm): At about the same time Middle Eastern terrorists were kidnapping American citizens in Lebanon during the 1980s, there was a kidnapping (or an attempted kidnapping) of a Soviet citizen. The KGB responded by murdering all the relatives of the suspected kidnapper. When the word got around that this would be the uniform response to all kidnappings, there were no more attempts to kidnap Soviet citizens. Whether this story is true or apocryphal, it makes the point: A nation that is prepared to use *any* means to prevent or deter suicide terrorism can be more effective than a nation that must fight "with one hand tied behind its back"[51] because of moral or legal constraints. It may well be that a case-utilitarian argument, weighing the cost and benefits of killing relatives *in one specific situation*, such as when a credible threat to kill one relative of the kidnapper could save the lives of ten kidnap victims, could be made for choosing the lesser of the evils. (If such a threat were deemed permissible, would it then be permissible to carry it out if the first suicide terrorist were not deterred—perhaps because he did not believe that a democracy would carry out such a threat— in order to assure the next terrorist that the threat was real?) It would be far more difficult, however, to justify such an action on a rule-utilitarian basis, weighing the costs and benefits of accepting a general rule permitting the killing of innocent relatives to save the lives of victims. That a democracy should not deliberately kill an innocent person seems to many to be one of those absolutes that should never be violated, regardless of the stakes. Attorney Nathan Lewin, who argued that killing the families of suicide bombers might be a necessary deterrent,[52] received harsh criticism for his stance,[53] including from me.[54] The intentional killing of an entirely innocent person is a line I do not believe a democracy should cross. Dostoyevsky posed the problem in a famous dialogue between Ivan Karamazov and his brother Alyosha in *The Brothers Karamazov*. Ivan put Alyosha to the test: "[I]magine that you yourself are building the edifice of human destiny with the object of making people happy in the finale, of giving them peace at last, but for that you must inevitably and unavoidably torture just one tiny creature, that same child who was beating her chest with her little fist, and raise your edifice on the foundation of her unrequited tears—would you agree to be the architect on such conditions? Tell me the truth." Alyosha replied without hesitation: "No, I would not agree."[55] The problem can be posed even more concretely in the context of the Holocaust. What if the Jewish underground had credibly believed that if by blowing up German kindergartens in Berlin, they could force the closure of the death camps—that the killing of a hundred innocent German children would save the lives of one million innocent Jewish children and adults? Would this be a morally permissible choice of evils? Kant would say no. Bentham would say yes. Alyosha would say no. Ivan would say yes. Those Jewish families that suffocated their own crying babies to prevent the Nazis from finding the rest of them said yes, and the rabbis agreed. The Catholic Church says no. This horrible no-win dilemma will never be resolved to the satisfaction of all moral people, but most will certainly agree that the willful killing of innocent people crosses a line that should be crossed, if ever, only in the most extreme situations. There are some, however, who argue that there is really no moral or practical difference between an action that willfully targets innocent people intending to kill them and an action that targets only the guilty but with full knowledge that innocent people will be killed "collaterally." The implications of this argument cuts both ways: For some the lack of a meaningful difference between willful and unintended killing of innocents cuts against the latter, while for others it cuts in favor of the former. The reality of course is that every society engages in self-protective actions against the guilty with full knowledge that some innocents may be killed in the process.

Although some have argued that preventive war, as distinguished from preemptive attacks, must be included among those actions that should always be categorically prohibited, that does not seem a plausible conclusion in an age of weapons of mass destruction, except if one engages in the word game of defining "preemptive attack" so broadly as to include at least some preventive wars. Certainly preemption is widely, if not universally, regarded as a proper option for a nation operating under the rule of law, at least in some circumstances—for example, when a threat is catastrophic and relatively certain, though nonimminent, and when the window of opportunity for effective prevention is quickly closing. Accordingly, we should now move to the next stage in constructing the jurisprudence—namely, to articulate principles, standards, and criteria for when preemptive action is warranted, as well as when and whether preventive war is justified.

Factors to Be Considered in Decisions to Engage in Preemptive and Preventive Military Action

If there are a wide array of preemptive and preventive actions that should be neither always prohibited nor always permitted, then it is essential that the criteria governing such actions be articulated and, to the extent possible, agreed to by the international community.

Primary among the factors that should be considered are the severity, certainty, and imminence of the threat, on the one hand, and the nature, scope, and duration of the contemplated preemptive actions, on the other. There is a considerable difference between a one-shot, decisive military strike, such as Israel's destruction of Iraq's nuclear reactor, and a full-blown military invasion followed by a lengthy occupation, such as the current situation in Iraq. Had the American military succeeded in its attempt to kill Saddam Hussein on the eve of the invasion, and had the subsequent invasion been deemed unnecessary, many people would have a different assessment of the propriety of such a preemptive strike. Even if the invasion had occurred, but without the need for a long-term occupation, there might be a different view.

Although the array of potential anticipatory military actions cannot be neatly lined up in a single continuum, it is possible to set them out in some orderly way, beginning with the least intrusive and moving to the most intrusive. The least intrusive end of any such continuum might consist of military or quasi-military actions that do not actually intrude physically into the territory of the enemy. These might include blockades and quarantines designed to prevent dangerous weapons or combatants from reaching the enemy. It might include security fences and other physical barriers on appropriate borders, as well as the mobilization of troops, no-fly zones, surveillance satellites, intelligence overflights, and spy networks.[56]

At the other end of the continuum would be full-scale invasions, occupations, destruction of the military capacity and infrastructure of the threatening enemy, and even nuclear attack.

Between these extremes lies a wide range of escalating military actions, including targeted killing of particularly dangerous individuals who qualify as "combatants," small-scale attacks on terrorist bases or other threatening enclaves, larger attacks against offensive weapons systems, and even larger-scale attacks on an entire air force, navy, or ground troops.

A related continuum would reflect the frequency of the preventive military action. Some require only a single attack, such as that which destroyed the Iraqi nuclear reactor.[57] Others require repeated attacks, such as the targeted killings of terrorists and their leaders. Some are episodic; others continuous, such as the building and maintaining of security barriers, checkpoints, and a long-term occupation designed to prevent remilitarization or the organization of terrorist cells.

Other obvious continua would relate to the certainty, severity, and immediacy of the feared attack. A one-dimensional standard of probable cause and imminence is inappropriate to the myriad risks that may be confronted by a democracy reasonably fearing a catastrophic first strike by an enemy. Even if the likelihood of a nuclear attack were statistically low—say, 5 percent—the number of casualties that could be inflicted in the unlikely event of such an attack must be factored into any moral or legal equation.[58] A small but significant risk of nonimminent nuclear attack may provide more justification for a preventive military action than would a large risk of an imminent but small-scale attack with conventional weapons. How to assess the appropriateness of preventive action designed to confront an unlikely but cataclysmic possibility is a daunting task. The likelihood of a false positive increases in proportion to the unlikelihood of the predicted event. But the risks involved in a false negative also increase. Much depends on the comparative consequences of false positives and false negatives.

To give an extreme example, if the military is seeking to test soldiers for eligibility to have access to a nuclear trigger, there is no real risk associated with false positives; it really doesn't matter how many soldiers are disqualified from such access since there is little stigma attached to disqualification and there is a virtually unlimited pool of potentially qualified soldiers. But the risk of false negatives is potentially catastrophic; giving an unstable or paranoid soldier access to a nuclear trigger could endanger millions of lives. It is a no-brainer, therefore, to err on the side of disqualification, all doubts should be resolved against a potential candidate. If there is even a 1 percent chance that a particular soldier might act irresponsibly, he should be assigned to less risky duty in which a mistake would cause little harm. This will result in a very high number of false positives (disqualified soldiers who would actually pose no risk), but it will also result in significantly diminishing the likelihood of false negatives (soldiers deemed qualified who would actually pose a risk). The trade-off is well worth it.

A counterexample was presented by an injunction granted during the 2004 Republican National Convention that prevented protesters from assembling in Central Park in New York City because there was a high probability that such a gathering would harm the grass in the park. Even if it were 95 percent likely that the grass would be damaged, that sort of damage is remediable, whereas the damage done to freedom of protest during a quadrennial presidential convention is irremediable. What Justice Louis D. Brandeis observed three-quarters of a century before the convention is as relevant today as it was then:

> [E]ven imminent danger cannot justify resort to prohibition of these functions essential to effective democracy, unless the evil apprehended is relatively serious. Prohibition of free speech and assembly is a measure so stringent that it would be inappropriate as the means for averting a relatively trivial harm to society. A police measure may be unconstitutional merely because the remedy, although effective as means of protection, is unduly harsh or oppressive. Thus, a State might, in the exercise of its police power, make any trespass upon the land of another a crime, regardless of the results or of the intent or purpose of the trespasser. It might, also, punish an attempt, a conspiracy, or an incitement to commit the trespass. But it is hardly conceivable that this Court would hold constitutional a statute which punished as a felony the mere voluntary assembly with a society formed to teach that pedestrians had the moral right to cross unenclosed, unposted, waste lands and to advocate their doing so, even if there was imminent danger that advocacy would lead to a trespass. The fact that speech is likely to result in some violence or in destruction of property is not enough to justify its suppression. There must be the probability of serious injury to the State. Among free men, the deterrents ordinarily to be applied to prevent crime are education and punishment for violations of the law, not abridgment of the rights of free speech and assembly.[59]

Justice Brandeis's reasoning is correct for two related reasons: First, the value we (and the First Amendment) place on freedom

of speech is so great—especially in the context of prior restraint—
that we properly demand that an extraordinary burden be met
before the government is empowered to censor, and second, this
burden simply cannot be met by invoking remediable risks to
property, such as trespassing or damaging the grass. Any contemplated governmental action that restrains the exercise of core
democratic liberties, such as freedom of speech or assembly, will
rarely be able to satisfy the stringent burden of proving that the
evil sought to be prevented is so serious, and so difficult to deter,
that the disfavored mechanism of prior restraint is constitutionally permissible. In this area, more than in others, we are willing
to tolerate many false negatives (speeches that we mistakenly
believe will not cause harm) in order to avoid even a small number of false positives (speeches that we mistakenly believe will
cause harm).[60]

There are, of course, obvious and important differences
between the stakes involved in ruining grass in a park and in preemptive or preventive military attacks. There are also differences
between full-scale military attacks, on the one hand, and focused
preemption, on the other. In deciding whether to authorize the
targeted killing of specific terrorists, especially if some "collateral"
deaths may result, various factors should be considered. They
should be as specific as possible. Some of the factors that should
go into a decision to engage in preemptive targeting include the
following:

How likely is it that the proposed target is a legitimate
   combatant?
   A.   Has he engaged in terrorism in the past? If so, how
        often and of what kind?
   B.   Is he currently involved in planning future terrorism? If
        so, how imminent? What is his precise role?

C. Will killing him prevent future acts of terrorism? Will it provoke other acts of terrorism?

D. How reliable is the intelligence on which the above assessments are made? Can accurate probability numbers be attached to them? If so, what are the probabilities?

Are there reasonable alternatives to killing him?

A. Can he be arrested or captured?

B. If so, at what risk to arresting soldiers or police officers?

C. Is he likely to submit to arrest or fight to the death?

D. If he does not submit, what is the likely casualty assessment?

E. What would be the political consequences of trying to apprehend him?

F. What would be the consequences of placing him on trial? Would it stimulate hostage-taking or other forms of terrorism?

How certain is it that the terrorist can be preemptively killed without undue risk to uninvolved others?

A. What is the likelihood that uninvolved enemy others may be killed or seriously injured if action is taken?

B. What is the likelihood that one's own civilians may be killed or seriously injured if action is not taken?

C. Can these risks to civilians—both enemy and one's own—be eliminated or reduced by placing the lives of one's own soldiers at risk?

D. How should a moral society compare the value of its own civilian lives to the value of enemy civilian lives? Of its own conscripted soldiers to enemy civilians? (The American decision to bomb Hiroshima and Nagasaki

was based explicitly on sacrificing Japanese civilian lives
to spare American military lives.)

E. Should the lives of all enemy civilians be valued the
same, or should a "continuum of civilianity" (or a
continuum of "involvement") be employed?

F. How reliable will any such continuum be, since it is far
more difficult to obtain reliable intelligence about
people marginally involved in terrorist activities.

G. Should it matter whether the dangerous actions being
undertaken by the target are legal or illegal (under the
domestic law of the state in which he is operating, under
international law, under the law of the targeting state)?

It would be virtually impossible in the real world to quantify
these variables with any degree of accuracy or precision, but it may
be valuable nonetheless to assign hypothetical numbers to them
for heuristic purposes.

Can a number be attached based on the reliability of intelligence,
the likelihood and imminence of the danger, the degree of
anticipated harm—e.g., 100 for 100 percent reliability, 100
percent certainty, 100 percent imminence, and 10 or more
certain deaths? This number would be reduced when
intelligence is less certain, harm is less imminent, and fewer
than 10 deaths likely (and raised if the number of likely
deaths to be prevented exceeds 10). A minimum total score
would be required for lethal action.

Can a number be assigned to the likelihood that the terrorist
could be apprehended without killing him or others?

A. Should different numbers be assigned to different
categories of potential casualties—e.g., the terrorist, his

supporters, police officers or soldiers, uninvolved adult
civilians, children?

B.   If so, what would these numbers be?

Can a number be assigned to the likelihood that uninvolved
persons may be killed or injured if targeted killing is
attempted?

A.   How many?

B.   How uninvolved on a scale of 10 (baby) to 1 (active
supporter)?

   A maximum total score would preclude action,
   except in extraordinary situations, such as nuclear
   terrorism.

Can the likelihood that uninvolved persons may be killed be
reduced by reducing the likelihood of killing the targeted
terrorist—e.g., smaller bomb, waiting for fewer people
nearby?

A.   How much of a reduction of collateral damage is
acceptable in order to reduce the likelihood of killing
the targeted terrorist by how much? This will depend on
the number assigned to the danger. The closer one gets
to 100, the higher the tolerance for the risks to
uninvolved people; the further one gets from 100 and
the closer to the minimum for action, the less tolerance
for the risks to uninvolved people.

I do not believe that these complex factors can be quantified in
real life with the degree of exactitude implied by the assignment
of numerical scores.[61] But it is a useful heuristic exercise to frame
the issues in a quantifiable manner so that rough weights can be
assigned to each of them. If the perfect is the enemy of the good,

then the exact is the enemy of the approximation, and approximation is often better than mere intuition in weighing choices of evil that involve assessments of risk and probabilistic outcomes.

This sort of exercise can be applied, with relevant adjustments, to other preemptive or preventive mechanisms, such as preventive detention, profiling, and quarantine. It is an important step in formulating a jurisprudence. Another essential step is to consider how to evaluate the costs in differing contexts of the mistakes that will inevitably be made. It is to that step that we now turn.

How to Think about Inevitable Mistakes

When the issue is one-dimensional—a simple prediction whether or not an individual (say, a suspected terrorist) will cause an identified harm (an act of terrorism) within a specified time period (say, a year)—the choices and outcomes can be represented by the following simple matrix:

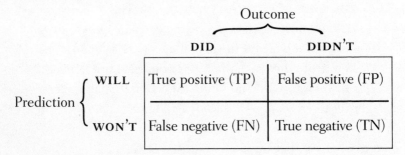

The words to the left of the boxes reflect the two predictions that can be made: (1) an individual will commit the harm or (2) he won't commit the harm. The words at the top of the boxes reflect the two possible outcomes (if we assume we can determine the actual outcomes): (1) he did commit the harm or (2) he didn't commit the harm. Combining the predictions with the outcomes produces four possible prediction outcome scenarios: If it is predicted that he will and he does, it is a true positive (TP); if it is predicted that he won't and he doesn't, it is a true negative (TN). Both these "true" scenarios represent accurate predictions. As for the possible inaccurate predictions, there are also two: If it is predicted that he will and he doesn't, it is a false positive (FP), and if it is predicted that he won't and he does, it is a false negative (FN). Sometimes as a matter of explicit policy we prefer one type of inaccuracy over another. For example, in the context of deciding if a criminal defendant committed the crime with which he stands charged, a guilty defendant who is wrongly acquitted is a false negative, whereas an innocent defendant who is wrongly convicted is a false positive. We prefer multiple false negatives to even a single false positive. This policy preference is encapsulated in the earlier cited principle that it is better that ten guilty defendants go free than that even one innocent defendant be wrongly convicted. (A similar preference governs decisions regarding prior restraint of speech, as illustrated by the quotation from Justice Brandeis.)

Numbers do matter, even in principled decisions, as Abraham reminded God during their negotiation over the sinners of Sodom.[62] It is right to shoot down a commercial jet with hundreds of innocent passengers in it if the jet is being flown toward a fully occupied large building that cannot be evacuated. That is so even if it is highly likely, but less than absolutely certain, that the plane is still in the hands of the hijackers. It is less clearly right to shoot down that same jet if it is being flown toward the Washington Monument at midnight when only a night watchman is in the monument. By similar reasoning, it is proper to bomb a military target close to a small number of civilians, but less proper to bomb a similar target adjacent to a large and fully occupied civilian hospital. That is the rule of proportionality enshrined in both morality and law. In a democracy these numbers, which reflect a society's values and preferences, should be decided by the people, subject to appropriate review by the courts. The maxim that it is better for ten guilty to go free than for one innocent to be wrongly convicted purports to reflect the values and preferences of most societies that operate under the rule of law.

There are several variables in the application of the maxim to suspected terrorists. The first is the number of potential victims if a false negative mistake is made—that is, if an actual terrorist is wrongly released. Consider the case of Mohamed Atta, who was allowed into the United States despite information linking him to terrorism. If he had been detained, it is certainly possible that the catastrophe of September 11 might have been averted. We will of course never know.

The failure to detain Atta was a failure of information coordination rather than a refusal to apply the maxim. But what if the relevant information had been known to those who did not detain him? To detain a suspect on the basis of the kind of vague and general information known to American officials would be to invite many false positive errors—that is, the detention of many people suspected of association with terrorism who, in fact, have no such association.[63] But that might be a cost worth incurring if it carried a significant possibility of preventing a mass-casualty terrorist attack.

This brings us to the second variable. If the consequence of a false positive error were to be the execution or targeted killing of an innocent person, that would raise the stakes considerably. But if the only consequence were a few weeks of erroneous preventive detention, unaccompanied by the risk of death or injury, the stakes would be considerably reduced. They do not, however, vanish. It is still costly, in moral as well as material currency, wrongfully to detain an innocent person for a matter of weeks. Those costs increase dramatically if the detained person is also abused, threatened, or tortured in an effort to elicit from him information about impending terrorist attacks. The costs also increase when those wrongly detained have been selected because they belong to a disfavored minority group, as occurs in racial, religious, or ethnic profiling. These and other costs must be weighed against the costs of a false negative error (the erroneous release of an actual terrorist). But who should be doing the weighing, and who should be striking the appropriate balance? This becomes a real challenge, especially when those who traditionally do the balancing represent the potential victims of false negative, rather than false positive, errors.

These are the kinds of issues we shall have to begin worrying about when potential terrorists with weapons of mass destruction pass through our legal system, as some inevitably will. We shall have to determine how many false positives we should be willing to tolerate in order to prevent how many false negatives. In order to implement any policy decisions we make in this regard, we shall also have to assess the accuracy of our predictive resources, accuracy in terms of correctly spotting potential terrorists and in terms of not incorrectly including innocent people in that target category. Although the maxim that prefers the acquittal of multiple criminals to the acquittal of one innocent is rooted specifically in the criminal trial, it has become a metaphor for the appropriate balance to be struck whenever security and liberty come into conflict. Whether or not the ratio should remain identical when different values are at stake, surely we must maintain our preference for liberty even in the face of the most pressing claims of security. But liberty, like security, is a matter of degree. It is also a matter of feel.

Preserving both the feel and the reality of freedom, when confronted with serious threats to security, is the true test of a democracy committed to the rule of law. Although freedom is more than the sum of individual restrictions and liberties, the specifics do matter, and our Constitution does impose constraints on some specific actions that a nation without a constitution might choose to take.

Accurately predicting retail harms by specific individuals is a difficult task, especially when the predicted act is infrequent. (In the first appendix to this book, I demonstrate this difficulty in the context of a specific predictive decision that was contemplated several years ago.)[64] The problem becomes even more difficult when the task is to predict the wholesale harms a nation or terrorist group may inflict in the absence of preventive steps as well as the harms that might be inflicted by taking preventive military action. The multiplicity of factors that must be considered in making such complex, conditional, and interactive predictions is difficult to enunciate and impossible to quantify with any degree of precision. Yet as I have previously argued, it is essential to try to think about these issues empirically as well as logically and morally.

Among the most difficult and complex decisions a democracy must make is whether to engage in a large-scale preventive or preemptive war of uncertain scope and duration. The considerations that must be factored into any such decision have been adumbrated earlier. The cost of making the wrong decision in a macromilitary context are far greater than the costs that are likely to be incurred in decisions involving individuals or small groups. That is even more reason for trying to articulate a jurisprudence of anticipatory self-defense for nation-states, as well as for trying to construct a jurismechanism to enforce the jurisprudence fairly.

Why a Jurisprudence of Preemption
and Prevention Is Needed

There is a desperate need in the world for a coherent and widely accepted jurisprudence of preemption and prevention, in the context of both self-defense and defense of others. There is also a pressing need for a neutral body or other fair mechanism to apply any such jurisprudence. Today both needs are lacking.[65] In the absence of a jurisprudence and jurismechanism, ad hoc decisions become the de facto rules.

A jurisprudence of preemption should be developed over time that reflects the multiplicity of factors that must be taken into account by decision makers contemplating preemptive-preventive military actions. It must also take into account the appropriate criteria for humanitarian intervention, either by the UN or by individual nations when collective action is impractical. These decisions should not be ad hoc, because decision makers tend to overvalue the risks to themselves and undervalue the costs to their enemies or others. Moreover, ad hoc decisions are generally made during a crisis when it is difficult to balance competing considerations. The virtue of a preexisting, widely accepted jurisprudence is that it can serve as a check on impulsive ad hoc decision making during crises. A related virtue of a preexisting jurisprudence is that it can be devised in a more neutral manner before it can be known who will be its immediate beneficiaries.[66] An ad hoc jurisprudence, on the other hand, tends to be a result-oriented rationalization for actions already decided upon. Objectifying the criteria will not necessarily eliminate this inherent bias, but it will at least require democracies that care about complying with legal and moral norms to justify their actions against some external standards that have been agreed to by outside sources.

The problem with objective standards, equally applicable across the board, is that neither all nations nor all leaders are equal when it comes to the actual danger presented by their access to WMDs. (The same is true of individuals in the context of self-defense.) Though neutral ex ante rules can reflect these differences to some degree, it is impossible for them to reflect the nuances that may be clear to all during an ongoing crisis. That is not a reason for dispensing with all efforts to formulate rules. It is merely a caveat calling for rules with some open-endedness that permit the exercise of reasonable discretion and flexibility in their application.

The need for a jurismechanism, a widely accepted and respected multinational institution capable of applying the jurisprudence to specific threats, is equally pressing and far more difficult to satisfy. The UN as presently constituted is not such an institution, especially when it comes to such unpopular nations and groups as Israel, Armenia, the Kurds, and Tibet (as contrasted with Palestinians, for example). Nor is the International Court of Justice in The Hague such a neutral tribunal; it is a UN organ, many of whose "judges" simply "vote" the narrow interests of their governments. Professor Eric Posner has documented this sad reality:

Why have countries abandoned the [International Court of Justice]? The most plausible answer is that they do not trust the judges to rule impartially, but expect them to vote the interests of the states of which they are citizens. Statistics bear out this conjecture. When their home countries are parties to litigation, judges vote in favor of them about 90 percent of the time. When their states are not parties, judges tend to vote for states that are more like their home states. Judges from wealthy states tend to vote in favor of wealthy states, and judges from poor states tend to vote in favor of poor states. In addition, judges from democracies appear to favor democracies; judges from authoritarian states appear to favor authoritarian states. This is not to say that the judges pay no attention to the law. But there is no question that politics matter. [67]

There is no realistic likelihood that this situation will improve any time soon. This reality does not obviate the need for substantive jurisprudence, it makes it even more compelling. A widely accepted international jurisprudence will impose domestic constraints on the unilateral actions of democracies committed to the rule of law since accepted international law is becoming part of the domestic law of many democracies.[68]

But the status of current international law remains seriously flawed. The Security Council's anachronistic mid-twentieth-century view of international law precludes a democracy threatened with nuclear annihilation (promised by religious Islamic zealots like those in charge of Iran) from taking proportional, preventive military action to dissipate the threat to its civilians. Under this benighted view, the United States, Russia, or Israel would not be able to take proactive steps against terrorist groups operating openly in foreign countries that threaten its civilians. They would have to wait until the terrorists attacked first, even if they were suicide bombers. At the very least they would have to wait until such an attack was imminent—if that could be known. This unrealistic perversion of international law must be changed to take into account situations in which deterrence simply cannot be counted on to work or where carrying out the deterrent threat would kill millions of innocent civilians. Democracies must be authorized to take preemptive military actions against grave threats to their survival or to their civilian population. As one commentator has put it, international law must not be deemed a "suicide pact."[69] It must authorize anticipatory self-defense when a nation reasonably believes that its "survival is at stake"[70] because "the survival of states will never be regarded as a matter of law."[71]

Although the difference between a surgical preemptive attack and an all-out preventive war is a matter of degree, and both are points along a wide continuum of anticipatory military actions, it is important to distinguish between these very different means of preventing anticipated harms. A threat that might justify the former would not necessarily justify the latter. Nor should employment of the former always be deemed unlawful because of fear that the slippery slope will inevitably lead from the former to the latter. Calibrated military preemption should be deemed lawful and morally proper when it is the only realistic alternative to absorbing an unacceptable first strike. As the risks grow more unacceptable, the level of lawful preemptive action should be authorized to move along the continuum, closer to full-scale preventive war.

Although military preemption has gotten a bad name among some following the attack on Iraq, it must remain an option in situations in which deterrence is unrealistic and the threat is sufficiently serious.[72]

Can a Comprehensive Jurisprudence of Prevention Be Developed?

It is now appropriate to return to the question posed in the Introduction. Do such apparently diverse preventive mechanisms as profiling, preventive detention, anticipatory mass inoculation, prior restraint of dangerous speech, preemptive military actions of various kinds, and full-scale preventive war share enough elements that a common, if rough, jurisprudence can be developed to help clarify the balancing judgments that must be made before those preventive actions are deemed justified? To put it more simply, is it possible to articulate a consistent and workable jurisprudence of a wide range of anticipatory governmental actions? Recall that although we do have a rough jurisprudence for one particularly serious type of after-the-fact governmental action, the imposition of criminal punishment, that jurisprudence is not generally deemed automatically applicable to all other serious after-the-fact governmental sanctions. The courts have distinguished, not always wisely, between criminal punishment and every other sanction, regardless of how punitive the sanction may feel to the one on whom it is imposed. This legal labeling game, as I have called it,[73] purports to derive its rules from the words of the Constitution and from the history of the common law.[74] Whatever its source, it produces results that often make little functional sense. As I have written elsewhere about the civil-criminal labeling game:

> The object of the civil-criminal labeling game is simple: the court must determine whether certain procedural safeguards, required by the Constitution in "all criminal prosecutions," apply to various proceedings. The rules are a bit more complex. The legislature enacts a statute that restricts the liberty of one player—variously called the defendant, patient, juvenile ward, deportee, et cetera. That player must then convince the court that the formal proceeding through which the state restricts his liberty is really a criminal prosecution. The state, on the other hand, must show that the proceeding is really civil. For support it often claims that the results of the proceeding help, rather than hurt, its opponent.
>
> In the course of this game's long history, prosecutors have succeeded with the help of the court, and all too often, without

the opposition of "defense" attorneys, in attaching the civil label
to a wide range of proceedings including commitment of juve-
niles, sex psychopaths, the mentally ill, alcoholics, drug addicts
and security risks. Likewise, sterilization, deportation, and revo-
cation of parole and probation proceedings are regarded as civil.
By attaching this label, the state has successfully denied defendants almost every important safeguard required in criminal trials. Invocation of this talismanic word has erased a veritable bill
of rights. As Alice said, "That's a great deal to make one word
[do]." To which Humpty Dumpty responded: "When I make a
word do a lot of work like that . . . I always pay it extra." Until
quite recently, this word must have been well paid indeed, for it
was doing the work of an army of jurists.[75]

Another labeling game more recently played by the Supreme
Court involves the distinction between regulatory and punitive
sanctions, as well as between preventive and punitive sanctions.
This is what the late Chief Justice William Rehnquist wrote in the
context of ruling that the pretrial preventive detention in a maximum security jail of a Mafia boss was not criminal punishment:

> As an initial matter, the mere fact that a person is detained does
> not inexorably lead to the conclusion that the government has
> imposed punishment. . . . To determine whether a restriction on
> liberty constitutes impermissible punishment or permissible reg-
> ulation, we first look to legislative intent. . . . Unless Congress
> expressly intended to impose punitive restrictions, the puni-
> tive/regulatory distinction turns on "whether an alternative pur-
> pose to which [the restriction] may rationally be connected is
> assignable for it, and whether it appears excessive in relation to
> the alternative purpose assigned [to it]. . . ."

Having set out these relatively meaningless criteria, the Court then applied them in a wooden manner that has broad and dangerous implications for other preventive mechanisms. It concluded:

> [T]he detention imposed by the Act falls on the regulatory side of the dichotomy. The legislative history of the Bail Reform Act clearly indicates that Congress did not formulate the pretrial detention provisions as punishment for dangerous individuals. . . . Congress instead perceived pretrial detention as a potential solution to a pressing societal problem. . . . There is no doubt that preventing danger to the community is a legitimate regulatory goal. . . . We have repeatedly held that the Government's regulatory interest in community safety can, in appropriate circumstances, outweigh an individual's liberty interest. For example, in times of war or insurrection, when society's interest is at its peak, the Government may detain individuals whom the Government believes to be dangerous. . . . Even outside the exigencies of war, we have found that sufficiently compelling governmental interests can justify detention of dangerous persons.[76]

This dichotomy between punishment, on the one hand, and "a potential solution to a pressing societal problem," on the other, fails to acknowledge the reality that punishment often *is* the solution to pressing social problems and that such solutions are often punitive in every sense of that word. Similarly, the purported dichotomy between "punishment for dangerous individuals" and "preventing danger to the community" fails to recognize the overlapping nature of these related mechanisms of social control.[77] In any event, these labeling games merely lead to the result-oriented negative conclusion that the constitutional jurisprudence governing criminal punishment is *not* applicable to preventive, preemptive, or other "regulatory" mechanisms, even when the look, smell, and sound are the same as criminal punishment. The cases that rely on these false dichotomies generally fail to articulate an alternative jurisprudence that should govern preventive or preemptive sanctions.

Since no meaningful jurisprudence of preemption or prevention has been constitutionalized—at least not to the extent that the criminal punishment system has been over the years—there exists more constitutional flexibility to devise and articulate a coherent, consistent, and functional jurisprudence of anticipatory governmental actions. Yet little has been done to fill this important need.

In order to construct a jurisprudence, one should first *complexify*, to assure that all the elements that warrant consideration are included. The next step is to try to *quantify* these elements, at least for heuristic purposes, in order to assess the proper weights that should be accorded to each. We should then *qualify* these results with the recognition that in real life there are too many ineffable factors to permit specific numbers to be assigned to the elements that should go into any preemptive or preventive decision. Finally, in order to make it feasible for decision makers to apply the jurisprudence to real-life decisions, we must *simplify* the above, recognizing that the law is a blunt instrument rather than a scalpel.

With these general considerations in mind, let us return to the original question, in its simple form: Is it possible to articulate a consistent and workable jurisprudence of anticipatory governmental action? The answer, I believe, is a qualified yes. Throughout this book and especially in this chapter, I have sought to outline such a jurisprudence. This outline is merely suggestive and general, since any systematic jurisprudence requires development over time and continuous testing by application to concrete situations. It requires democratic input from the citizens on the values and priorities of the society. With these caveats in mind, let us consider some of the broad elements that should go into a jurisprudence of prevention.

An important element of any jurisprudence relates to the burden of going forward. This burden is a reflection of several factors. What should the default position be? What are the comparative costs of the inevitable mistakes that will occur if action is taken or not taken? How should the costs of these variables be allocated? Should the burden be the same for all preventive decisions? Or should it depend on the values at stake in each category of cases? Who should decide these issues? Who should review such decisions?

I believe that most reasonable people will agree that in general a heavy burden must be borne by those advocating preventive governmental actions of the sorts discussed in this book. All such actions involve the imposition or at least risk of imposition of significant costs in terms of liberty, health, life, and other values. The highest potential costs are of course imposed by such macro actions as full-scale preventive war and preemptive military actions. But costs measured in lives and health are also at stake in mass inoculation programs, targeted killings, and other smaller-scale preventive interventions. Costs measured in dignity, liberty, and freedom are involved in any profiling, detention, or censorship decisions.

On the other side of the ledger are the costs—also measured in life, health, dignity, liberty, and freedom—of not taking preventive measures. In any situation, the costs of inaction may exceed the costs of action. But that does not necessarily mean there should not be a heavy burden of going forward with any preventive or preemptive action. It only means that the burden will be more easily met when the costs of inaction are very great. The bur-

den should remain high whenever the government is contemplating preventive action that poses significant risks to life, health, dignity, liberty, or freedom, if for no other reason than to demand
caution whenever the stakes are high and the likelihood of error
great. There are also other reasons, some of which have been previously suggested: There are dangers implicit in any allocation of
power to the government to intervene in the lives of people before
a harm has occurred. Requiring a harm, or at least a specified act,
as a precondition for the exercise of certain governmental powers
serves as an important check on the abuse of such powers. That
is why after-the-fact deterrence, rather than before-the-fact prevention, has generally been the default position in democracies.
Any government seeking to act contrary to this democratic norm
should have to satisfy a significant burden. The burden should be
especially high whenever a government is contemplating preventive action taken in self-defense against perceived enemies
because governments will generally overestimate (or overstate) the
dangers to themselves and their citizens while underestimating (or
understating) the risks to those who are perceived as posing the
danger. The burden should be somewhat lower when the contemplated action is humanitarian in nature—that is, designed to
protect others—because the risks of over- and underestimation
are not as great. The same may be true when a democracy is contemplating preventive action against all or large segments of its
own citizens, actions such as mass inoculation or quarantine. The
risks of over- and underestimation are also not as great in such situations, so long as no invidious factors, such as race, religion, ethnicity, and national origin, are being employed.

There is in Harvard Square a sign by an environmental group
that reads: INDICATION OF HARM, NOT PROOF OF HARM, IS OUR CALL
TO ACTION. This is, essentially, the precautionary principle, as
developed in Europe, primarily in the context of environmental

and other related hazards. The action contemplated by this group is also preventive, but it does not necessarily involve the same sorts of risks to life or liberty that are entailed in anticipatory self-defense. It seems to be limited to expenditures of money, legislative restrictions on pollution, and the like. The burden of going forward with these kinds of actions should of course be lower, as should the burden on private, as contrasted with governmental, actions.

The burden should be highest when the government contemplates action that endangers innocent lives, even if it does so to protect innocent lives. That heavy burden should be most readily satisfied by a showing that failure to take the action endangers even more innocent lives. The lives of innocent civilians should be valued more highly than the lives of aggressors or military enemies. Reasonable people can disagree about what comparative value to place on the lives of one's own soldiers as compared with the lives of enemy civilians. (This calculus may well depend on the precise nature of the civilian's "civilianality": Is he a baby or a totally uninvolved adult? Or is he an active supporter of the aggressor?) These kinds of judgments should be made democratically and with accountability.

The burden should be somewhat lower when the contemplated action endangers liberty and other important values, but not life. Moreover, if the contemplated action has a high likelihood of saving civilian lives at the potential temporary cost of some liberty (or other important values short of life), then the value of the saved lives should generally be deemed higher than the value of the lost liberty.

Because the values vary so greatly in each situation, it is impossible to come up with an aphorism analogous to the "better ten guilty" rule that mandates the very high burden of proof in criminal cases. But if one could hold constant the values at stake—say, one life for one life or one "unit" of liberty for one "unit" of liberty—it might be reasonable for a democracy to try to attach a number to the burden. It is not better that the government risk killing one innocent civilian in order to potentially save one other innocent civilian. Inaction in the face of equipoise is probably wise counsel. But what if risking the life of one innocent civilian were required to save potentially two or three or five innocent civilians? Is that ratio high enough to justify highly risky, but potentially beneficial, preventive action? How much weight should be accorded the default position of inaction? Of the law of unintended consequences? Of inevitable errors in the calculation of probabilities? Of the moral cost of the government's ever taking lives? Of the moral distinction, sometimes made, between culpability for acts and omissions? Of the psychological burden of responsibility for actively taking a life?

The answers to the questions will vary with the different values at stake in different kinds of preemptive and preventive decisions. Some suggested answers have been outlined in prior pages on which the relevant factors were enumerated and even quantified (for heuristic purposes). To that extent, a single narrow jurisprudence will not adequately cover the diverse array of preventive mechanisms now in use and likely to be introduced in the future. But this is true, to some degree, of after-the-fact deterrence sanctions as well. There *is* no one law governing all things.

Other than the "better ten" rule and some constitutionally required procedural safeguards, the wide array of different tragic-choice-of-evils questions posed by after-the-fact sanctions are also not amenable to a single, narrow jurisprudential answer. But the broad issues involving the allocation of burdens and the acceptable ratios of false positives and negatives do have some common denominators.

These are the sorts of choice-of-evil questions too rarely

debated openly in democratic societies. We answer them more often implicitly by our actions than explicitly by our votes.[78]

Every time a government acts preventively in a manner that implicates life and liberty, it implicitly answers these and other daunting questions about values. It is the role of a jurisprudence to force these value choices into the open, so that they can be made explicitly and democratically. The specific numbers—the acceptable ratios of false positives to false negatives—must ultimately be assigned by the people. The choices will often be painful ones that most people would prefer not to have to make. But that option is unavailable, since inaction too is a choice of values, as Samantha Power has so powerfully argued in the context of our collective failures in preventing genocide.[79]

Other choices, beyond those involving burdens and how to meet them, relate to permissible and impermissible preventive mechanisms for democratic societies committed to the rule of law. Just as not every after-the-fact punishment is permissible, regardless of its effectiveness, so too not every preventive mechanism is permissible, even if it is believed to be quite effective. Democracies must indeed fight terrorism and other evils with one hand tied behind their backs.

It is the role of a jurisprudence to draw difficult lines, to choose between evils, to make such tragic choices—or at least to establish frameworks and mechanisms for making and reviewing these kinds of decisions.

In the end any jurisprudence will inevitably reflect the broad value choices of a society. In eclectic, heterogeneous democracies, no jurisprudence will ever reflect a single ideology or worldview. Nor should it. It should incorporate Benthamite utilitarian principles that weigh costs against benefits, but it should also reflect some Kantian imperatives and absolutes. The experiences of the diverse peoples and groups that constitute any polity must figure into any widely accepted jurisprudence. Process, politics, and compromise will produce some inconsistency, as they have in every other area of governance. The jurisprudence that emerges will be a work in process, a dynamic process rather than a static product. If a camel is a horse produced by a committee, then the resulting jurisprudence may resemble a lumbering dromedary more than a sleek equine. But we live in a barren desert today when it comes to the rules governing preemption and prevention. A camel would be a useful start.

In August 1972, I wrote an article for the American Bar Association Journal *that dealt with the mathematics of prediction and especially the difficulty of accurately predicting relatively rare events without incurring large numbers of false positives. In 1975, I applied my analysis to the use of karyotypes in predicting criminal behavior. I reproduce these articles here (in slightly edited form) because they are relevant to many decisions involving preventive or preemptive governmental actions based on probabilistic predictions.*

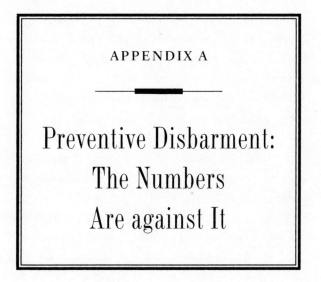

APPENDIX A

Preventive Disbarment: The Numbers Are against It

I n the early 1970s—during the heyday of the civil rights and antiwar protests in which many lawyers participated—a committee of the Section of Legal Education and Admissions to the Bar of the American Bar Association recommended that research studies be undertaken "to determine whether character traits can

be usefully tested prior to application for admission to the bar. . . ."
The following studies were specifically proposed:

> A. An interdisciplinary inquiry into what is now being done or
> projected in other professions or businesses: . . .
> > (1) To identify those significant elements of character that
> > may predictably give rise to misconduct in violation of
> > professional responsibilities.
> > (2) To estimate the capacity of those inimical elements to
> > persist despite the maturing process of the individual and
> > the impact of the stabilizing influence of legal education.
> B. A "hindsight" study of selected cases of proved dereliction of
> lawyers to ascertain whether any discoverable predictive
> information could have been obtained at the law student
> level by feasible questionnaires or investigation; and if so,
> what type of inquiry would have been fruitful.

The stated objects of these studies are to determine whether
it is "within the present state of the art to devise a test which can
be administered to 35,000 or 40,000 22-year-old men and women
each year and which will develop any genuinely useful information as to their future conduct and integrity in the practice of law?"
Presumably, if an "accurate" predictive test can be devised, it
would be used preventively against persons "who in fact have
character deficiencies which would deny them admission or
which in later years would lead to disciplinary action by the bar."
The report continued: "This in turn would avoid the distressing
and sometimes tragic problem of a student becoming aware of this
hurdle only after he has invested three or four years of his life in
acquiring a legal education."

The report, which was approved by the council of the Section,
did not specify the precise consequences that might follow from

predicted "future derilections." It simpy proposed "leaving to the 50 jurisdictions whatever supplemental inquiry or investigation each might wish to make. . . ." But the concerns that appear to have given rise to the proposal suggest that those who "fail" the predictive test might be weeded out of the "competition for a legal education and ultimate admission to the bar" at an early state or might be "deterred" from entering the competition. The report cited the growing number of applicants for the approximately 36,000 first-year law school seats (80,000 in 1971 and 100,000 in 1972). These figures, according to the report, "have raised increasing concern over the adequacy of present procedures to be sure that those best qualified, both from the standpoint of intellect and motivation and from the standpoint of proper moral character attributes, are the ones who succeed in the competition for a legal education and ultimate admission to the bar."

The committee acknowledged that it did not know the answer to the question it posed: whether an accurate predictive test can be devised. Pointing to the work that is currently "going on in a variety of fields to come up with some answers to the enigma of predictability of human behavior," it conceded that it "certainly is not adequately informed as to the nature of success of such efforts." It expressed the hope, however, that the studies it has proposed "might move [the committee] from sheer guesswork and individual opinion to a more solid footing."

What Is the Feasibility of Carrying Out These Studies?

The report raises many troubling issues of policy and constitutionality, some of which were discussed in a letter to the President of the American Bar Association from the deans of eight leading law schools. This article will not, however, consider those issues; it will focus instead on the empirical feasibility of carrying out studies of the kind proposed and on the utility of the results that the studies might produce. I respectfully offer some caveats in the hope that they may contribute—albeit in a limited way—to the consideration of the committee's proposal or other similar proposals.

The report suggested that the "career background of selected offenders" be studied in depth in order to determine "whether there are any patterns or discernible factual matters which might have been discovered at the time of admission to law school and upon which probable future derelictions could have been predicted."

Hindsight studies of this kind, if properly conducted, are a useful first step in the construction of a prediction index. But no hindsight study of an offender group can by itself produce reliable predictive criteria. Even if a study were to reveal that every past offender possessed certain characteristics in common, it would still not follow that all—or even most—persons who possessed them would become offenders.

This is so for two important reasons. First, these characteristics may not be sufficiently discriminating: that is, they might not only be present in all or most offenders but also in a substantial number of nonoffenders. For example, it may well be true that a large percentage of present heroin addicts previously smoked marijuana; but it is also true that a very small percentage of marijuana smokers become heroin addicts. It may be true that a significant percentage of certain kinds of criminals have XYY chromosomes; but it does not follow that a significant percentage of persons with those chromosomes will become criminals.

The second reason is that the characteristics the study succeeded in isolating might be associated with offenders only in the small past sample and not generally with offenders in other population groups. The sample employed in the hindsight study may have been unique in certain respects. For example, the famous hindsight study of delinquency conducted by Professors Sheldon and Eleanor Glueck was conducted among Boston immigrants of predominantly Irish descent. Considerable doubts have been expressed about its applicability to other populations. The risk of uniqueness is especially great if the original sample is relatively small, as it would necessarily be in the study at issue. Moreover, the characteristics associated with offenders may change over a period of time, especially when attitudes are changing as quickly as they seem to be at present.

Before data derived from a hindsight study can validly be applied to other populations, a prospective validation study should be conducted. The predictive characteristics derived from the hindsight sample should be applied to another population that includes potential offenders and nonoffenders. On the basis of these characteristics, predictions should be made about the future performance of the members of the new group, but these predictions should be kept secret. If they were revealed—to predicted offenders or bar association officials—the validation study would be skewed by the power of self-fulfilling prophecy.

The careers of the new group should then be followed over a number of years—ideally an entire professional career, but at least ten or fifteen years. The actual performance of the group then would have to be matched with the predictions. Only then could it be determined—and even then only tentatively—whether the factor or factors associated with offenders and nonoffenders in the hindsight group were truly characteristic of the general relevant population.

Another but less reliable validation technique would be to apply the predictive characteristics derived from the original sample study to other "past" groups that included both offenders and nonoffenders. If the characteristics succeeded in "postdicting" the past offenders, then there would be some assurance that the original group was not unique.

If the data from a hindsight study were used, without validation, to disqualify law students from further pursuing their careers, then only one aspect of the predictive index would ever be validated. Failures in spotting potential offenders—the false negatives—would be exposed; but few or none of the false positives—those erroneously disqualified—would be exposed, as they would have no opportunity to engage in the predicted conduct. The higher visibility of the failure to spot violators might then incline the testers to expand the category of those to be disqualified.

Unsolvable Dilemma of the Excessive False Positives

Even if these methodological problems could be overcome, there would still be considerable difficulty in usefully applying the resulting predictive index to the population at issue. This can be demonstrated by imagining that a hindsight study was conducted in which the "education and career background" of 1,000 past offenders were studied. Imagine further that the study was enormously successful: that it isolated a number of characteristics that were present in most of the offenders and absent in most of the nonoffenders. For purposes of this analysis, let us postulate that 80 per cent of the offenders possessed one or more of these characteristics and that 80 per cent of the control sample of nonoffenders lacked these characteristics.

It is extremely unlikely in real life that a cluster of characteristics could be discerned to be present in so high a percentage of offenders and absent in so high a percentage of nonoffenders. This is so for the obvious reason, *inter alia*, that people commit offenses out of a very wide range of motives. In many instances, an offense may be committed by someone with an exemplary past record—recall Dean Landis's tax conviction; in other instances, persons who seem to have the ideal profile for delinquency in fact never engage in this conduct.

Indeed, Jerome Carlin in his empirical study *Lawyers' Ethics* concluded that "situational" factors play a major role in determining whether a lawyer will violate ethical norms. These situational factors—the size and status of his firm, the nature of his clientele, the level of governmental agency with which he deals—would be most difficult to forecast during a student's first year in law school. Psychologists and other professionals who have tried to construct prediction indexes have been somewhat successful in predicting cognitive performance, such as academic success, but notoriously unsuccessful in predicting such things as "future character derelictions or vulnerability to temptation" (to use the report's words).

Thus, it is extremely unlikely that characteristics could be discovered that are present in 80 per cent of the offenders and absent in 80 per cent of the nonoffenders. But for purposes of this analysis, it will be assumed that 80 per cent of the past offenders possessed the characteristics and that 80 per cent of the nonoffenders lacked it.

The reason it would be difficult to apply even this highly "accurate" prediction index to the population at issue inheres in the extremely low ratio of potential violators to nonviolators among first-year law students. The population, according to the report, consists of "35,000 or 40,000 22 year-old men and women." Although precise information is not available as to the number of disciplinary proceedings annually, they are, in the words of an American Bar Foundation report, "certainly small in relation to the number of lawyers." Despite the "increasing attention to the problem of discipline of lawyers . . . the number of disbarments and forced resignations is probably still less than 150 per year." This constitutes approximately three quarters of 1 per cent of the yearly new admissions to the Bar. Over the past ten years, there have been fewer than 1,600 lawyers disbarred. This constitutes approximately one half of 1 per cent of the 300,000 currently practicing in the United States. There are no reliable statistics on the number of applicants annually denied admission to the Bar for "character" deficiencies, but the number is probably no more than fifty. This brings the relevant figure to less than 200 per year, or about 1 per cent of the new admissions.

To avoid any charge of understating the case in favor of prediction, the figure will be raised to 5 per cent: it will be assumed that 5 per cent of the 40,000 first-year students to whom the test would be administered will commit conduct resulting in official professional discipline or be denied admission to the Bar. The extreme exaggeration of this figure is illustrated by applying it to the entering class of Harvard Law School: 5 per cent of that class is more than twenty-five students. Surely nowhere near that number will be denied admission or disbarred during their legal careers.

It may be that the committee is seeking to cast its predictive net wider than disbarable conduct and conduct or character deficiencies that would deny the applicant admission to the Bar. It may be seeking to predict all unethical conduct—that is, conduct that now results in reprimand or that goes undetected or unpunished. There is, of course, no reliable estimate of the extent of undetected unethical behavior among lawyers. Mr. Carlin in his book estimates that it may be as high as 22 per cent of the lawyers practicing in New York City, but he also says that "fewer than 2 per cent of lawyers who violate the generally accepted norms of the bar are formally handled by the official disciplinary machinery; only about 0.02 per cent are publicly sanctioned by being disbarred, suspended or censured." It would be unrealistic in the extreme, therefore, to attempt to predict all violations of ethical norms. The 5 per cent figure certainly covers all violations that are publicly sanctioned by disbarment, suspension or censure. (To the extent that the studies would be seeking to "predict" the existence of those character traits that are currently used to disqualify applicants for admission to the Bar—as distinguished from predicting disbarable conduct itself—then the studies would be attempting a compound prediction, since many of the traits that now disqualify are themselves predictive of ultimate misconduct.)

Applying the 80 per cent factors to the population at issue would produce the following results: 80 per cent of the potential offenders would be correctly spotted. This would come to about 1,600 (40,000 × .05 × .80). Eighty per cent of the future nonoffenders would be spotted as well. This would come to 30,400 (40,000 × .95 × .80). But 20 per cent of the potential offenders would be missed: 400 potential offenders would manage to sneak by. More significant, 20 per cent of the nonoffenders would be incorrectly identified as offenders. And here the percentages are extremely misleading. When the figure of 20 per cent is converted into absolute numbers, it turns out that a total of 7,600 students would be identified erroneously as offenders (40,000 × .95 × .20).

Put another way, if a test 80 per cent accurate for offenders and nonoffenders is administered to a group of 40,000 with a "base rate expectancy" of 5 per cent, the result will be 30,800 "passing" scores and 9,200 "failing" scores. The 30,800 passing scores will include 30,400 students who would not commit offenses (these are the true negatives), and 400 who would commit offenses (these are the false negatives). The 9,200 failures will include 1,600 students who would commit offenses (these are the true positives), and 7,600 who would not commit offenses (these are the false positives).

The problem is that it is impossible, under the predictive index being used, to tell the difference between the true positives and the false positives or between the true negatives and false negatives. Either all of the 9,200, or none of them, should be disqualified. If all of the 9,200 were to be prevented or discouraged from continuing their legal education, 1,600 cases of future misconduct would have been prevented but at a cost of 7,600 persons who would not commit misconduct being kept out of the legal profession. This would constitute overprediction of almost five to one.

But, it might be asked, could not the number of false positives (students erroneously predicted to be offenders) be reduced if there were a willingness to sacrifice some efficiency in spotting future offenders? After all, spotting 80 per cent of future offenders is pretty high. What if we were satisfied to spot only 60 or even 20 per cent of future offenders, would there still be so many false positives? The answer is no. The number of false positives could be reduced, if there were also a willingness to reduce the number of true positives, that is, the number of potential offenders correctly spotted. But the number of false positives—in both percentage and absolute terms—would still remain quite high, under the population at issue here.

This can be demonstrated by hypothesizing that a four-factor index is employed to achieve 80 per cent accuracy in identifying offenders and nonoffenders. Assuming that each of these factors were of equal predictive significance, there presumably would be

a reduction of about 25 per cent in the accuracy of the index's ability to spot future violators if one of the factors were converted from
a "failing" criterion to a "passing" one—or put another way, if the
"cutting line" were raised. There might also be an improvement of
about 25 per cent in the index's ability to predict nonoffenders.

Assume, for instance, that past record of dishonesty would no
longer result in a failure. Obviously, some but not all persons with
that record would become offenders. The elimination of the
factor would result in a smaller number—and percentage—of
failures among those taking the test. Included in the new group
of "passers" would be some who, under the old test, would have
been correctly identified as offenders and some who would have been
incorrectly so identified.

What would the numbers look like under this new and more
conservative index? Only 60 per cent of the potential offenders
would be identified (80 per cent × .75). This would come to 1,200
of 2,000. But approximately 85 per cent of the nonoffenders
would now be correctly identified. (The increase of 5 per cent is
25 per cent of the original 20 per cent inaccuracy.) This would still
leave 5,700 false positives—students incorrectly identified as
future offenders.

If one other factor were converted from a failing criterion to a
passing one—if the cutting line were raised even higher—the
number of future offenders correctly identified would be reduced
to 800 (less than half), but the test would still produce about 3,800
false positives. If three of the four factors were converted, thus
reducing the number of spotted future offenders to 400 of 2,000
(or a mere 20 per cent), the test would still produce 1,600 false
positives. Even if the cutting line were raised further so that 99
per cent of all persons who failed would become offenders, there
would still be approximately 380 false positives.

It is, of course, theoretically possible to reduce the number of false positives to any number desired by continuing to raise the cutting line until only "certain" future offenders were included. But that would probably bring the percentage of offenders spotted down below 1 per cent. It is unlikely that it would then be thought worth the effort to identify so small a percentage of future violators, especially since they would be the most obvious ones who probably would be weeded out by current practices.

There is simply no way to reduce the number or percentage of false positives to manageable figures, while still spotting any significant number or percentage of true positives. The reason for this inheres in the mathematics of the situation: whenever the base rate expectancy for a predicted human act is very low or very high—say, below 10 per cent or above 90 per cent—it becomes extremely difficult to spot those who would commit the act without also including a large number of false positives. And since the percentage of future offenders among the entering law school classes is extremely low—certainly not more than 5 per cent—it is not feasible to develop predictive criteria capable of sorting out the future offenders from the future nonoffenders.

The dilemma inherent in predicting disbarable conduct among first-year law students is illustrated in the accompanying table.

	#F	TP	FP	#P	TN	FN		
CUTTING LINE I (All persons with any one of the negative characteristics)	9,200	1,600	7,600	30,800	30,400	400	80%	80%
CUTTING LINE II (All persons with any two)	6,900	1,200	5,700	33,100	32,300	800	60%	85%
CUTTING LINE III (All with any three)	4,600	800	3,800	35,400	34,200	1,200	40%	90%
CUTTING LINE IV (All with all four)	2,300	400	1,900	37,700	36,100	1,600	20%	95%

Column headers (diagonal, left to right):

- TOTAL NUMBER WHO WOULD "FAIL" UNDER A GIVEN CUTTING LINE
- NUMBER WHO WOULD BE CORRECTLY IDENTIFIED AS FUTURE OFFENDERS (TRUE POSITIVES)
- NUMBER INCORRECTLY IDENTIFIED AS FUTURE OFFENDERS (FALSE POSITIVES)
- TOTAL NUMBER WHO "PASS" UNDER A GIVEN CUTTING LINE
- NUMBER WHO WOULD BE CORRECTLY IDENTIFIED AS FUTURE NON-OFFENDERS (TRUE NEGATIVES)
- NUMBER WHO WOULD BE INCORRECTLY IDENTIFIED AS NON-OFFENDERS (FALSE NEGATIVES)
- PERCENT OF VIOLATORS CORRECTLY IDENTIFIED*
- PERCENT OF NON-VIOLATORS CORRECTLY SPOTTED*

Total number of people being tested = 40,000 (#F + #P = 40,000).

Total number of anticipated future offenders (base rate expectancy) = 2,000
   (TP + FN = 2,000).

Total number of anticipated future non-offenders = 38,000 (FP + TN = 38,000).

*[There is no fixed mathematical relationship between the percentage decrease in accuracy of an index's ability to spot offenders and the increase in its ability to predict non-offenders. The figures used in the table are, in the author's view a fair reflection of what might realistically be expected.]

Clinical Versus Statistical Prediction

The predictive test, of course, need not be used to disqualify auto matically all those who fail it. It could be used simply as a screening mechanism to isolate from the large population a smaller group that could then be further interviewed and investigated. Only those who "failed" these additional "tests" would then be disqualified or discouraged from further pursuit of a legal career. Would not this variation reduce the number of false positives even further?

The short answer to this question—a question which raises a series of complex considerations—is that this variation might well reduce the number of false positives, but it would do so in essentially the same way that raising the cutting line of an objective test would do it. In other words, the decision by an interviewer or investigator to "pass" certain students who had "failed" the written test is conceptually parallel to the introduction of a new cutting line that has the effect of passing some who would have failed under a different cutting line.

Many people do not view it this way, because they regard the introduction of the human element—the interviewer or investigator—as an improvement, as an increase in sophistication and subtlety over the mechanically scored test. They believe that the human agency is capable of doing what the test is incapable of doing—using insight and experience to distinguish the true from the false positives within the population that failed the test.

But the available data lend no support to this belief. Indeed, in 1957, Paul Meehl, a distinguished psychologist and a clinician, wrote a book, *Clinical versus Statistical Prediction*, that summarized the literature comparing the accuracy of statistical predictions (those made by mechanically scored tests) and clinical

predictions (those made by individual experts). His conclusion—
one that is now widely accepted as confirmed—was:

> As of today there are 27 empirical studies in the literature which
> made some meaningful comparison between the predictive suc-
> cess of the clinician and the statistician. . . . Of these 27 studies,
> 17 show a definite superiority for the statistical method; 10 show
> the methods to be of about equal efficiency; none of them show
> the clinician prediction better. . . . I have some reservations
> about these studies; I do not believe they are optimally designed
> to exhibit the clinician at his best; but I submit that it is high time
> that those who are so sure the "right kind of study" will exhibit
> the clinician's prowess, should do this right kind of study and
> back up their claim with evidence.

A more recent comparison, published in 1966, also found that of
forty studies examined, the actuarial technique was always equal
or superior to the clinical mode. A paper published in 2002 sum-
marizing the studies made after Meehl's book concluded: "Since
1954 [the publication of Meehl's book], almost every non-
ambiguous study that has compared the reliability of clinical and
actuarial predictions has supported Meehl's conclusion."[1]

There is thus no objective evidence to support the claim that
the introduction of an interviewer or investigator would increase
the accuracy of the predictions made by a mechanically scored
test. There is some evidence that it might actually decrease its
accuracy. Introducing an interviewer may well result in more of a
sacrifice in the number of true positives spotted to achieve the
same reduction in the number of false positives. In any event, even
if the clinical prediction were as good as or even better than the
statistical prediction, it is clear that every increase in accuracy in

avoiding false positives could be achieved only at the cost of a decrease in accuracy in spotting future violators.

It is, of course, possible that an investigation would produce more information about applicants that would improve the accuracy of the prediction, *i.e.*, that would lower the percentage of false positives by a greater degree than it would reduce the percentage of offenders spotted. But numerous studies have demonstrated that the accuracy of predictions does not necessarily increase— indeed, it sometimes decreases—as the result of more information being made available to the predicter.

It is important to note that this is not a case in which some competitive selection must take place anyway, and one additional factor is merely being thrown into the calculus. Once a student is admitted to law school, no further process of competitive selection is contemplated before he is admitted to the Bar. To be sure, there are processes of disqualification (for instance, failure in law school, on the bar examination or in the character examination), but that is a different matter. The proposal of the committee of the Section of Legal Education and Admissions to the Bar would have been somewhat more defensible empirically, although it still would have been vulnerable on numerous grounds, if the predictive tests were to be administered to all law school applicants, and the results used as an aid in the competitive selection process. But in the last analysis, any attempt to predict attorney misconduct, whether among first-year law students or law school applicants, is necessarily doomed to failure.

As long as we are dealing with a population that includes so small a proportion of future violators, it will not be possible to spot any significant proportion of those violators without erroneously including a far larger number of "false positives." This, in a nutshell, is the dilemma of attempting to predict rare human occurrences. And this is the dilemma that will inevitably plague the studies proposed by the committee.

Unless the legal profession is prepared for the "preventive disbarment" of large numbers of young students who might, if permitted to pursue their careers, practice law with distinction, it should not encourage the development of tests designed to predict potential character defects or misconduct among lawyers at an early stage in their legal education.

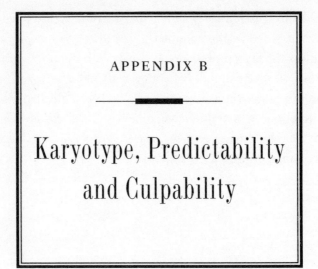

APPENDIX B

Karyotype, Predictability and Culpability

I t has been suggested that the presence of the XYY karyotype in a man may be associated with—and consequently predictive of—certain kinds of violent crime.

One can sympathize with efforts to predict and prevent crimes before they occur, rather than to wait until the victim lies dead.

But as Alice in Wonderland understood, "There's a mistake somewhere—"[1]

There are at least two mistakes prevalent in current discussions of the XYY karyotype that this essay will focus on: The first concerns whether the presence of such karyotype, alone or in combination with other factors, should be deemed predictive of violent crime; the second concerns whether the presence of such karyotype, alone or in combination with other factors, should be deemed an excusing or mitigating condition in assessing criminal responsibility.

First a few words of introduction: In 1961, the first report of a 47, XYY human appeared in a letter by Sandberg et al.[2] The XYY characteristic or karyotype is a chromosome abnormality in which a man has 47 as compared to the normal 46 chromosomes. It is the result of non-disjunction, or the failure of the chromosomes to properly separate during the meiotic division which gives rise to the sperm. This phenomenon remained but a biological curiosity until the paper in *Nature* in 1965 by Jacobs et al.[3] which associated this extra Y chromosome with tall stature, mental retardation, and aggressive behavior. Thus began a long series of studies attempting to substantiate or disprove this claim, which, if true, would have the most profound consequences for society.

The original Jacobs study in England justifiably caused much commotion, as it found 7 XYY males in a mental hospital of 197 patients when previously only 11 XYY males had been identified throughout the world. A number of retrospective validation studies confirmed the higher incidence, but nowhere near the 7 out of 197 of the Jacobs study. Aggregating 12 studies[4] of mental subnormals and mental hospital patients, yields a rate of approximately 10 XYY males out of 8,500 or 0.12% of the subnormal population. The alleged association of XYY and violence naturally led investigators to criminal populations in prisons. Putting together the data from 16 separate studies, there is an incidence of approximately 55 out of 17,500 or 0.32% of inmates who are XYY. More information is necessary, however, before it is possible to judge the significance of these data. The incidence rates are worthless until we know the natural incidence of XYY in the total male population. Three studies of consecutively born males have found a population rate of 12 out of 6,746 or 0.18%, somewhat higher than the incidence in mental hospitals and somewhat more than one-half the incidence in prison.

Since the validation studies have all been retrospective, they tell us very little about the percentage of XYY individuals in the total population that will become aggressive, much less become prison inmates. This latter figure is crucial to establishing any sort of reliable predictive criteria. At present there is no published data on a prospective study of XYY individuals, although such studies are in progress. Walzer, for example, has been examining every newborn male at a hospital in Boston for several years and is keeping track of all the XYY children. If the study is permitted to continue, these subjects will be followed into maturity so as to get as complete a report as possible. For ethical reasons, Walzer is informing the families about the nature of what they are studying in the children. From a purely experimental point of view this threatens to contaminate the results, but is necessary for the reason that parents have a right to know what is being measured in their children.[5]

Methodological problems aside, there would still be great problems in the application of the data to a group of XYY males for predictive purposes. Using the data above, if the United States has a population of 110,000,000 males, it will have approximately 200,000 males with the XYY karyotype. If there are 1,000,000 American males who have at one time commited a seriously violent crime, then by these incidence rates 3,200 of them have the XYY karyotype. Thus, to line up all XYY males and try to predict which of them will be criminally violent without any other information, one would have to select 3,200 out of 200,000 or a mere 1.5%. To predict that all the XYY persons will be violent would result in a false positive rate of 98.4%.

These data may very well later be proved inaccurate. If the incidence of the XYY individual is either greater in prison populations or lower in the total population than presently believed, the predictability of violence or criminality in XYY individuals would increase proportionately. Thus, if the total population incidence were actually half of the estimate in use here there would only be

100,000 males in the United States with the XYY karyotype. For a target population of 1,000,000 criminals this would increase the prediction accuracy to 3.2%; that would still result in an unacceptably high false positive rate for virtually any program of incarceration or serious constraint on liberty.

To show how far from the mark we currently are, hypothesize the following situation:

Assume that 1 out of 200 in prison has an XYY karyotype.

Assume that 1 out of 10,000 in normal population has such a karyotype. Under this hypothetical situation—which exaggerates any likely predictive strength of the XYY karyotype—the incidence of the alleged predictor would be 50 times greater in the prison than in the normal population. The total population of normal males (110,000,000) would include only 11,000 XYY males; the hypothetical prison population (1,000,000) would include 5,000 XYY males. If all the XYY individuals were to be confined, there would still be more than twice as many false positives as true positives (16,000 confined of which 11,000 were false positives and 5,000 true positives). Moreover, only a small amount of the potential target population (less than one-half of 1%) would have been correctly identified. Even if one were to expand the target population 10-fold to include all persons who will ever engage in any serious violence, the predictive utility of the XYY karyotype would prove unsatisfactory. Assume that 10,000,000 American males would fit into this expanded category. Assume—an even more unlikely situation—that the ratio of XYY males in this expanded target group remained the same as in the original target group (1 out of 200). Now the number of XYY males in the target group would increase to 10,000 (1/200 × 10,000,000) and the number of XYY's in the normal population would decrease slightly to 10,100 (1/10,00 × 101,000,000). Thus, the total number of persons confined under an XYY preventive confinement program would come to 20,100 of whom 10,000 would be true positives and 10,100 would be false positives. Even under this absolutely unreachable plateau, the number of false positives would slightly exceed the number of true positives.

There is simply no way to reduce the number or percentage of false positives to manageable figures, while still spotting any significant number or percentage of true positives. The reason for this inheres in the mathematics of the situation: whenever the base rate expectancy for a predicted human act is low, it becomes extremely difficult to spot those who would commit the act without also including a large number of false positives—unless, of course, the predictor being employed is far more discriminating than the XYY karyotype is ever likely to be. And since the percentage of American males who will engage in seriously violent conduct is relatively low, it is not feasible to use the XYY karyotype as a predictive criterion capable of sorting out the future offenders from the future non-offenders. Nor is it likely that the XYY karyotype, even in combination with other factors, could be used to predict violence. Current efforts at violence prediction—employing sophisticated and multifaceted approaches—have also produced extraordinarily large numbers and percentages of false positives. There is simply no hard evidence establishing that any combination of factors can accurately spot a large percentage of future violent criminals without also including an unsatisfactorily large number and percentage of false positives.[6]

On the opposite side of the coin from the prediction problem is the question what to do with the defendant who has committed a serious violent crime and who claims—in defense or in mitigation—that he is affected with an XYY karyotype. Even if such a karyotype does not have predictive significance, it can be argued, that does not mean it should not be deemed an excusing or mitigating condition. After all, such a condition would help the bearer of the XYY karyotype, would it not? The answer to that question is complex, both as it relates to the particular criminal defendant raising the XYY karyotype as a defense, and as it relates to the general class of persons afflicted with that abnormality. As to the particular individual: since there is no known cure for this type of chromosomal abnormality, the likely result of a successful "chromosomal defense" would be long term—perhaps lifetime—confinement.

As to the general class of XYY males, there has always been a direct relationship between a class's lack of criminal accountability and the power of the state to confine that class preventively. The relationship is a natural one: most people believe, and probably always have, that someone who has committed a serious crime and who continues to be dangerous should be incapacitated in some manner. Accordingly, if the formal criminal process is incapable of dealing with him effectively, then he must be dealt with by some other, perhaps less formal but equally effective, mechanism of control.

Even if a dangerous "madman" has not "yet" committed a serious crime, the fact that he could not be held answerable for any future criminality would suggest the need for preventive intervention. After all, an important assumption underlying most criminal punishment is that the threat of its imposition will, in most cases, deter potential criminals. When that assumption is negated—when there is no threat of criminal punishment or when the potential crime-doer is seen as incapable of exercising choice in a rational manner—then a need is perceived for some other mechanism of social control. Thus, there has always been a direct relationship between the size and nature of the category of persons deemed criminally nonresponsible and the size and nature of the category of persons regarded as preventively confinable. This relationship has been most direct, and most easily observable, in the context of madmen who have committed criminal acts and been acquitted by reason of insanity, or found incompetent to stand trial. But there has also been a significant relationship in the context of what has come to be called "civil commitment," i.e., the confinement of insane persons who have not "yet" engaged in criminal behavior, but who are thought "likely" to do so in the future.

Blackstone tied the power to confine the mentally ill directly to the lack of answerability and responsibility in the formal criminal process:

> In the case of absolute madmen, *as they are not answerable for their actions*, they should not be permitted the liberty of acting, unless under proper control; and, in particular, they ought not be suffered to go loose, to the terror of the king's subjects. It was the doctrine of our ancient law, that persons deprived of their reason might be confined till they recovered their senses, without waiting for the forms of a commission or other special authority from the crown. . . . [7]

My fear is that if the XYY karyotype came to be recognized as an excusing or mitigating condition, this would create increasing pressure to preventively confine persons with such karyotypes.

Conclusion

The XYY karyotype is an intriguing phenomenon in search of employment. It is the thesis of this essay that the time is not ripe for it to find any employment in the service of crime prevention or criminal responsibility. Nor is there any basis for expecting that such a time is close at hand. Further research should not, however, be throttled in the name of misguided certainty that chromosomal abnormality is a blind alley, or misguided fear of the consequences of a finding that there is a relationship between such abnormality and violence. We should be vigilant to control the uses to which scientific research may be put, while at the same time remaining vigilant to the dangers of scientific censorship.

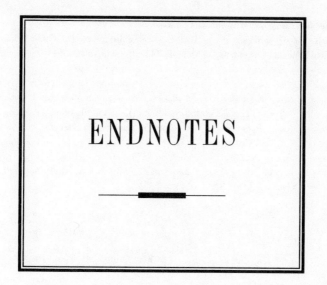

ENDNOTES

INTRODUCTION

1. Curt Anderson, "Aschroft Cites 'Monumental Progress' in U.S. War on Terrorism," Associated Press, February 13, 2003.
2. Ibid.
3. Transcript of Senate Judiciary Committee confirmation hearing; accessible at http://www.nytimes.com/2005/01/06/politics/06TEXT-GONZALES.html.
4. Deuteronomy 21:18.
5. Lombroso believed that criminality was inherited and that someone could be born a criminal—that criminals possessed physical defects characteristic of primitive animals. As a result, one could identify a criminal from physical traits like the size of his jaw or the shape of his nose.
6. Sheldon and Eleanor Glueck, my former colleagues at Harvard and pioneers in the prediction of juvenile delinquency, maintained that they could spot potential criminals at an early age by observing aspects of their family life, and some biologists now assert, on the basis of rather flimsy evidence, that they could identify potential criminals by examining the chromosomal structure of their cells. Alan M. Dershowitz, *Shouting Fire: Civil Liberties in a Turbulent Age* (New York: Little Brown, 2002), p. 235.
7. Edward Rothstein, "Museum Review: The Tainted Science of Nazi Atrocities," *New York Times,* January 8, 2005, p. B7.
8. Ibid. Even one of Hitler's own relatives, a forty-nine-year-old woman identified as

Aloisia V., was gassed as an "idiotic progeny" on December 6, 1940. She apparently suffered from schizophrenia and other illnesses. Susanna Loof, "Hitler Relative Was Gassed in Nazi Program to Kill Mentally Ill People, Historians Say," Associated Press, January 18, 2005.

9. Rothstein, op. cit.

10. The problem with this approach is that even if 90 percent of certain types of criminals have a particular genetic marker, it may also be true that only 1 percent of people with that marker will become criminals. See Alan M. Dershowitz, "Karyotype, Predictability and Culpability," in *Genetics and the Law*, ed. Aubrey Milunsky and George J. Annas (New York: Plenum Press, 1976), pp. 63–71. See Appendix B, p. 268.

11. Cass R. Sunstein, *Laws of Fear: Beyond the Precautionary Principle* (New York: Cambridge University Press, 2005), p. 15.

12. Ibid., p. 13.

13. "The Year in Ideas: A to Z," *New York Times Magazine*, December 9, 2001, p. 92.

14. Sunstein, op. cit., p. 4 (notes omitted).

15. Ibid., p. 14.

16. Lewis Carroll, *The Annotated Alice* (New York: Norton, 2000), pp. 196–98.

17. *Everett v. Ribbands*, 2 Q.B. 198 (1952), p. 206.

18. There are morally *un*acceptable tactics, such as the killings of innocent relatives of suicide bombers that could deter some such suicide terrorists, but no democracy should employ such tactics.

19. William Blackstone, *Commentaries on the Laws of England* (Oxford: Clarendon Press, 1769), vol. 4, p. 25; accessible at http://www.yale.edu/lawweb/avalon/blackstone/bk4ch2.htm.

20. See p. 175 for a discussion of the statement made by Hashem Rafsanjani, the former president of Iran, suggesting that it might be worth it to drop a nuclear bomb on Israel, killing five million Jews, even if Israel's retaliation would kill fifteen million Iranian Muslims.

21. "In Defense of Deterrence," *New York Times*, September 10, 2002, p. A24.

22. Ibid. International law probably prohibits retaliation against civilians for an attack on civilians. See p. 74. Thus the entire theory of tit-for-tat deterrence may well be technically illegal.

23. Ibid.

24. Ibid.

25. Ibid.

26. To be sure, Germany was in violation of its treaty obligations, but as the international reaction to the American invasion of Iraq shows, mere violation of treaties is not always seen as a justification for military action.

27. See pp. 146–47 for a discussion of the decision of the International Criminal Tribunal for Rwanda.

28. "Some Prior Restraints Squeaked by in Past Year, Says PLI Panel," *Media Law Reporter*, vol. 30, no. 46 (November 26, 2002); accessible at http://ipcenter.bna.com/pic2/ip.nsf/id/BNAP-5G5L3N?OpenDocument.

29. For an analysis of variations on this maxim, see Alexander Volokh, "*n* Guilty Men," *University of Pennsylvania Law Review*, vol. 146 (1997), pp. 173–216.

30. Constructing a jurisprudence requires complexification, quantification, qualification, and simplification. See p. 244.

31. The nature of the harm includes both its qualitative and quantitative aspects. Each can be placed on continua. For example, death would be at one end, with inconvenience at the other end. Multiple deaths are an obviously serious harm, warranting considerable costs and inconveniences. But if inconvenience for millions is weighed against one death, reasonable people might disagree about how to strike the balance. For example, a decision to raise the speed limit from 55 mph to 65 mph may be seen as weighing the convenience of many more heavily than the potential loss of some lives.

32. This oversimplifies reality. In the real world, there will often be a range of intermediate steps between doing nothing and taking strong preemptive measures that could be taken and that might reduce, but not eliminate, the feared harm.

33. These costs could include various categories of human life, such as enemy soldiers, one's own soldiers, enemy civilians, etc. It could also include financial costs, political costs, and other such factors. Some costs will be short-term, others longer-term. Some will be easily calculable, others less so. Sometimes the criteria for determining "success" will be obvious. Other times it will not be.

34. Seriousness of the harm is a product of its nature (e.g., death), degree (e.g., how many deaths), irrevocability (death is more irrevocable than minor physical injury or temporary economic consequences), and other such factors.

35. *United States v. Dennis*, 183 F.2d 201, 212 (2d Cir. 1950). This effort at constructing a formula for balancing relevant factors in the free speech context followed by three years a similar effort to quantify a complex problem in the context of maritime torts:

> [T]here is no general rule to determine when the absence of a bargee or other attendant will make the owner of the barge liable for injuries to other vessels if she breaks away from her moorings. However, in any cases where he would be so liable for injuries to others obviously he must reduce his damages proportionately, if the injury is to his own barge. It becomes apparent why there can be no such general rule, when we consider the grounds for such a liability. Since there are occasions when every vessel will break from her moorings, and since, if she does, she becomes a menace to those about her; the owner's duty, as in other similar situations, to provide against resulting injuries is a function of three variables: (1) the probability that she will break away; (2) the gravity of the resulting injury, if she does; (3) the burden of adequate precautions. Possibly it serves to bring this notion into relief to state it in algebraic terms: if the probability be called P; the injury, L; and the burden, B; liability depends upon whether B is less than L multiplied by P: i.e., whether B less than PL. Applied to the situation at bar, the likelihood that a barge will break from her fasts and the damage she will do, vary with the place and time; for example, if a storm threatens, the danger is greater;

> so it is, if she is in a crowded harbor where moored barges are constantly being shifted about. On the other hand, the barge must not be the bargee's prison, even though he lives aboard; he must go ashore at times.

United States v. Carroll Towing Co., Inc., 159 F.2d 169, 173 (2d Cir. 1969). This decision, like *United States v. Dennis*, was written by Judge Learned Hand.

36. See Sunstein, op. cit. See also *Brandenburg v. Ohio*, 395 U.S. 444 (1969).

37. *Vargas-Figueroa v. Saldana*, 826 F.2d 160, 162 (1st Cir. 1987). Justice Breyer wrote this opinion when he was on the Court of Appeals. A common formulation is the following: "(1) that plaintiff will suffer irreparable injury if the injunction is not granted; (2) that such injury outweighs any harm which granting injunctive relief would inflict on the defendant; (3) that plaintiff has exhibited a likelihood of success on the merits; and (4) that the public interest will not be adversely affected by the granting of the injunction." *Women's Community Health Center, Inc. v. Cohen*, 477 F. Supp. 542, 544 (D. Me. 1979).

38. This decision might cover a range of different attacks, from wholesale nuclear to retail terrorist killings.

39. As we shall see in Chapter 5, there may be important differences between wars that are preemptive and those that are preventive.

40. This decision may cover steps as diverse as committing sexual psychopaths to institutions and the targeted killing of unarrestable ticking bomb terrorists.

41. There are of course many past reconstructions that can be confirmed by incontrovertible and self-proving evidence, but there are many that cannot.

42. There are interesting epistemological issues about what is meant by there being a 90 percent likelihood that a given event, which either occurred (100 percent) or did not occur (0 percent), may have occurred. What I mean is that if thousands of decisions were made on the basis of this quality and quantity of evidence they would turn out be correct (to the extent that can be known) 90 percent of the time. I am not aware of any good, double-blind experiments that ask subjects to make predictive and retrospective decisions (will or did a given event occur?) based on comparable information, complexity, temporal proximity, and likelihood. For example, subjects could be given a detailed history of a somewhat psychopathic person. Half could then be asked to determine, on the basis of this information, whether he *had* committed a specific crime (say, rape, robbery, or murder) within the past year. The other half could be asked to predict whether he *would* commit such a crime within the next year. To add complexity to this issue, any "good" predictor of crime would want to know whether the person had committed recent past crimes, since the past is the best predictor of the future, at least when it comes to certain kinds of crimes. The contrary is probably also true: If a person *will* commit certain types of crime in the future, it is more likely that he *has* committed other crimes in the past. For certain types of unique crime—e.g., passion killing of a particular love-hate object and highly situational crimes—neither of these relationships will necessarily hold true. Since most conclusions that a person did, in fact, commit a past crime are themselves probabilistic, this adds a further com-

plexity to any predictive decision based on past conduct. This is prevalent in literature on predicting pretrial violence in the context of setting bail. See, for example, Thomas Bak, "Pretrial Release Behavior of Defendants Whom the U.S. Attorney Wished to Detain," *American Journal of Criminal Law*, vol. 30 (2002–03), pp. 45–74. I predict that such experiments would show—or if any have been conducted, I postdict they have shown—little difference in *actual* outcomes, though the subjects might be more confident in their retrospective than in their predictive judgments. There are numerous experiments that purport to compare predictive and postdictive decisions but not quite in this way. See Paul E. Meehl, *Clinical versus Statistical Prediction: A Theoretical Analysis and a Review of the Evidence* (Minneapolis: University of Minnesota Press, 1954).

43. See *United States v. Booker*, 125 S.Ct. 738 (2005).
44. See Chapter 7.
45. Mishnah Peah 1:1.
46. Genesis 18:23–27, 29–33.
47. Maimonides articulated a similar principle hundreds of years before Blackstone: "If we do not punish on very strong probabilities, nothing can happen other than that a sinner be freed; but if punishment be done on probability and opinion it is possible that one day we might kill an innocent man—and it is better and more desirable to free a thousand sinners, than ever to kill one innocent." Maimonides, *Sefer HaMitzvot*, Negative Commandments no. 290, quoted in Nachum L. Rabinovitch, "Probability and Statistical Inference in Ancient and Medieval Jewish Literature," diss., University of Toronto, 1971, p. 157.
48. As we shall see, preventive and preemptive wars are distinguished largely by the temporal proximity of the feared attack. See p. 59.
49. Exodus 22:2.
50. Talmud Sanhedrin 72a.
51. Haim Cohen, *Dangerous Halakhah*, p. 42; accessible at http://www.come-and-hear.com/supplement/free-judaism-cohen.rtf.
52. Ibid.
53. Ibid., p. 31.
54. Shlomo Shamir, "Had It Been Mitzna, They Would Have Gone Nuts," *Ha'aretz*, May 18, 2005; accessible at http://www.jpef.net/may05/Had%20it%20been.pdf.
55. See, for example, Alan M. Dershowitz, "Preventive Confinement: A Suggested Framework for Constitutional Analysis," *Texas Law Review*, vol. 51 (1973), pp. 1277–1324; Alan Dershowitz, "The Origins of Preventive Confinement in Anglo-American Law," *University of Cincinnati Law Review*, vol. 43 (1974), pp. 1–60, and 781–846; Alan M. Dershowitz, "Indeterminate Confinement: Letting the Therapy Fit the Harm," *University of Pennsylvania Law Review*, vol. 123 (1974), pp. 297–339; and Alan M. Dershowitz, "Psychiatry in the Legal Process: A Knife That Cuts Both Ways," *Trial* (February–March 1968), pp. 29–33.
56. See, for example, Dershowitz, *Shouting Fire*, loc. cit., pp. 233–45; and Dershowitz, "Preventive Confinement," loc. cit.

57. See, for example, Dershowitz, *Shouting Fire,* loc. cit., pp. 431–56 (originally published in 1971); Ibid., pp. 416–30 (originally published in the *Nation* [March 15, 1971]).

58. See, for example, Dershowitz, "Karyotype, Predictability and Culpability," loc. cit.; and Dershowitz, "Preventive Disbarment: The Numbers Are against It," *American Bar Association Journal,* vol. 58 (August 1972), pp. 815–19. (See the appendices to this book.)

59. See, for example, Dershowitz, "Psychiatry in the Legal Process," loc. cit.; Dershowitz, "Imprisonment by Judicial Hunch: Case against Pretrial Preventive Detention," *Prison Journal,* vol. 50 (1970), pp. 12–22; and Dershowitz, "Preventive Detention: Social Threat," *Trial* (December–January 1969–1970), pp. 22–26.

60. See, for example, Dershowitz, "The Origins of Preventive Confinement in Anglo-American Law," loc. cit.

CHAPTER I.

A BRIEF HISTORY OF PREEMPTION, PREVENTION, AND PREDICTION IN THE CONTEXT OF INDIVIDUAL CRIME

1. William Blackstone, *Commentaries on the Laws of England* (Oxford: Clarendon Press, 1769), vol. 4, p. 248; accessible at http://www.yale.edu/lawweb/avalon/blackstone/bk4ch18.htm.

2. *Maung Hla Gyan v. Commissioner,* Burma Law Reps. 764 (1948), p. 766.

3. A slew of nations have borrowed from the Anglo-American legal system. Kenya, Switzerland, South Africa, the Czech Republic, and the Marshall Islands are but a few examples. Iraq's constitution will also reflect Anglo-American legal principles because the United States played an important role in overseeing it. See Neil Mac-Donald, "Iraq Constitution Will Draw Heavily From Transitional Law, Says Zoellick," *Financial Times,* May 20, 2005, p. 9.

4. Oliver Wendell Holmes, Jr., *The Common Law* (Boston: Little, Brown, 1881), pp. 46, 43.

5. Blackstone, op. cit., vol. 4, p. 249; accessible at http://www.yale.edu/lawweb/avalon/blackstone/bk4ch18.htm.

6. Jerome Hall, a leading theoretician, echoed Wharton in asserting that ours is a "legal order which does not recognize prevention as a sufficient ground of punishment. . . ." Jerome Hall, *General Principles of Criminal Law* (Indianapolis: Bobbs-Merrill, 1960), p. 219. Francis Wharton, *Treatise on Criminal Law* (Rochester: Lawyers Co-operative Publishing Company, 1932), p. 2.

7. Caesar Bonesana, Marquis Beccaria, *An Essay on Crimes and Punishments* (Philadelphia: Nicklin, 1819), pp. 148, 47.

8. Immanuel Kant, *Metaphysical Elements of Justice* (Indianapolis: Hackett, 1999), p. 138. To allay all doubts that this principle was indeed a "categorical imperative," Kant constructed his oft-quoted hypothetical: "Even if a civil society were to dissolve itself

by common agreement of all its members (for example, if the people inhabiting an island decided to separate and disperse themselves around the world), the last murderer remaining in prison must first be executed. . . ." Ibid., p. 140.

9. Indeed, Holmes espoused, in rather categorical terms, an "external" theory that abjured prying into motives and tendencies and focused almost single-mindedly on inducing "external conformity to rule." Oliver Wendell Holmes, Jr., *The Common Law* (Boston: Little, Brown, 1881), p. 49.

10. Ibid., p. 46.

11. Blackstone, op. cit., p. 249.

12. Even Wharton, who proposed an "absolute" theory of punishment, under which "crime as crime must be punished," acknowledged that all theories of guilt must ultimately "rest more or less on the danger of crime to society" and that "one of the objects of penal discipline" is to place the offender "in a condition in which he cannot be guilty of future mischief." Francis Wharton, *Wharton's Criminal Law* (Rochester: Lawyers Co-operative Publishing Company, 1932), vol. 2, p. 12. Professor Hall, who insists on the commission of past "harm" as a condition to imposing criminal punishment, would also consider future "dangerousness" as relevant in some contexts. Hall, p. 222.

13. Frederick Pollock and Frederic William Maitland, *The History of English Law* (Cambridge: Cambridge University Press 1898), vol. 2, p. 475.

14. Code of Hammurabi, sections 116, 209–10, and 229–30; accessible at http://www.wsu.edu/~dee/MESO/CODE.HTM.

15. Payment of this bot could, under certain circumstances and for "emendable" crimes, satisfy the victims and the state. It was also somewhat preventive, insofar as any painful response is preventive, in that it made crime expensive and thus presumably reduced its frequency.

16. Pollock and Maitland, op. cit., vol. 2, p. 478. This practice was described as follows:

> Though we must not speculate about a time in which there was no law, the evidence which comes to us from England and elsewhere invites us to think of a time when law was weak, and its weakness was displayed by a ready recourse to outlawry. It could not measure its blows; he who defied it was outside its sphere; he was outlaw. He who breaks the law has gone to war with the community; the community goes to war with him. It is the right and duty of every man to pursue him, to ravage his land, to burn his house, to hunt him down like a wild beast and slay him; for a wild beast he is; not merely is he a "friendless man," he is a wolf. Even in the thirteenth century, when outlawry had lost its exterminating character and had become an engine for compelling the contumacious to abide the judgment of the courts, this old state of things was not forgotten; *Caput great lupinum*—in these words the courts decreed outlawry.

Ibid., vol. 2, p. 449.

17. This argument has been repeatedly offered against efforts to construct a jurisprudence of torture. See, for example, Richard H. Weisberg, "Loose Professionalism, or Why

Lawyers Take the Lead on Torture," in *Torture: A Collection*, ed., Sanford Levinson,(Oxford: Oxford University Press, 2004), pp. 299–305.

18. Roscoe Pound, Introduction to Raymond Saleilles, *The Individualization of Punishment* (Boston: Little, Brown 1911), p. XI.

19. "Dispose" is a particularly apt word because for generations dangerous people were simply disposed of outside the formal legal system, without much concern for the niceties of the formal legal system. See pp. 39–40.

20. *Williamson v. United States*, 184 F.2d 280 (2d Cir. 1950), p. 280. See also Albin Eser, "The Principle of Harm in the Concept of Crime," 4 *Duquesne Law Review*, 345 (1965–66), p. 436.

21. Pollock and Maitland, op. cit., vol. 2, p. 507.

22. Ibid., vol. 2, p. 508, n. 4. If the authors meant to include the period after the Norman Conquest, then they were plainly in error, as is demonstrated in J. G. Bellamy, *The Law of Treason in England in the Later Middle Ages* (Cambridge: Cambridge University Press, 1970). Bellamy gives numerous early illustrations of a very broad construction of both "high treason" and "petty treason." See, for example, J. G. Bellamy, *The Law of Treason in England in the Later Middle Ages*, 1st paperback ed. (Cambridge: Cambridge University Press, 2004), pp. 61, 130, 132, 133, 135.

23. Attributed to C.J. Brian at "the end of the middle ages," quoted in Dershowitz, "Preventive Confinement," op. cit., p.10.

24. Jerome Hall, "Criminal Attempt—A Study of Foundation of Criminal Liability," *Yale Law Journal*, vol. 49 (1940), p. 791. Hall cites Henry de Bracton for the proposition that harm was caused before the criminal liability could be imposed: "For what harm did the attempt cause, since the injury took no effect." Sir Travers Twiss, ed., *Henrici de Bracton de Legibus et Consuetudinibus Angliae* (London: Longman & Co., 1879), vol. 2, p. 337. He then summarized the thirteenth-century compiler's views as follows: "Bracton plainly reveals a strong bias against penalizing any conduct short of action which resulted in actual injury, and 'injury' had crude, physical denotation set by the then-proscribed felonies." Hall, op. cit., p. 791.

25. Such an act would of course have been recognized as an assault at a certain stage in the development of the law.

26. Deuteronomy 17:6. The Bible does provide for the execution of a "stubborn and rebellious" child: "And they shall say unto the elders of his city, This our son is stubborn and rebellious, he will not obey our voice; he is a glutton and a drunkard. And all the men of his city shall stone him with stones, that he die. . . ." Deuteronomy 21:20–21. The Talmud suggests that rebellious sons were not actually executed. Rabbi Jonathan said "he had once seen such a one and sat on his grave" (Sanhedrin 71a). The Talmud itself made it virtually impossible to execute a rebellious son, since he had to be thirteen years of age to bear criminal responsibility but still young enough to be a "son" and not a man. Professor Menachem Elon views the biblical rule as "intended to limit the powers of the *paterfamilias*: the head of the household could no longer punish the defiant son himself, according to his own whim, but had to bring him before the elders (i.e., judges) for punishment. In earlier laws (e.g., Hammurabi Code nos. 168, 169) only the father had to be defied; in biblical law, it must be both father and mother."

See generally Menachem Elon, *The Principles of Jewish Law* (Jerusalem: Encyclopaedia Judaica, 1974), p. 491.

27. Talmud Sanhedrin 81b.

28. The Bible also prescribes "cities of refuge" designed to prevent blood avengers from taking revenge against innocent people who had accidentally killed. See Numbers 35:9–34. Recent research suggests that the urge for revenge may well have a genetic component. See Benedict Carey, "Payback Time: Why Revenge Tastes So Sweet," *New York Times*, July 27, 2004, p. F1. Even if this is true, it does not follow that law should not try to channel it in morally proper directions, as it sought to do with regard to the biblical cities of refuge.

29. This has been true in modern times with regard to bail. When it was relatively easy to deny pretrial release to dangerous defendants, we did not need an explicit system of preventive detention. As the law made it more difficult to use bail in this way, the need for preventive detention increased. See William F. Duker, "The Right to Bail: A Historical Inquiry," *Albany Law Review*, vol. 42 (1977), pp. 33–120.

30. *Williamson v. United States*, 184 F.2d 280, 282 (2d Cir. 1950). See also 18 USC § 3043 (1970).

31. Pollock and Maitland suggest that during the Anglo-Saxon period, "great difficulty was found both in obtaining specific evidence of offenses, and in compelling accused and suspected persons to submit themselves to justice. . . ." Pollock and Maitland, op. cit., vol. 1, p. 49. This may help explain a provision, apparently originating during that period, against persons described as "frequently accused." Ibid., vol. 1, p. 50. Such a person could be arrested "and treated as an outlaw if he failed to give security. . . ." Ibid. The "oldest dooms" provided penalties for "plotting" against the king, even though the act of plotting did not in itself produce any harm. Charles Austin Beard, *The Office of Justice of the Peace in England: in Its Origin and Development* (New York: Columbia University Press, 1904), pp. 13–14. Under the later Saxon kings and certainly by the time of the Norman Conquest, preventive laws were enacted whereby "all men were bound to combine themselves in associations of ten, each of whom was security for the good behavior of the rest. . . ." James Stephen, *A History of the Criminal Law of England* (London: Macmillan, 1883), vol. 1, p. 65.

In early times the tithing group was an effective way of both preventing crime and apprehending criminals, particularly in small villages. An early writer describes the tithing groups as follows: "In the Saxon times, every hundred was divided into ten districts or tithings, each tithing made up of ten Friborgs, each Friborg of ten families, and within every such tithing, there were tithing-men to examine and determine all lesser causes between villages and neighbors, but to refer all greater matters to the Superior Courts." Thomas Blount, *Glossographia Anglicana Nova: or a Dictionary Interpreting Such Hard Words of Whatever Language as Are Presently Used in the English Tongue with Their Etymologies, Definition, etc.* (London: D. Brown, 1707), quoted in Dershowitz, "Origins of Preventive Confinement in Anglo-American Law," loc. cit., p. 13, n. 40. The tithing group was held as surety for its members. If a member of the tithing group was accused of a crime, the entire group was responsible for producing the suspect under penalty of a rather heavy amercement, or fine. As Pollock and Maitland write, "The strict enforcement of these rules is abundantly proved by the rolls of the itinerant justices. When an accused person is not produced, his township is amerced if he was not in a tithing . . . , and, if he was in a tithing, then that tithing is amerced." Pollock and Maitland, op. cit., vol. 1, pp. 568–69.

A similar, though later, device—watch and ward—was developed in the thirteenth century. This system, consolidated in 1285 by the Statute of Winchester, put the town or village on watch, especially during times of political unrest. The villagers were to watch for any suspicious-looking persons, and any stranger who could not give a good account of himself was to be pursued with "hue and cry." For a good account of the uses of watch and ward, extending back to times before the statutory enactment, see F. M. Powicke, *King Henry III and the Lord Edward: The Community of the Realm in the Thirteenth Century* (Oxford: Clarendon Press, 1947).

32. Pollock and Maitland, op. cit., vol. 1, p. 154.

33. The degree to which the Great Charter spoke to rights, especially the right of trial by jury ("by peers") is unclear. The charter did seek to guarantee the continuance of the king's writs, such as novel disseisin, mort d'ancestor, simply because royal justice was more efficient than either local justice or self-help. See Doris M. Stenton, *English Justice between the Norman Conquest and the Great Charter, 1066–1215* (Philadelphia: American Philosophical Society, 1964). Indeed, the main thrust of the Great Charter was probably to maintain these writs and to end the abuse by the king of the traditional feudal incidents, especially wardship and relief. It is manifest that the rights to which the charter spoke were limited in application to a small proportion of the population. As Professor Samuel Thorne has written, "For a formula of politics, some theory of the state, we search it [the Great Charter] in vain. What we find instead—speaking generally, for its miscellaneous provisions cannot be summed up in a phrase—is a series of clauses regulating the relations between the king and the men of his realm. These latter are in general the tenants-in-chief, those who hold their great fiefs directly of the king, but the interests of others less exalted are not disregarded." Samuel E. Thorne, "What Magna Carta Was," in *The Great Charter*, ed. Samuel E. Thorne et al. (New York: Pantheon, 1965), p. 3.

The chapter of the charter usually cited as the guarantor of rights, at least in criminal prosecutions, is Chapter 39, which reads: "No freeman shall be taken or [and] imprisoned or disseised or exiled or in any way destroyed, nor will we go upon him nor send upon him, except by lawful judgment of his peers or [and] by the law of the land." Quoted in Thorne et al., op. cit., p. 132. This was clearly an exclusive right, and it seems at first to be limited to "peers"—that is, tenants in chief. The development into a general right appears to have been quite slow. Professor Faith Thompson writes:

Taking the fourteenth century as a whole, the sources examined reveal more references to chapter 29 [39] than to any other one provision of the charter. Moreover, it becomes apparent that this famous provision had its reputation pretty well established in these years and that there was less of novelty in later interpretations than is commonly supposed. In this period the *per judicium parium* was still appealed to as a guarantee "[t]hat execution should be preceded by a judgment." It was believed to confer trial as well as judgment by peers, and trial in which lawful procedure must be observed. In this period the *liber homo* lost whatever aristocratic connotation it had ever had and was construed as equivalent to "any freeman" or even "anyone, whoever it may be."

Faith Thompson, *Magna Carta: Its Role in the Making of the English Constitution, 1300–1629* (Minneapolis: University of Minnesota Press, 1948), p. 69.

The Magna Carta, however, was not without the bigotry of its times. For example, Chapters 10 and 11 provide: "If one who has borrowed from the Jews any sum, great or small, die before that loan be repaid, the debt shall not bear interest. . . . And if anyone die indebted to the Jews, his wife shall have her dower and pay nothing of that debt. . . ." Quoted in Thorne et al., op. cit., p. 119.

34. Pollock and Maitland expressed the belief that during this era crimes of violence were common and "the criminal law was exceedingly inefficient." Pollock and Maitland, op. cit., vol. 1, p. 557 (citing figures for the years 1221, 1256, and 1279), quoted in Dershowitz, "Preventive Confinement," op. cit., p. 15.

35. This language comes from Michael Dalton, *The Countrey Justice* (London: printed for the Societie of Stationers, 1661), describing the traditional function of the conservator of the peace.

36. By the time the Assize of Clarendon was issued (1166), it certainly could no longer be said, if ever it could, that the criminal law was exclusively or even predominantly retrospective in focus. Henry II's assize directed, "for the keeping of the peace and the maintenance of justice, that enquiry be made in every county . . . whether any man . . . is suspected or rumoured to be a robber or murderer or a receiver of robbers or murderers. . . . And let the justices enquire into this, and the Sheriffs also." Translated and reprinted in A. K. R. Kiralfy, *A Source Book of English Law* 1 (London: Sweet & Matwell, 1957). This and other twelfth-century enactments do not reflect an entirely retrospective system of justice based exclusively on revenge for completed harms, as some commentators would have it. A retrospective system would of course provide for the punishment of murderers, robbers, and arsonists, but it would not necessarily "insure enquiry" or search out all persons "suspected or rumoured" to have committed these crimes in the distant past. Enquiry and searching out, as well as "exile" and "pledges," are forward-looking, preventive techniques designed to reduce the frequency of future crimes; they are not backward-looking techniques designed exclusively to expiate past harms.

   Ten years later, in the Assize of Northampton, the list of crimes to be searched out was expanded to include larceny, forgery, and arson; the punishments were made more severe as well (including loss of hand and foot if the suspect passed the ordeal, and death if he failed it). The 1176 edict also provided for "pledges" if the defendant "came clean through"; if, however, he was "suspected of murder or other foul felony by the general opinion of the county," even if he "came clean," then "he must go into exile within forty days. . . ."

37. Beard, op. cit., p. 17. Legal historian John Bellamy wrote: "The forerunner of these justices was the keeper of the peace, who first emerged in the guise of a local military lieutenant during the civil war of 1263–5. Edward I on two occasions appointed keepers of the peace in each county to assist the sheriff, but it was his son who first issued regular commissions to them. Until 1329 the keepers had power only to record breaches of the peace, but in that year and then intermittently until 1389 when the duty was made permanent, the keepers and their successors, the justices of the peace, were empowered to determine felonies and trespasses." John Bellamy, *Crime and Public Order in England in the Later Middle Ages* (London: Routledge & Kegan Paul 1973), pp. 94–95.

38. Beard, op. cit., p. 18.

39. Ibid., p. 21. These conservators were also authorized to arrest and commit to the nearest "gaol" all "disturbers of the peace," a catchall phrase that was apparently intended to include dangerous individuals who could not be convicted of specific past offenses. In the Commission of 1313, specific reference was made to persons "who were suspected notoriously"; these persons were to "be kept in custody." By the end of Edward II's reign the conservators were authorized to disperse "seditious assemblies" and to punish, according to their discretion, all "malefactors" and "all those who were disobedient or contrary." Ibid., pp. 27–28. Preventive sanctions took a variety of forms. Although large-scale imprisonment did not begin until many centuries later, confinement in jails and dungeons was employed against dangerous persons.

40. Ibid., p. 41.

41. Ibid., p. 41. The justices were "duly to punish" those who could not comply. The express purpose of this statute was to prevent people from being put in the peril of rioters, rebels, and other blemishers of the peace.

42. As with many other markers throughout history, it may well have been true that a large proportion of criminals had these markers, but it was probably also true that only a small proportion of people with these markers became serious criminals. See below.

43. Ibid., pp. 86–87. All first offenders were to be whipped; second offenders were "to be whipped, set in pillory and lose an ear"; and third offenders were to be whipped, set in pillory, "and lose the other ear."

44. Ibid., p. 88.

45. Ibid., pp. 91–92.

46. That they have been used in a preventive way by modern-day police has been recognized by court decisions. For example, in *Papachristou v. Jacksonville*, 405 U.S. 156, 169 (1972), the Supreme Court acknowledged: "Future criminality . . . is the common justification for . . . vagrancy statutes." Such statutes are deemed necessary "to deter vagabondage and prevent crimes." See also *Johnson v. State*, 202 So. 2d 852 (Fla. 1967); *Smith v. State*, 239 So. 2d 250, 251 (Fla. 1970); *Ricks v. District of Columbia*, 414 F.2d 1097 (D.C. Cir. 1968).

47. Alan Macfarlane, *Witchcraft in Tudor and Stuart England: A Regional and Comparative study* (New York: Harper, 1970), p. 158 (citations omitted). Witchcraft prosecutions apparently constituted a significant proportion of the trials at certain times.

Macfarlane has found that over the period 1560–1680, a rather large span of time, witchcraft indictments constituted 5 percent of all the criminal proceedings at the Essex Assizes. The trial of witchcraft was second only to the trial of thieves in the number of frequency at the Essex court. As Macfarlane wrote, "It was no peripheral, abnormal crime, but of central importance. As has been demonstrated, there were few years when indictments did not occur." Ibid., p. 30. For similar ideas on the relationship between witchcraft prosecutions and other criminality, see George F. Black, *Calendar of Cases of Witchcraft in Scotland 1510 to 1727* (New York: New York Public Library, 1938).

48. Michael Dalton (d. 1648) was the author of two legal works of high repute in the seventeenth century, including *The Countrey Justice*. The available evidence suggests that Dalton was never a barrister-at-law, was not a member of Lincoln's Inn (although he dedicates *The Countrey Justice* to the masters of that society) or a master of Chancery, as is sometimes supposed. *Dictionary of National Biography,* ed. L. Stephen and S. Lee (1917), vol. 5, pp. 435–36. It is quite likely that Dalton's work is a precise and accurate portrayal of the duties of a justice of the peace during the time in which he lived, though it must be noted that *The Countrey Justice* was written at a time (1618) of both centralization and political uncertainty. Another source, A. Fitzherbert, *L'Office et Auctoryte des Justyces de Peas* (1538), is more historical, though less detailed. See W. Lambarde, *Eirenarcha: Or, of the Office of the Justice of Peace* (1581).

49. Dalton, op. cit., p. 7.

50. Ibid.

51. Ibid., p. 2, quoted in Dershowitz, "The Origins of Preventive Confinement in Anglo-American Law," loc. cit., p. 20 (emphasis added).

52. Ibid., p. 4 (emphasis added).

53. Ibid., p. 171 (emphasis added).

54. Ibid., p. 189 (emphasis added).

55. Ibid., p. 158 (emphasis added).

56. Ibid., p. 161.

57. Ibid., p. 192. The authority to bind on to "good behaviour" or to keep the peace was an important tool that seems to have been employed frequently by the justices of the peace (though Dalton never explicitly gave figures). The mechanism was simple: Any individual (with some special and limited exceptions) could come before a justice of the peace and demand that another named individual (also with some exceptions) be required to "find sureties for the peace"; the complainant had to swear that he or she was "afraid of" harm from the person complained of; this fear might derive from hostile or threatening acts, such as an "offer" or "threat" to strike, the bearing of weapons, or "an unusual number of servants or attendants. . . ." Further, the fear might derive from circumstances or reputation—for example, "if one hath received a wound," the justice of peace might require a surety "until the wound be cured and the malice be over." If the justice of peace found the fear to be reasonable, he "may by word command the same party to find sureties for the peace." Ibid., pp. 158, 161, 163–65, in Dershowitz, "Origins," loc. cit., p. 21.

58. Ibid., p. 165. These old laws were the predecessors to current orders of protection, injunctions against threatening persons, and stalking laws. Dalton did not make clear how long a person might be confined to jail "for default of sureties." He did, however, specify certain circumstances under which release should be ordered: "after he that demanded the peace against him happen to die, or shall release the peace . . . for after such death or release, there seemeth no cause to continue the other in prison." Ibid., p. 167. But the implication seems to be that absent an occurrence that eliminated, or reduced, the fear that prompted the demand for sureties, there would be no release so long as the danger continued. In practice, there may well have been informal, or even formal, limits on the duration of the confinement. If satisfactory sureties were found, the person complained against was released on recognizance. However, recognizance was forfeited by the commission of any actual breach of the peace or even any threat of or "menacing" breach. Ibid. p. 177, in Dershowitz, "Origins," loc. cit., p. 22.

59. Ibid., pp. 362–63.

60. Much has been written, especially in recent years, about the jurisdiction of the justices of the peace over vagrants, rogues, and vagabonds. The crime prevention aspects of these laws have only recently come back into focus; previously, attention centered on their economic—poor law—aspects. See, for example, *Ricks v. District of Columbia*, 414 F.2d 1097 (D.C. Cir. 1968). The two aspects were obviously related.

61. Dalton, op. cit., p. 35 in Dershowitz, "Origins," loc. cit., p. 23.

62. Ibid., pp. 36, 158.

63. Ibid., p. 65.

64. Ibid.

65. Ibid., p. 216, in Dershowitz, "Origins," loc. cit., pp. 23–24 (emphasis added).

66. Ibid., p. 217, in Dershowitz, "Origins," loc. cit., p. 24. An overt act was apparently required to convert an unlawful assembly into a "Rout": "If after their first meeting, they shall ride, go, or move forward toward the execution of any such act (whether they put their intended purpose in execution, or not) this is a Rout." The progression from inchoate to substantive crime is nicely illustrated by the next sentence: "And if they execute any such thing indeed, then it is a Riot."

67. Ibid., p. 110. It is significant that the justice of the peace could not punish them by "fine, without an enquiry, which enquiry must be by a jury, and before two Justices of the Peace," but a single justice was empowered to take "preventive action," even if that preventive action took the form of imprisonment or forfeiture of expensive weapons and armor. Ibid., p. 111.

68. Ibid., p. 339. The "fighting words" doctrine excluded words inherently likely to provoke a violent reaction, those likely to cause a fight, from the protection of the First Amendment. See *Chaplinsky v. New Hampshire*, 315 U.S. (1942), p. 568.

69. Ibid., pp. 371–72, in Dershowitz, "Origins," loc. cit., p. 25. In addition to these characterological items of evidence, which are as probative of future dangerousness as of past guilt, there were some items that specifically related to the past offense of which the defendant was suspected. Among these were:

If he hath any blood about him
. . . or that his weapon be bloody. . . .
. . . [he] is blushing, looking downwards, silence, trembling.
The bleeding of the dead body in his presence [an "old wives' tale" current in early times]
If he fled . . .
If he were the first that found the party Murdered.

70. The punishments for conviction of most past felonies was execution. It is not surprising therefore that the procedural and evidentiary requirements were more demanding.

71. Dalton, op. cit., p. 331, in Dershowitz, "Origins," loc. cit., p. 26 (emphasis added).

72. W. Blackstone, op. cit., vol. 4, p. 352; accessible at http://www.yale.edu/lawweb/ avalon/blackstone/bk4ch18.htm. Blackstone was paraphrasing earlier formulations of this principle.

73. Ibid., p. 253; accessible at http://www.yale.edu/lawweb/avalon/blackstone/bk4ch18.htm.

74. Ibid., p. 249; accessible at http://www.yale.edu/lawweb/avalon/blackstone/bk4ch18 .htm. Though Blackstone reiterated Dalton's view that no past crime was required before a person could be made to give sureties, he departed from Dalton in suggesting that a crime—or at least an act—was probably required before a recognizance would be deemed forfeited: "But not by barely giving fresh cause of suspicion of that which perhaps may never actually happen: for, though it is just to compel suspected persons to give security to the public against misbehavior that is apprehended; yet it would be hard, upon such suspicion, without the proof of any actual crime, to punish them by a forfeiture of their recognizance." Ibid., p. 254; accessible at http://www.yale.edu/lawweb/avalon/blackstone/bk4ch18.htm. Blackstone did not discuss the hardship of the person who was imprisoned, though merely suspected of future wrongdoing, because of his inability to produce sureties.

75. Ibid., vol. 4, p. 248 (emphasis added); accessible at http://www.yale.edu/lawweb/ avalon/blackstone/bk4ch18.htm. Blackstone was wrong in suggesting that preventive justice was unique to English law. All legal systems have had analogous provisions. For example, the Carolina, a German ordinance promulgated in 1532, included at least two preventive provisions: Section 176 dealt with "detention of persons of whom crime and evil must, upon manifest ground, be anticipated," and Section 195 provided for sureties upon "sufficient indication of bad intention regarding future criminal harm." See John H. Langbein, *Prosecuting Crime in the Renaissance: England, Germany, France* (Cambridge: Harvard University Press, 1974).

76. Blackstone, op. cit., vol. 4, p. 249; accessible at http://www.yale.edu/lawweb/avalon/ blackstone/bk4ch18.htm. Even this division is too sharp, at least as a factual matter, since it is likely that in a great many instances the "probable suspicion" about a future crime was in fact based upon a suspicion's falling short of the proof required for conviction of a "crime actually committed by the party" in the past. For an elaboration of this point, see Dershowitz, "Preventive Confinement," loc. cit., pp. 1288–93.

77. Dalton, op. cit., p. 331.

78. "Howard recounts many examples of prison doctors and, of course, prison personnel and their relatives who had died of prison fever. Its consequences were so widely known and feared that they would deter even the most faithful wife, the fondest father from prison visits, according to Howard, who added that in the beginning he always changed his clothes and bathed after every prison inspection. In Taunton, in 1730, according to Howard, a handful of prisoners infected the judges, the prosecutor, the sheriff and several hundred townspeople; all died. And in 1750 the Lord Mayor of London caught the disease and succumbed to it." Torsten Eriksson, *The Reformers: An Historical Survey of Pioneer Experiments in the Treatment of Criminals* (New York: Elsevier, 1976), pp. 34–35.

79. *Conductor Generalis, or the Office, Duty and Authority of Justices of the Peace* (revised and adapted to the United States of America, 1794), p. 346. Hereinafter cited as *Conductor Generalis*.

80. Ibid., p. 336. In describing the powers of the JPs in Kentucky, an 1804 treatise suggests that preventive confinement could not be employed unless the dangerous person had committed some act, such as "threatened to do . . . injury, or lain in wait" or "contend . . . with hot words, or shall go about with unusual weapons. . . ."

81. By the middle of the nineteenth century several eastern cities had well-paid, well-developed police departments charged with taking direct preventive measures. When announcing changes in the organization of the municipal police force in 1837, Boston Mayor Samuel Eliot said that the new men "would not be expected to pay for themselves through fees and other concessions but would be given regular wages, at the rate of two dollars a day. Unlike the watch, they would work in the daytime, full time. And most important, although less clear, they would be a 'preventive force.' " Roger Lane, *Policing the City: Boston 1822–1885* (Cambridge: Harvard University Press, 1967), p. 35.

At the same time in the settled but still rural areas of the Midwest, the justice of the peace was the principal crime prevention officer, but by this time he usually took action only after a complaint, and his authority was limited by long-established court systems. See Merle Curti, *The Making of an American Community: A Case Study of Democracy in a Frontier County* (Stanford: Stanford University Press, 1959), pp. 305–06. On the edge of the frontier local sheriffs had relatively complete autonomy to take any action, whether it be preventive confinement or preventive execution. A historian of the western frontier wrote:

> If a man does wrong, you chastise him. Chastisement can take any form that you think is necessary to hold him in line. One of the acceptable forms is murder. . . .
>
> Of course, one reason that this simplistic attitude toward settlement of problems prevailed on the frontier was a physical one of lack of jails. Where do you put a man when you possibly have no place to put yourself? To be neat and economical, you must put him away. This may mean tying him to a tree and leaving him to starve or be stung to death; if he has been real mean, you might like to

wrap him in rawhide and then let the sun shrink the rawhide slowly around him until he is gradually strangled. . . .

What do you do with a man whose crime may not really warrant execution? Either you execute him anyway, stifling your doubts, or you let him go.

Joe B. Frantz, "The Frontier Tradition: An Invitation to Violence," in *Violence in America: Historical and Comparative Perspectives*, ed. Hugh Graham and Ted Gurr (New York: Bantam, 1969), p. 130.

82. Like first offenders in noncapital crimes, the mentally ill were divided into two general categories, those who were strangers and those who belonged. The strangers were excluded, while those who belonged were cared for within their communities. To the colonial townsman, "insanity was really no different from any other disability; its victim, unable to support himself, took his place as one more among the needy." David J. Rothman, *The Discovery of the Asylum: Social Order and Disorder in the New Republic* (New York: Walter de Gruyter, 2002), p. 4. Thus, although "some assemblies passed laws for a special group like the insane," most of the colonies grouped the insane among other "diverse vagrant and indigent persons." Ibid., pp. 4, 23. The cause of their dependency—whether it be mental illness, physical disease, or poverty—made little difference; dependency, whatever its cause, made one either an undesirable stranger, to be excluded if possible, or an expensive burden to be borne.

A number of colonies enacted early laws providing that "when and so often as it shall happen any person to be naturally wanting of understanding, so as to be uncapable to provide for him or herself," and in the absence of relatives and property, the town "was to provide for his relief." Ibid., p. 4. The "relief" sometimes took the form of paying for the erection of an improvised asylum, as illustrated by what may be the first recorded case dealing with the mentally ill in Pennsylvania. That case, decided in 1676, provided: "Jan Vorelissen, of Amesland, Complayning to ye Court that his son Erik is bereft of his naturall Senses and is turned quyt madd and yt, he being a poore man is not able to maintaine him; Ordered: yt three or four persons bee hired to build a little block-house at Amesland for to put in the said madman." Albert Deutsch, *The Mentally Ill in America: A History of Their Care and Treatment from Colonial Times* (New York: Columbia University Press, 1962), p. 42. In other instances, the relief was merely an order that the town marshal be paid a weekly sum by the church workers "for to Subsist" the dangerous "Madman in Prison" until "he shall Recover his senses." Ibid., p. 42.

Despite some charitable instincts reflected in the early records, there can be little doubt that the primary purpose behind confinement of the mentally ill in the colonies was neither treatment nor the prospect of cure; it was to preserve peace.

The preventive nature of confining the dangerous mentally ill, and its relationship to other preventive measures, are strongly suggested by the New York statute of February 9, 1788, probably the earliest systematic legislative effort to regulate the community's response to mental illness, poverty, and minor criminal behavior. Laws of New York 1778–1792, chapter 31 § 6 (2 Greenleaf), pp. 52–54. The statute began by describing a class not of acts but of persons who "shall be deemed and adjudged disorderly persons." Its preventive focus is illustrated by the group first mentioned: "all persons who threatened to run away and leave their wives and children to the town or city." The second category included "all persons who shall unlawfully return to the city or town from whence they shall respectively have been legally removed," an implementation of the settlement, banishment, and warning-out laws, which were also preventive in nature. The remaining categories included those people typically the subject of vagrancy and disorderly person (or conduct) statutes: the "idle"; those who "go about from door to door"; "all jugglers" and persons "pretending to tell fortunes"; prostitutes; and finally, "all persons wandering abroad . . . and not giving a good account of themselves." The next section of the statute specified the places to which such persons might be confined (the "gaol," "bridewell," or "house of correction"), the duration of their confinement ("not exceeding six months"), and the punishments that could be administered to recalcitrant prisoners in order to "correct" their misbehavior ("whipping").

The sixth section of the act, which dealt with the "furiously mad," stated:

And whereas there are sometimes persons, who by lunacy or otherwise, are furiously mad, or are so far disordered in their senses that they may be dangerous to be permitted to go abroad; Therefore, be it further acted . . . That it shall and may be lawful for any two or more justices of the peace, where such lunatic or mad person shall be found, by warrant under their hands and seals, directed to the constables and overseers of the poor of the city or town, or some of them, to cause such person to be apprehended and kept safely locked up in some secure place within such city, . . . and, if such justices shall find it necessary, to be there chained, . . . and if the last legal place of settlement of such person shall not be in such city or county, then such person shall be sent to the place of his or her last settlement, in the manner directed in and by the laws relating to the poor, and shall be locked up or chained, . . . this act . . . shall not . . . restrain or abridge the power of authority of the chancellor . . . touching or concerning such lunatics; or to refrain or prevent any friend or relation of such lunatic, from taking them under their own care and protection.

Laws of New York 1778–1792, chapter 31 § 6 (2 Greenleaf), pp. 52–54.

That section also briefly encapsulated the history of the treatment of the dangerously mentally ill from colonial times to the turn of the nineteenth century. The focus was on the "furiously mad" who "may be dangerous to be permitted to go abroad." These concepts were regarded as self-defining, not requiring further legislative specification. The justices of the peace, who had a wide preventive jurisdiction over disturbers of the peace, were empowered to "lock up" the dangerously insane in "some secure place," though no specific buildings were allocated for this purpose. They were also empowered to order the inmate to be "chained." If he was a stranger, he was to be "sent to the place of his or her last settlement," just as if he were subject to the poor laws. Finally, the alternative methods of treating the mentally ill—having the chancellor appoint a guardian or having the family care for its unfortunate member—were specifically reaffirmed by the act. Ibid.

In its origins, therefore, the locking up of the mentally ill was a paradigmatic case of preventive confinement. Its function was to prevent the occurrence of anticipated conduct of a dangerous or disturbing nature. Nothing positive was expected of the confinement; it was simply regarded as a necessary and convenient way of removing—of isolating—persons whose presence in the community was deemed intolerable or dangerous. It was a kind of inward banishment; its intent was simply to build a wall, a total separation, between those who were "normal" and those who were disturbingly disturbed.

Similar walls were erected to exclude other disturbers of the peace, the poor, the minor criminal, the vagrant, the vagabond, and the contagiously ill. In each of these cases, whatever meager efforts were made to treat the underlying causes of the disability were incidental to the primary aim of prevention through isolation. The fact of the disability, not the special circumstances that caused it, led the community to isolate the unfortunate person. Likewise, the function of his custodian was simply to provide custody—nothing more and nothing less.

What is often forgotten in current discussions of confinement of the mentally ill is that its historical origins, both in Britain and in this country, had little to do with treatment or cure. Confinement of the insane preceded the development of modern psychiatry. The mental asylum came before the mental doctor. Indeed, the pre-Jacksonian statutes authorizing the incarceration of the insane generally make no mention of doctors, either as expert witnesses or as custodians of the asylums, and contemporaneous records establish that doctors were not, in fact, relied upon for either purpose. Nor were they regularly used in insanity defense cases. The mentally ill, like the poor, the vagabond, and the minor criminal, were not confined because of the illness they had but rather because of what they did and what it was expected ("predicted" is the word of a later generation) they would do. It did not require a doctor or any other kind of expert—or so it was thought—to tell the community which people needed to be confined.

Laws regulating the confinement of the insane, like other preventive laws, were relatively unstructured and informal until the middle of the nineteenth century. The forms of the law that were regarded as important in the formal system of criminal justice—trial by jury, rigorous rules of evidence, specific charges, carefully defined criteria—were replaced by virtually untrammeled discretion lodged in the justices of the peace. Operative phrases such as "if they think convenient" and "if such justices shall find it necessary" were employed in the statutes. Still, the threat to liberty created by the existence of such unregulated discretion was not as great as it might seem since the jurisdiction of the justice of the peace in most cases was limited by the amount of the fine and the duration of the confinement that could be imposed without formal trial.

With regard to the mentally ill, however, there were no express statutory limits placed on the duration of their confinements.

83. The confinement of defendants acquitted by reason of insanity is also a way of hold-ing past criminals who cannot be convicted. (In the modern context, it is clear that sex-ual psychopathy and defective delinquency statutes are often used against "known" criminals who cannot be convicted because of evidenciary inadequacies or the like.)

84. But this balloon phenomenon does not operate in isolation from other social dynam-ics. For example, it is well recognized that available spaces in custodial institutions will generally be filled even if the actual need for confinement has decreased. Thus, after the large asylums and jails were built in nineteenth-century America, they remained filled even after their exaggerated promises had been exposed as hollow. There are of course exceptions to both rules.

85. One example of a judicial effort to address these issues is found in Judge Bazelon's opinion in *Cross v. Harris*, 418 F.2d 1095 (D.C. Cir. 1969). See also *Park v. Munici-pal Judge*, 427 P.2d 642, 645 (Nev. 1967).

86. Introduction to Saleilles, op. cit., p. xi.

87. To follow through on these metaphors, we have not addressed the questions of whether a pound of prevention (measured in human confinement or other invasions of liberty) is worth an ounce (or a pound, or a ton) of cure (measured in human life). Or whether it pays to use nine stitches to save one.

CHAPTER 2.

PREEMPTIVE MILITARY ACTION:
FROM SURGICAL STRIKE TO ALL-OUT WAR

1. Gareth Evans, "When Is It Right to Fight?" *Survival*, vol. 46, no. 3 (summer 2004), p. 65; accessible at http://www.cfr.org/pdf/59–1.pdf.

2. For a discussion of this biblical episode, see Alan M. Dershowitz, *The Genesis of Jus-tice: Ten Stories of Biblical Injustice That Led to the Ten Commandments and Modern Law* (New York: Warner, 2000), pp. 147–64.

3. Even the domestic law of self-defense, which generally disallows the preemptive use of deadly force, does not require an individual to wait until his attacker actually strikes his first blow. It authorizes the use of proportional force to prevent an imminent deadly assault. See the Model Penal Code: "[T]he use of force upon or toward another per-son is justifiable when the actor believes that such force is immediately necessary for the purpose of protecting himself against the use of unlawful force by such other per-son on the present occasion." Model Penal Code § 3.04(1).

4. Other preventive attacks include, at least according to some commentators, the mas-sacre of the clan of Shechem by Jacob's sons Shimon and Levi. Although this text of Genesis (Chapter 34) describes the killings as revenge for the rape of Jacob's daugh-ter, some commentators, ever eager to defend the actions of biblical heroes, argue that the clan of Shechem was thought to be planning an attack on the family of Jacob. Another more enlightened example of preventive action from the Bible is the com-

mand to build cities of refuge into which the accidental killer might go to prevent an avenger from killing him. See Numbers 35:9–34.

5. The decision to kill the Jews can also be seen as preventive since Haman warned the king that the Jews did not obey his laws and therefore might be seen as dangerous to him.

6. In the citadel of Susa, "the Jews killed and destroyed five hundred men," including the ten sons of Haman. In all, the Jews killed more than "seventy-five thousand of them but did not lay their hands on the plunder." For this reason, the Jews celebrate the holiday of Purim "as the time when the Jews got relief from their enemies." Mordechai was to be remembered throughout history "because he worked for the good of his people and spoke up for the welfare of the Jews." Esther 3:8, 3:13, 8:8, 8:11, 9:1, 9:2, 9:4, 9:5.

7. They were not praised by God because God is not mentioned in this account. Indeed, this is the only book of the Jewish Bible in which God is never mentioned. But its inclusion in the Bible has been interpreted as bestowing acceptance on the actions of its heroes, Mordechai and Esther. Because of the absence of God in the narrative, the Book of Esther has become the "bible" of some secular Jewish nationalists and advocates of Jewish self-defense.

8. Edward Gibbon, *The Decline and Fall of the Roman Empire* (New York: Modern Library, 2005), pp. 587–88.

9. Machiavelli well understood the paradox of early intervention: The earlier the intervention, the higher the likelihood of false positives; the later the intervention, the higher the likelihood of false negatives. Niccolo Machiavelli, *The Prince*, ed. and tr. David Woottan (Indianapolis/Cambridge: Hacket Publishing Co., 1995).

10. Ibid., p. 11.

11. Quoted by Ken Adelman, "Six Degrees of Preemption," *Washington Post*, September 29, 2002, p. B2.

12. John Dryden, *Absalom and Achitopel* (London: J.T. & W. Davis, 1682), quoted in William C. Bradford, "'The Duty to Defend Them': A Natural Law Justification for the Bush Doctrine of Preventive War," *Notre Dame Law Review*, vol. 79 (2004), p. 1372. I wish to acknowledge Professor Bradford's article in which I found several quotations that I have used in this book. Although I do not subscribe to his natural law approach, I find his analysis and research useful and insightful.

13. John Locke, *Two Treatises of Government* (Cambridge: Cambridge University Press, 1988), p. 274, quoted in Bradford, op. cit., p. 1431.

14. Hugo Grotius, *De Jure Belli ac Pacis Libri Tres*, tr. Francis W. Kelsey, vol. 2, *The Classics of International Law*, ed. James Brown Scott (Oxford: Oxford University Press, 1925), p. 176, quoted in Bradford, op. cit., p. 1433.

15. Samuel von Pufendorf, *De officio hominis et civis juxta legem naturalem libri duo*, tr. Frank Gardner (Oxford: Oxford University Press, 1927), p. 32, quoted in Bradford, op. cit., pp. 1433–34.

16. Alan M. Dershowitz, *Why Terrorism Works: Understanding the Threat, Responding to the Challenge* (New Haven: Yale University Press, 2002), pp. 155–57.

17. See Thomas Hobbes, *Leviathan*, ch. XXI.

18. John Curtis Perry, *The Flight of the Romanovs* (New York: Basic Books, 1999), p. 21.
19. A similar account appears in Sophocles's *Oedipus Rex*, in which Oedipus's father has been told by the oracle that his son will kill him.
20. Quoted by Ruth Wedgwood, "Six Degrees of Preemption," *Washington Post*, September 29, 2002, p. B2.
21. See Winston Churchill, *The Gathering Storm* (Boston: Houghton Mifflin, 1948), pp. 15–16, 244–49. See also William L. Shirer, *The Rise and Fall of the Third Reich: A History of Nazi Germany* (New York: Touchstone, 1990), pp. 297–300.
22. Quoted in Paul Johnson, *Modern Times: The World from the Twenties to the Eighties* (New York: Perennial, 1983), p. 341.
23. See Shirer, op. cit., pp. 299–300:

> Though they were alarmed, Britain and France had not lifted a finger to prevent Hitler from violating the peace treaty by rearming Germany and by reoccupying the Rhineland; they had been unable to stop Mussolini in Abyssinia. And now, as the year 1937 began, they were cutting a sorry figure by their futile gestures to prevent Germany and Italy from determining the outcome of the Spanish Civil War. Everyone knew what Italy and Germany were doing in Spain to assure Franco's victory. Yet the governments of London and Paris continued for years to engage in empty diplomatic negotiations with Berlin and Rome to assure "non-intervention" in Spain. It was a sport which seems to have amused the German dictator and which certainly increased his contempt for the stumbling political leaders of France and Britain—"little worms," he would shortly call them on a historic occasion when he again humbled the two Western democracies with the greatest of ease.
>
> Neither Great Britain and France, their governments and their peoples, nor the majority of the German people seemed to realize as 1937 began that almost all that Hitler had done in his first four years was a preparation for war.

24. Historian Charles A. Beard believed that Roosevelt conducted foreign affairs (before declaring war against Japan and Germany) "as a maneuver to a foreign country into firing the shot that brought on war." Quoted in Leonard Baker, *Roosevelt and Pearl Harbor* (New York: Macmillan, 1970), p. vii.
25. See Robert Stinnett, *Day of Deceit: The Truth about FDR and Pearl Harbor* (New York: Touchstone, 2000).
26. David Alan Rosenberg, a specialist in the American national security establishment in the twentieth century and a professorial lecturer with Temple University's history department, made comments about such a preventive attack in an interview with PBS:

> The Soviet Union explodes an atomic bomb in August of 1949. It's disclosed to the world in September. In the spring and summer of 1950, the Joint Chiefs of Staff do some consideration of an additional targeting category. And in August of 1950, the Joint Chiefs lay on the Strategic Air Command the requirement to in

fact also to begin targeting Soviet capability to deliver nuclear weapons against the United States and its allies. And this is one of the great drivers of any kind of nuclear competition between the United States and the Soviet Union, at least on the America side. And that is the requirement to be able, under the right circumstances, to launch a disarming first strike against the Soviet Union. A preemptive strike, not a preventive war but a preemptive strike against Soviet nuclear capability.

"Race for the Superbomb," transcript of interview with David Alan Rosenberg; available at http://www.pbs.org/wgbh/amex/bomb/filmmore/reference/interview/rosenberg02 .html.

In *The Evolution of Nuclear Strategy*, Lawrence Freedman also discusses the debates surrounding a preventive attack:

In 1954, the feasibility of an attack upon Soviet nuclear installations was even reported to have been discussed at the level of the National Security Council. Public advocacy of preventive war was not encouraged amongst serving officers though the sentiment could, now and again, be detected. It was a minority opinion. Though it was generally felt that the Soviet Union would have few qualms about suddenly launching an unprovoked attack if the moment was considered right, it was equally generally thought that it would be quite out of character, given the prevailing morality and constitutional provisions, for the US ever to do such a thing. . . . The other alternative was taken more seriously. This was *pre-emptive* war. . . . Preventive war advocacy was based on a concern over an historical shift in the military balance. Any moment before that shift had been completed would be favourable for a strike; any moment after completion would be unfavourable. Pre-emptive war was, on the other hand, tied to a specific situation, most likely to arise after the completion of the historical shift, when there were strong grounds for believing that a Soviet strike was imminent. The second difference followed from the first. Preventive war would be based upon straightforward strategic superiority. Pre-emptive war would be launched in all probability against an enemy of equivalent strength if slower in movement.

Lawrence Freedman, *The Evolution of Nuclear Strategy* (Hampshire, U.K.: Palgrove Macmillan 2003), pp. 119–20.

A preemptive attack on nascent Chinese military nuclear facilities had also been considered:

In 1963, Gen. Maxwell Taylor, then chairman of the Joint Chiefs of Staff, planned Unconventional Warfare Program BRAVO. It called for the United States to prevent the People's Republic from building a nuclear weapon by launching a secret attack against a weapons plant in north central China. The attack was to be carried out by a nonnuclear bombing mission or a 100-man sabotage team made up of Chinese Nationalists.

The plan was vetoed on the urging of the State Department. China went forward with its nuclear weapons program, exploding its first device . . . at its Lop Nor test site on Oct. 16, 1964.

Jim Wilson, "Greatest Secrets of the Cold War," *Popular Mechanics* (April 1, 1998); accessible at http://www.popularmechanics.com/science/defense/1281171.html.

27. Franklin Delano Roosevelt, Fireside Chat (September 11, 1941), quoted in Robert Debs Heinl, Jr., ed., *Dictionary of Military and Naval Quotations* (Annapolis: United States Naval Institute Press, 1966), p. 247, quoted in Bradford, op. cit., p. 1440.

28. See John Lewis Gaddis, *We Now Know: Rethinking Cold War History* (Oxford: Oxford University Press, 1997), pp. 98, 103.

29. As a child I was certainly led to believe a nuclear attack was possible. We participated in duck and cover drills. Some people built shelters.

30. See Robert F. Kennedy, *Thirteen Days: A Memoir of the Cuban Missile Crisis* (New York: Norton, 1999), pp. 82–83; and Max Frankel, *High Noon in the Cold War: Kennedy, Khrushchev, and the Cuban Missile Crisis* (New York: Presidio, 2004), pp. 133–38. Some argue that the United States did, in fact and in law, wage a preemptive attack since a naval blockade is deemed to be an act of aggression. See Max Boot, "The Bush Doctrine Lives," *Weekly Standard*, February 16, 2004. The U.S. invasions of the Dominican Republic in 1965 and of Granada in 1983 were sought to be justified as preventive in nature, as was the death of Salvador Allende in 1973. See Charles Mohr, "President Sends Marines to Rescue Citizens of U.S. from Dominican Fighting," *New York Times*, April 29, 1965, p. 1; Michael Powell, "How America Picks Its Fights," *Washington Post*, March 25, 2003, p. C1; and Neil A. Lewis, "Delight over Coup Is Evident in Transcripts," *New York Times*, May 28, 2004, p. A17.

31. Christopher Torchia, "S. Korean: U.S. Weighed Attack on North," Associated Press, January 18, 2003.

32. See Jacqueline Cabasso and John Burroughs, "Lessons of Hiroshima: A Response to Kristof," Lawyer's Committee on Nuclear Policy, August 8, 2003; accessible at http://www.lcnp.org/wcourt/lessonsofHiroshima.htm.

33. "Legality of the Threat or Use of Nuclear Weapons: Advisory Opinion of July 8, 1996," ICJ Reports 1996, General List No. 95, paragraph 67; accessible at http://www.icj-cij.org/icjwww/icases/iunan/iunanframe.htm.

34. Ibid., paragraph 97.

35. Ibid., § (2)(D).

36. See International Committee of the Red Cross, "Basic Rules of the Geneva Conventions and Their Additional Protocols," summary, 1988; accessible at http://www.icrc.org/WEB/ENG/siteeng0.nsf/htmlall/p0365?OpenDocument&style=Custo_Final.4&View=defaultBody2.

37. The seven judges in favor were from Algeria, Germany, Hungary, Madagascar, China, Russia, and Italy. The seven judges opposed were from Sierra Leone, United Kingdom, United States, Japan, France, Guyana, and Sri Lanka. See "The Judges of the I.C.J. (1996–2000)," *World Court Digest*; accessible at http://www.virtual-institute.de/en/wcd.cfm?judges03.cfm.

38. "Legality of the Threat or Use of Nuclear Weapons," loc. cit., § (2)(E).
39. "Legality of the Threat or Use of Nuclear Weapons: Advisory Opinion of July 8, 1996, Dissenting Opinion of Vice-President Schwebel"; accessible at http://www.icj-cij .org/icjwww/icases/iunan/iunanframe.htm.
40. Ibid.
41. Ibid.
42. A "belligerent reprisal" is defined as "an enforcement measure under the law of armed conflict consisting of an act which would otherwise be unlawful but which is justified as a response to the unlawful acts of an enemy. The sole purpose of a reprisal is to induce the enemy to cease its illegal activity and to comply with the law of armed conflict. Reprisals may be taken against enemy armed forces, enemy civilians other than those in occupied territory, and enemy property." U.S. Navy, *The Commander's Handbook on the Law of Naval Operations* (Norfolk: Department of the Navy, 1995), § 6.2.3; accessible at http://www.nwc.navy.mil/ILD/NWP%201-14M%20(3%20of%205).pdf. As the definition itself states, the allowance of using force against enemy civilians as part of a belligerent reprisal would otherwise be illegal and conflicts with the general prohibition against targeting civilians.

CHAPTER 3.
PREEMPTION AND NONPREEMPTION
IN THE ARAB-ISRAELI CONFLICT—
ITS RELEVANCE TO U.S. POLICY

1. See Chapter 5.
2. See Michael Walzer, *Just and Unjust Wars* (New York: Basic Books, 2000).
3. I have studied Israel's approach to preemption since 1970, when I spent several weeks at Hebrew University researching and writing about administrative (or preventive) detention of suspected terrorists. More recently I researched targeted killings of terrorist leaders, during visits in December 2003, January 2004, and June 2005.
4. For some of Israel's enemies, a military defeat can constitute a political victory. See Abraham Rabinovich, *The Yom Kippur War: The Epic Encounter that Transformed the Middle East* (New York: Schocken, 2004), p. 507.
5. See Alan Dershowitz, *The Case for Peace: How the Arab-Israeli Conflict Can Be Resolved* (Hoboken: Wiley, 2005), pp. 91, 115–16, 143–48.
6. William C. Bradford, "'The Duty to Defend Them': A Natural Law Justification for the Bush Doctrine of Preventive War," *Notre Dame Law Review*, vol. 79 (2004), p. 1469.
7. "Remarks by the Honorable Dean Acheson," *American Society of International Law Proceedings*, vol. 57 (1963), pp. 13, 14, quoted ibid., p. 1470.
8. Dershowitz, op. cit., pp. 102–04.
9. Quoted in Alan Dershowitz, *The Case for Israel* (Hoboken: Wiley, 2003), p. 187.

10. Israel often uses retaliation as a cover for preemptive actions. After the September 1972 killings of nine Israeli Olympic athletes, Prime Minister Golda Meir approved of the assassinations of leaders of Black September, the group that carried out the massacre at the Olympics. These assassinations were "wholesale vengeance," but they also served "as a deterrent." Ian Black and Benny Morris, *Israel's Secret Wars: A History of Israel's Intelligence Services* (New York: Grove, 1991), p. 272. It is likely that many of those who were assassinated would otherwise have lived to plan and execute more attacks on Israelis.

11. Ahron Bregman, *Israel's Wars*, 2nd ed. (London and New York: Routledge, 2002), p. 35.

12. Black and Morris, op. cit., p. 128.

13. Ibid.

14. Ibid., p. 56.

15. "The fedayeen raids against Israel and the cycle of counter-raids they precipitated were the main cause of the IDF [Israel Defense Forces] invasion of the Sinai peninsula on 29 October 1956, the eastern flank of the Anglo-French-Israeli attack on Egypt known as the Suez Campaign. The immediate trigger for the Israeli offensive was the fear of Egypt's military capability, which, it was believed, would shortly be vastly increased as a result of the Egyptian-Czech arms deal of 1955. The IDF commanders feared that the dozens of modern, Soviet-made fighter aircraft, bombers, tanks and guns that began to pour into Egypt would dramatically tip the military scales against Israel within months, and that a preemptive strike was necessary for survival." Black and Morris, op. cit., p. 126.

16. Benny Morris, *Righteous Victims: A History of the Zionist-Arab Conflict* (New York: Vintage, 2001), pp. 297–98.

17. Bregman, op. cit., p. 75.

18. See pp. 82–83, 85.

19. Quoted in Dershowitz, *The Case for Israel*, loc. cit., p. 92.

20. Michael B. Oren, *Six Days of War: June 1967 and the Making of the Modern Middle East* (Oxford: Oxford University Press, 2002), pp. 186–87.

21. Samir A. Mutawi, *Jordan in the 1967 War* (Cambridge: Cambridge University Press, 1987), p. 124.

22. See Oren, op. cit., pp. 305–06.

23. Warner D. Farr, "The Third Temple's Holy of Holies: Israel's Nuclear Weapons," Counterproliferation Papers, Future Warfare Series No. 2; accessible at http://www.au.af.mil/au/awc/awcgate/cpc-pubs/farr.htm.

24. Michael Karpin, *The Bomb in the Basement* (New York: Simon & Schuster, 2006), p. 276 (of uncorrected proofs).

25. Oren, op. cit., p. 82. Some have argued, with the benefit of hindsight, that it is possible that absent Israel's first strike, there would have been no 1967 war. Even if that were true, and it is impossible to be certain that it is, Israel's actions must be judged on the basis of what it knew and reasonably believed *at the time*. As prime minister of

Israel Menachem Begin spoke about the uncertainty Israel faced and its motives in launching its preemptive strike: "In June 1967, we again had a choice. The Egyptian Army concentrations in the Sinai approaches do not prove that Nasser was really about to attack us. We must be honest with ourselves. We decided to attack him. This was a war of self-defense in the noblest sense of the term. The Government of National Unity then established decided unanimously: we will take the initiative and attack the enemy, drive him back, and thus assure the security of Israel and the future of the nation." "Excerpts from Begin Speech at National Defense College," *New York Times*, August 21, 1982, p. 6.

26. See Oren, op. cit., p. 306: "Casualty rates . . . among civilians was remarkably low [because] much of the fighting took place far from major population centers."

27. Ibid., pp. 162–64.

28. Michael Walzer, *Just and Unjust Wars* (New York: Basic Books, 2000), pp. 83–86.

29. Ibid.

30. Ibid., p. 84.

31. See also Eric Hammel, *Six Days in June: How Israel Won the 1967 Arab-Israeli War* (Pacifica, Calif.: Pacifica Press, 2001), p. 29: "[T]he bluff . . . Nasser commenced on May 13, 1967 ensured that the inevitable war would commence sooner rather than later."

32. See, for example, *Washington v. Hazlett*, 113 N.W. (1907), pp. 371, 380–81; and *Washington v. Wanrow*, 88 Wash. 2d 221, 559 P.2d (1977), p. 548.

33. Steven J. Rosen and Martin Indyk, "The Temptation to Pre-empt in a Fifth Arab-Israeli War," *Orbis* (Summer 1976), p. 270.

34. Rabinovich, op. cit., p. 87.

35. Rosen and Indyk, op. cit., p. 272.

36. Ibid., p. 273. Even in the planning stages for a possible war, preemption was essentially taken off the table:

> In the wake of the 1967 victory new elements were introduced into Israel's calculus. The capture of Sinai, the West Bank and the Golan Heights for the first time provided her with strategic depth and with what her leaders regarded as defensible borders. Thus it was believed that pre-emption was no longer a military necessity. Moreover, the political costs of pre-emption had risen considerably, as America sought stability in the region as a precondition for a negotiated settlement. Accordingly, Defense Minister Dayan ordered the IDF to rely primarily on a non-pre-emptive strategy. Instead, the Israeli forces depended on early warning of any Arab intention to attack to allow time for mobilization.

Ibid., p. 270.

37. Rabinovich, op. cit. p. 89.

38. Ibid., p. 454. Some have questioned this assessment. See p. 304, n. 50.

39. There were times during the Yom Kippur War when Moshe Dayan and others feared

for the survival of Israel. Abraham Rabinovich wrote: "What [Dayan] sensed now was Israel's mortality and it shook him. He was gripped, he would later write, by an anxiety he had never before known." Ibid., p. 218.

40. Ibid., p. 491.

41. To put the losses into comparative perspective, Israel "lost almost three times as many men per capita in nineteen days as did the United States in Vietnam in close to a decade." Ibid., p. 498.

42. Many of the Israeli casualties of the 1967 war occurred on the Jordanian front, and they might have been avoided or reduced had Israel taken preemptive action against Jordan.

43. "Arab casualties as given by a western analyst were 8,528 dead and 19,450 wounded. Israel estimated Arab casualties to be almost twice those figures—15,000 dead . . . and 35,000 wounded. . . ." Rabinovich, op. cit., p. 497.

44. Oren, op. cit., p. 305

45. Rosen and Indyk, op. cit., p. 272

46. It might also have prevented the subsequent peace treaty between Egypt and Israel— or perhaps facilitated it. No one can know for certain. The contingencies of history, especially military history, always leave much to speculation.

47. Rabinovich, op. cit., p. 55.

48. Ibid., p. 507. At least in the short term. He was assassinated several years later by Islamic fundamentalists.

49. This issue is complicated by the fact that Israel did not even call up all its reserve soldiers in the days leading up to the Yom Kippur attack, as it did in 1967. General Elazar estimated that "if we had mobilized, the war would have lasted three, four, six days." Ibid., p. 489. Mobilization, especially by Israel, which relies on reserves, can itself be viewed as a preemptive tactic—or at least as a combination of preemption and deterrence.

50. It turned out, ironically, that "[a]t the initial meeting of the policy makers [in Washington at the beginning of the war], most participants presumed that Israel had started the war"—probably because of its preemptive actions in 1967. Ibid., p. 322. This and other factors have led some experts to conclude that Meir was wrong to refuse preemption because of fear of American reaction. "Two influential exponents of this line of reasoning, Edward Luttwak and Walter Laqueur, have denigrated the political costs of pre-emption in arguing: '. . . the moral issue of who fired first did not after all make any difference. Rather the reverse. Most governments blandly accused the Israelis of being aggressors. Clearly only the United States mattered, and it remains an open question whether an Israeli air strike against Arab forces whose offensive had entered the operational phase would have made much of a difference to American opinion.'" Rosen and Indyk, op. cit., p. 275.

51. Shimon Peres, *From These Men: Seven Founders of the State of Israel* (New York: Wyndham, 1979), p. 55, quoted in Bradford, op. cit., p. 1457.

52. For an interesting analysis of how an "abundance of information" may have led Israel "to intelligence hubris," see Efraim Halevy, "In Defense of the Intelligence Services," *Economist*, July 29, 2004.

53. Walzer sought to revise the preexisting paradigm in light of his conclusion justifying Israeli preemption in the Six-Day War:

> To say that [Israel's preemption was justified], however, is to suggest a major revision of the legalist paradigm. For it means that aggression can be made out not only in the absence of a military attack or invasion but in the (probable) absence of any immediate intention to launch such an attack or invasion. The general formula must go something like this: states may use military force in the threats of war, whenever the failure to do so would seriously risk their territorial integrity or political independence. Under such circumstances it can fairly be said that they have been forced to fight and that they are the victims of aggression. Since there are no police upon whom they can call, the moment at which states are forced to fight probably comes sooner than it would for individuals in a settled domestic society. But if we imagine an unstable society, like the "wild-west" of American fiction, the analogy can be restated: a state under threat is like an individual hunted by an enemy who has announced his intention of killing or injuring him. Surely such a person may surprise his hunter, if he is able to do so. The formula is permissive, but it implies restrictions that can usefully be unpacked only with reference to particular cases. It is obvious, for example, that measures short of war are preferable to war itself whenever they hold out the hope of similar or nearly similar effectiveness. But what those measures might be, or how long they must be tried, cannot be a matter of *a priori* stipulation. In the case of the Six Day war, the "asymmetry in the structure of forces" set a time limit on diplomatic efforts that would have no relevance to conflicts involving other sorts of states and armies. A general rule containing words like "seriously" opens a broad path for human judgment—which it is, no doubt, the purpose of the legalist paradigm to narrow or block altogether. But it is a fact of our moral life that political leaders make such judgments, and that once they are made the rest of us do not uniformly condemn them. Rather, we weigh and evaluate their actions on the basis of criteria like those I have tried to describe. When we do that we are acknowledging that there are threats with which no nation can be expected to live. And that acknowledgment is an important part of our understanding of aggression.

Walzer, op. cit., p. 85.

54. UN Secretary-General Kurt Waldheim called Israel's rescue of the hostages a "serious violation of Uganda's national sovereignty." Kathleen Teltsch, "U.S. Wants U.N. to Debate Hijacking as Well as Israeli Raid," *New York Times*, July 8, 1976, p. 4.

55. A successful rescue was expected to result in twenty Israeli fatalities. See Zeev Maoz, "The Decision to Raid Entebbe: Decision Analysis Applied to Crisis Behavior," *Journal of Conflict Resolution*, vol. 25, no. 4 (December 1981), p. 698.

56. The Israeli soldier who was killed was the older brother of Israel's future prime minister Benjamin Netanyahu. Yehonatan Netanyahu, the leader of the raiding party, was shot by a sniper as the mission was being completed.

57. It is quite informative to read the actual text of the resolution, especially recalling that the president of Uganda, Idi Amin, was actively complicit with the hijackers and personally ordered the murder of an elderly Jewish woman who had been taken to a hospital following the hijacking:

> The Assembly of Heads of State and Government of the Organization of African Unity, meeting in its Thirteenth Ordinary Session at Port Louis, Mauritius, from 2nd to 6th July 1976,
>
> *Having heard* the statement of the Minister of Foreign Affairs of the Republic of Uganda;
>
> *Deeply alarmed* about the Israeli aggression on Uganda which constitutes a threat to international peace and security;
>
> *Considering* that an aggression against one OAU Member State, is aggression against all Member States requiring collective measure to repel it;
>
> *Believing* that such aggression results from the policy of cooperation between Israel and South Africa which aims at threatening the independence and territorial integrity of all African and Arab States and to undermine the aim of Africa to liberate the territories which are still under colonialism and racist domination in the Southern part of Africa.
>
> 1. *Strongly condemns* the Israeli aggression against the sovereignty and territorial integrity of Uganda; the deliberate killing and injuring of people and wanton destruction of property; and for having thwarted the humanitarian efforts by the President of Uganda to have the hostages released;
>
> 2. *Calls* for an immediate meeting of the United Nations Security Council with a view to taking all appropriate measures against Israel, including measures under Chapter 7 of the United Nations Charter;
>
> 3. *Expresses* its full support to Uganda and its appreciation to its president for the humanitarian role he has played;
>
> 4. *Decides* to send a message of solidarity, support and condolence to the President and people of Uganda; and
>
> 5. *Calls upon* all African States to intensify their efforts in order to isolate Israel and compel her to change her aggressive policy;
>
> 6. *Calls upon* Member States of the OAU to assist Uganda to retrieve much of what she has lost;
>
> 7. *Mandates* the Current Chairman of the Council of Ministers and Guinea and Egypt to assist Uganda in putting the case before the Security Council.

AHG/Res.83 (XII), Resolution on Israel Aggression Against Uganda; accessible at http://www.iss.co.za.AF/RegOrg/unity_to_union/pdfs/oau/hog/mHoGAssembly 1976.pdf

58. Maoz, op. cit.

59. This act of separating the hostages along primarily religious lines reminded many of the notorious "selections" that led many to their deaths at Auschwitz. It generated

emotional reaction in Israel and may have contributed to the decision to take military action. Ibid., p. 688

60. Ibid., p. 689.
61. Maoz wrote:

> The evidence suggests that complex outcomes were decomposed into distinct elements, that conditions of dependence and interdependence among elements were determined and processed accordingly, and that the combination of those elements into an overall estimate intuitively approximated optimal methods such as Bayesian analysis. . . . Base rates were not ignored; on the contrary, they were clearly incorporated into the estimation process. This is best illustrated by the use of background evidence regarding previous operations of Hadad's organization in combination with current evidence regarding the behavior of the hijackers toward the hostages. This combination allowed the decision makers to assess the credibility of the hijackers' threats. Moreover, there is no evidence to suggest that unequal weights were assigned to data supporting favorable outcomes relative to data supporting unfavorable outcomes. The decision makers were equally receptive to "bad news"—for instance Amin's refusal to cooperate with Israel— as they were with respect to "good news."
>
> Given the enormous time pressure the decision makers experienced, and given the overwhelming quantity of information they were required to process, the quality of the revision process was remarkably high.

Ibid., pp. 695–96.
62. Ibid., p. 695.
63. Ibid., p. 704.
64. Michael Reisman, "Assessing Claims to Revise the Laws of War," *American Journal of International Law*, vol. 97, no. 1 (2003), pp. 82–90.
65. Quoted in Shlomo Nakdimon, *First Strike: The Exclusive Story of How Israel Foiled Iraq's Attempt to Get the Bomb* (New York: Summit, 1987), p. 156.
66. Shlomo Nakdimon, *First Strike* (New York: Summit, 1987), p. 156.
67. See, generally, Michael Karpin, *The Bomb in the Basement* (New York: Simon & Schuster, 2006).
68. See statement of Arthur Goldberg, pp. 98–99.
69. See Richard Posner, *Catastrophe* (Oxford: Oxford University Press, 2004) for an interesting analysis of decision making in the face of unlikely but potentially catastrophic threats.
70. Nakdimon, op. cit., pp. 239–40.
71. Ibid., p. 232.
72. Ibid., p. 317.
73. Ibid., pp. 274–75 and 276. Thus, even if mutually assured destruction is lawful (but see the International Court of Justice opinion, pp. 71–72), moral leaders might be hesitant to retaliate against civilian population centers.

74. Michael Walzer, *Arguing about War* (New Haven: Yale University Press, 2004), p. 147.

75. "Six Degrees of Preemption," *Washington Post*, September 29, 2002, p. B2.

76. Ibid.

77. One possible reason for this attitude was the fact that the United States was supporting Iraq at the time in its war against Iran.

78. Margaret Thatcher, "Don't Go Wobbly," *Wall Street Journal*, June 17, 2002.

79. After the war began, the "Iron Lady" changed her mind again, calling the war a mistake and criticizing Tony Blair for involving Great Britain in a "mission without end for years." Chris Mclaughlin, "Maggie's Mauling for Blair," *Sunday Mirror*, September 21, 2003; accessible at http://www.sundaymirror.co.uk/news/news/page.cfm?objectid =13431916&method=full&siteid=106694.

80. Nakdimon, op. cit., p. 269 (emphasis added).

81. Ibid. pp. 257–58.

82. Ibid., pp. 256–57.

83. This argument was made by Walter Sullivan, among others. Walter Sullivan, "U.S. Expert Disputes Israelis on Reactor," *New York Times*, June 25, 1981, p. A9. Another *New York Times* article soon after the bombing reported that it would have been much more hazardous to bomb a reactor that had already gone critical. Walter Sullivan, "Hazard from Debris Considered Limited," *New York Times*, June 9, 1981, p. A9. See also Richard Wilson, "Israel Stopped No Iraqi A-Bomb Production," *New York Times*, June 14, 1984, p. A22.

84. Nakdimon, op. cit., p. 262.

85. Israel did bomb the outskirts of Beirut in an effort to destroy terrorist enclaves, and early in its history it took retaliatory action against enemy villages. Lee Hockstader, "Israeli Bombs Hit Targets near Beirut," *Washington Post*, June 25, 1999, p. A21; and Benny Morris, *Righteous Victims: A History of the Zionist-Arab Conflict* (New York: Vintage, 2001), pp. 276–77. But it did not bomb Cairo, Amman, Baghdad, or Damascus in retaliation for bombs dropped on its cities.

86. It is of course uncertain what Israel would actually do in the event of a nuclear attack on one of its cities. This uncertainty itself provides some deterrent impact.

87. See Machiavelli, pp. 63–64.

88. Bregman, op. cit., pp. 159–60.

89. Ibid., p. 175.

90. Ibid., pp. 176–78.

CHAPTER 4.
PREVENTIVE MEASURES AGAINST TERRORISM

1. It is of course possible that a leader of a nation may be willing to die and to take many of his citizens with him. See statement of Hashemi Rafsanjani, p. 175.

2. Defence of the Realm Consolidation Act, November 27, 1914; accessible at http:

//www.nationalarchives.gov.uk/pathways/firstworldwar/transcripts/first_world_war/ defence_ofthe-realm.htm.

3. See generally Stephen J. Schulhofer, "Checks and Balances in Wartime: American, British and Israeli Experiences," *Michigan Law Review,* vol. 102 (2004), pp. 1906–58.

4. *A(FC) v Home Secretary* [2004] UKHL 56; accessible at http://news.bbc.co.uk/1/ shared/bsp/hi/pdfs/16_12_04_detainees.pdf.

5. Mark Oliver and Sarah Left, "Law Lords Back Terror Detainees," *Guardian*, December 16, 2004; accessible at http://www.guardian.co.uk/terrorism/story/0,12780,1374967,00.html.

6. "UK Court Rejects Terror Detentions," CNN, December 16, 2004; accessible at http://edition.cnn.com/2004/WORLD/europe/12/16/britain.detention/.

7. John Deane, "Blair Defends Terror Suspects Crackdown," *Press Association,* September 16, 2005.

8. Ibid.

9. Ibid.

10. "Blair unveils new anti-terrorism plans," *Xinhua News Agency,* August 5, 2005. After concern was expressed that terror suspects would face "torture and inhuman treatment" by the countries to which they are deported, the British Home Office reportedly signed a treaty with Jordan, declaring that those deported by Britain will not be sentenced to death or mistreated. Ibid.

11. Ibid.

12. Alan Cowell, "Britain Considers Lengthening Time for Holding Terror Suspects," *New York Times,* August 10, 2005, p. 8.

13. Ibid.

14. Ibid.

15. Human Rights Watch, "UK: Detention Plan Amounts to Punishment Without Trial. Draft Antiterrorism Law Raises Serious Human Rights Concerns," London, September 16, 2005, accessible at http://www.hrw.org/english/docs/2005/09/16/uk11751.htm.

16. Raymond Bonner, "Australia to Present Strict Antiterrorism Statute," *New York Times*, November 3, 2005, p. 6.

17. Shortly after Lincoln issued his "incarceration proclamation," an obscure Marylander named John Merryman, whose loyalties were apparently with the South, was roused from his bed at two in the morning, taken to Fort McHenry, and imprisoned there under military guard. A writ of habeas corpus was sought from the chief justice of the United States, Roger B. Taney, a Lincoln antagonist and author of the infamous *Dred Scott* decision. Taney's opinion gave Lincoln a failing grade in constitutional law. "I had supposed it to be one of those points in constitutional law upon which there was no difference of opinion," he commented sarcastically, "that the privilege of the writ could not be suspended, except by act of Congress." But though the chief justice ordered Merryman released, he remained confined. The general in charge of the fort simply denied the marshal permission to serve the necessary papers, and Lincoln took no official notice of the opinion (which was personally transmitted to him by order of the Court).

18. Congress enacted a statute giving President Lincoln even more authority to suspend constitutional safeguards than he had requested. And so when Lambdin Milligan was

arrested in Indiana on October 5, 1864, there was little doubt that the privilege of the writ of habeas corpus had been properly suspended. Not content to detain him, the military authorities decided to try Milligan, a civilian, before a military commission, which promptly sentenced him to hang. By the time the case worked its way up to the Supreme Court, the war was over, and in the words of Justice David Davis, "now that the public safety is assured, this question . . . can be discussed and decided without passion or the admixture of any element not required to form a legal judgment."

19. *Ex parte Milligan*, 71 U.S. (4 Wall.) (1866), p. 2.

20. *Moyer v. Peabody*, 212 U.S. 78, 84 (1909). Although Justice Holmes intimated that the Court might not sustain a detention of undue duration, his uncritical legitimation of the governor's exercise of extraordinary power was a clear invitation to abuse. And abuse was not long in coming. Numerous governors invoked the magic phrase "martial law" as a kind of "household remedy" to accomplish such diverse and illegitimate ends as closing a racetrack, manipulating a primary election, keeping a neighborhood segregated, and—most often—settling labor strikes to the advantage of management. It was inevitable that the Supreme Court could not long tolerate such bogus declarations of martial law. The case that finally wore the Court's patience arose in the East Texas oil fields during the early years of the Depression. The governor declared martial law and ordered restrictions on the production of oil in an effort to raise its price. There were no riots or violence, nor were any troops employed. Martial law was invoked simply to accomplish economic ends. The Supreme Court enjoined the governor's action, reasoning that unless it did so, "the fiat of a state Governor, and not the Constitution of the United States, would be the supreme law of the land." Alan M. Dershowitz, *Shouting Fire* (New York: Little, Brown, 2002), p. 422.

21. The civilian governor handed the reins of government over to the military only after receiving assurances that civilian control would be restored as soon as the immediate emergency was over—within days or, at most, weeks. Relative calm returned quickly to the islands as the threat of renewed attack dissipated. Places of amusement and saloons were permitted to open in February 1942, and life returned to near normality after the U.S. victory at Midway removed any realistic threat of invasion. But the military still insisted that the civil courts remain closed and the writ of habeas corpus remain suspended. Over the next years a considerable battle ensued between the ousted civilian officials and the governing generals. It culminated in a contempt citation issued by a federal judge against the commanding general followed by an order issued by the general threatening to court-martial the judge if he persisted in issuing writs of habeas corpus.

22. *Duncan v. Kahanamoku*, 327 U.S. 304, 316–17 (1946).

23. Virtually all of them born here, since residents who emigrated from Japan were ineligible for American citizenship under the racial prohibitions then on the statute books.

24. This is the claim of the Japanese American Citizens League, and I know of no allegations to the contrary.

25. Quoted in Bill Hosokawa, *Nisei: The Quiet Americans* (New York: Norton, 1969), pp. 287–88.

26. Ibid., p. 260.

27. Virtually no exceptions were made; those detained included veterans of World War I, future soldiers who were to die fighting in the famous 442nd Regimental Combat Team (the Nisei Brigade), and lifelong members of the American Legion (whose monthly publication advocated "putting American Japanese on some Pacific island").

28. Professor Mark Tushnet has defended *Korematsu* on experiential grounds, writing "that *Korematsu* was part of a process of social learning that both diminishes contemporary threats to civil liberties in our present situation and reproduces a framework of constitutionalism that ensures that such threats will be a permanent part of the constitutional landscape. . . . I have tried to explain how decision-makers faced with what they understood to be a threat to the nation might engage in actions that in retrospective seem quite unjustified." Mark Tushnet, "Defending *Korematsu?*: Reflections on Civil Liberties in Wartime," *Wisconsin Law Review* (2003), p. 274.

29. Quoted in Dershowitz, op. cit., pp. 420–23, 440–42.

30. I have argued elsewhere that Justice Robert Jackson was wrong when he made the following observations:

> Much is said of the danger to liberty from the Army program for deporting and detaining these citizens of Japanese extraction. But a judicial construction of the due process clause that will sustain this order is a far more subtle blow to liberty than the promulgation of the order itself. A military order, however unconstitutional, is not apt to last longer than the military emergency. Even during that period a succeeding commander may revoke it all. But once a juridical opinion rationalizes such an order to show that it conforms to the Constitution, or rather rationalizes the Constitution to show that the Constitution sanctions such an order, the Court for all time has validated the principle of racial discrimination in criminal procedure and of transplanting American citizens. The principle then lies about like a loaded weapon ready for the hand of any authority that can bring forward a plausible claim of an urgent need. Every repetition imbeds that principle more deeply in our law and thinking and expands it to new purposes. All who observe the work of courts are familiar with what Judge Cardozo described as "the tendency of a principle to expand itself to the limit of its logic." A military commander may overstep the bounds of constitutionality, and it is an incident. But if we review and approve, that passing incident becomes the doctrine of the Constitution. There it has a generative power of its own, and all that it creates will be in its own image.

Korematsu v. United States, 323 U.S. 214 (1944), pp. 245–46 (note omitted). This is what I have argued in response:

> Experience has not necessarily proved Jackson's fear . . . to be well founded. The very fact that the Supreme Court expressly validated the detentions contributed to its condemnation by the verdict of history. Today the Supreme Court's deci-

sion in *Korematsu* stands alongside decisions such as *Dred Scott, Plessy v. Ferguson*, and *Buck v. Bell* in the High Court's Hall of Infamy. Though never formally overruled, and even occasionally cited, *Korematsu* serves as a negative precedent—mistaken ruling not ever to be repeated in future cases. Had the Supreme Court merely allowed the executive decision to stand without judicial review, a far more dangerous precedent might have been established: namely, that executive decisions during times of emergency will escape review by the Supreme Court. That far broader and more dangerous precedent would then lie about "like a loaded weapon" ready to be used by a dictator without fear of judicial review. That comes close to the current situation, in which the administration denies it is acting unlawfully, while aggressively resisting any judicial review of its actions with regard to terrorism.

Alan Dershowitz, "Tortured Reasoning," in *Torture: A Collection*, ed. Sanford Levinson (Oxford: Oxford University Press, 2004), pp. 268–69.

31. In *Rasul v. Bush*, 124 S.Ct. 2686 (2004), the Supreme Court ruled that foreign-born detainees at Guantánamo Bay can challenge their captivity in the U.S. judicial system.

32. According to the Israel Defense Forces, there were 135 successful terrorist attacks in Israel between October 2000 and November 2004, while 431 potential terrorist attacks were thwarted during that period. See "Suicide Bomber Attacks Carried-Out vs. Attacks Prevented" link at http://www1.idf.il/dover/site/mainpage.asp?sl=EN&id=22&docid=16703.EN&unit=10.

33. Following the Oslo Accords, Israel vacated the West Bank population centers to a large degree but reoccupied most of them following the renewal of terrorism in 2001.

34. Emergency Powers (Detention) Law, 5739–1979.

35. There exists, under U.S. law, a statutory framework for dealing with some such issues. See 18 U.S.C. 4001. But it does not cover all such issues. See Philip B. Heymann and Juliette N. Kayyem, *Protecting Liberty in an Age of Terror* (Cambridge, Mass.: MIT Press, 2005), pp. 41–52.

36. The references were to a case then under consideration.

37. See Dershowitz, *Shouting Fire*, loc. cit., pp. 431–56.

38. See *Hamdi v. Rumsfeld*, 124 S.Ct. 2633 (2004).

39. Laura King, "Israel to Delay Pullout from Gaza," *Los Angeles Times*, May 10, 2005, p. A4.

40. *Williamson v. United States*, 184 F.2d 280, 282 (2d Cir. 1950). See also Albin Eser, "The Principle of 'Harm' in the Concept of Crime: A Comparative Analysis of the Criminally Protected Legal Interests," *Duquesne University Law Review* (1965–1966), 345–417.

41. 18 U.S.C. § 4001 (a). In 1970 Congress also repealed the McCarran Act, which had been on the books for twenty years. The statute authorized during periods of internal security emergency the preventive confinement of persons who there was "reasonable

ground to believe . . . probably will commit or conspire with other to commit espionage or sabotage. . . ." The statute cataloged "evidentiary matters" that should be considered in making this decision. Not surprisingly, the matters consisted primarily of
suspected past actions, such as (1) whether "such person has knowledge of or has
received or given instruction or assignment in the espionage, counterespionage, or sabotage service," (2) "any past . . . acts of espionage or sabotage," or (3) "activity in the
espionage or sabotage operations of, or the holding at any time after January 1, 1949,
of membership in, the Communist Party of the United States. . . ." Acts within the
first category would of course constitute serious crimes if they could be proved. The
McCarran Act thus employed "preventive" detention in this category of cases to dis-
pense with the rigorous requirements of proving past criminality. Acts in the second
category would also be crimes, unless they had already been punished or the statute
of limitation had run. Preventive detention was thus being employed to circumvent
the double jeopardy and ex post facto prohibitions of the Constitution. Acts in the
third category, if not covered by the first two, would consist of membership in an organization that a statute of doubtful constitutionality had made criminal. The act thus
used preventive detention to avoid a possible judicial decision that membership could
not be criminalized.

 The McCarran Act differed in fundamental respects from the preventive action
taken against the Japanese-Americans. The former attempted primarily to confine individuals whose past suspected acts of espionage, sabotage, or membership in hostile
organizations made them dangerous; the latter to confine an entire group without regard
to individual past acts. Inclusion in the former category required a voluntary act; inclusion in the latter required merely an involuntary and unchangeable "birth status."

42. Professor Martha Minow has written: "The actual number of detainees held by the
 United States since September 11 is difficult to verify because the government has
 treated this matter as too sensitive for disclosure. One estimate made indicates 2200
 detainees within the United States, 800 at Guantanamo Bay, and 50,000 in Iraq and
 Afghanistan." Martha Minow, "What Is the Greatest Evil? Book Review of *The Lesser
 Evil*, by Michael Ignatieff," *Harvard Law Review*, vol. 118, no. 7 (May 2005), pp.
 2134–35, n. 2.

43. These "witnesses" would of course have a Fifth Amendment privilege against self-
 incrimination with regard to their own crimes that could be trumped only by a grant
 of derivative use immunity. See *Kastigar v. United States*, 406 U.S. 441 (1972).

44. Alan Dershowitz, "'Stretch Points' of Liberty," *Nation*, March 15, 1971, pp. 329–34.

45. Landau Commission, "The Report of the Commission of Inquiry Concerning Methods of Investigation by the General Security Service of Hostile Terrorist Activity,"
 October 1987.

46. Or a waiver by the person being questioned.

47. See *Chavez v. Martinez*, 538 U.S. 760 (2003).

48. This mechanism brings up the extraordinarily controversial, and emotional, issue of
 what is euphemistically called highly coercive interrogation techniques and what has

been colloquially labeled "torture lite." The scandal at Abu Ghraib prison in Iraq focused the attention of the world on this problem.

In December 2004 a report entitled "Long-term Legal Strategy Project for Preserving Security and Democratic Freedoms in the War on Terrorism" was issued by Harvard's Kennedy School of Government. Among the subjects the report covered was the preventive detention of suspected terrorists who could not be brought to trial without endangering national security. The distinguished group responsible for the report recommended an approach to preventive detention not very different from that employed by Great Britain and Israel. "On an *ex parte* showing to a court that, despite the Classified Information Procedure Act, a trial would currently be impossible without a severe loss of National Security secrets, and evidence that cannot be revealed in public demonstrating that release of the detainee would significantly endanger the lives of others," the judge can order the preventive detention of the suspect "for a period of up to two years." (The detention can be authorized for only ninety days and can be renewed for up to two years.)

Beyond some general language regarding burdens of proof, the report provided few specifics on the nature of the evidence required—would hearsay suffice?—or about the number of false positives the process should be willing to tolerate in order to prevent possible acts of terrorism of what magnitude. (Double false positives are likely under any such procedure; the suspect may be innocent of the past crimes of which he is suspected and may not commit the future crimes that he is predicted to commit.) Even more disappointing was the report's refusal to face up to the issue of precisely what sorts of extraordinary interrogation measures, short of outright torture, it was willing to accept. For example, it has been widely reported that "water boarding" has been used by American intelligence officials against some high-value sources. This technique places the subject on a board and lowers his head into water until he experiences the sensation of nearly drowning. It is repeated until the subject indicates a willingness to cooperate. Is this an acceptable tactic in extraordinary cases? Does it constitute torture? Is it "better" or "worse" than the nonlethal infliction of excruciating pain? Is it permissible under our law and treaty obligations? Instead of answering these currently pressing and very real questions, the report left them to the political process, which is supposed to determine which specific measures are acceptable under what circumstances. Heymann and Kayyem, op. cit., pp. 23–32. These difficult and controversial issues would justify an entire book of their own.

49. In December 2004 Britain's high court ruled in an 8–1 decision that indefinite detention of terror suspects was a human rights violation and therefore impermissible. *A v. Secretary of State for the Home Department* (2004) UKHL 56; accessible at http://www .publications.parliament.uk/pa/ld200405/ldjudgmt/jd041216/a&oth-l.htm.

50. Ian Black and Benny Harris, *Israel's Secret Wars: A History of Israel's Intelligence Services* (New York: Grove, 1991), pp. 194–96.

51. For a more critical assessment of this operation, see Michael Karpin, *The Bomb in the Basement* (New York: Simon & Schuster, 2006).

52. Gordon Thomas, *Gideon's Spies* (New York: St. Martin's, 1999), pp. 123–24.

53. Ibid., p. 123.

54. For an account of this decision, see Alan M. Dershowitz, *Why Terrorism Works: Understanding the Threat, Responding to the Challenge* (New Haven: Yale University Press, 2002), pp. 41–50.

55. Black and Morris, op. cit., p. 272.

56. They are combatants because they are part of a paramilitary insurgency, but they are not POWs because they themselves do not follow the laws of war in their targeting of civilians. Professor Rotunda contends that not all detainees should be considered prisoners of war. The basic rights afforded to POWs under the Geneva Convention are applicable only to "lawful combatants." As such, he has written "unlawful combatants," such as terrorists who do not abide by the international rules of engagement, should not be considered POWs, unless "they file a declaration with the Swiss government accepting the obligations of the [Geneva Convention]." Ronald D. Rotunda, "No POWs," *National Review Online*, January 29, 2002; accessible at http://www.nationalreview.com/comment/comment-rotunda012902.shtml.

57. Yoram Dinstein, *The Conduct of Hostilities under the Law of International Armed Conflict* (Cambridge: Cambridge University Press, 2004), p. 29.

58. According to B'Tselem, the Israeli Information Center for Human Rights in the Occupied Territories, between September 29, 2000, and September 30, 2005, 300 Palestinians were killed during the course of an assassination. Of that total, 191 were assassination targets. See http://www.btselem.org/English/Statistics/Casualties.asp. As I wrote in *The Case for Peace*: "In June 2005, I interviewed the commander of the Israeli Air Force, General Elyezer Shkedy, about targeted killings and civilian casualties. He told me that until the beginning of 2004, the ratio of terrorists to civilians killed by targeted bombings was approximately 1:1. But as a result of sophisticated technological improvements, that ratio changed dramatically between early 2004 and 2005 to twelve terrorists killed for every civilian killed." Alan Dershowitz, *The Case for Peace* (Hoboken: Wiley, 2005), p. 78.

59. A common variation on this paradigm involves an armed terrorist about to enter a Jewish settlement in Gaza. This variation no longer exists now that Israel has abandoned its settlements in Gaza.

60. See Alan Dershowitz, "Should This Man Be Assassinated? Israel Is Perfectly within Its Rights to Execute Its Terrorist Enemies," *Toronto Globe & Mail*, September 16, 2003.

61. John Howard, Australia's prime minister, "repeatedly has said his government would attack militants overseas if they were planning to strike Australian interests and the host country refused to act. . . . Mr. Howard instituted the policy after a bomb attack in Bali two years ago killed dozens of Australian tourists, and other attacks and threats from Islamic militants based in Indonesia." Phil Mercer, "Tensions Rise over Australia's Pre-Emptive Strike Policy ahead of ASEAN Summit," Voice of America, November 26, 2004; accessible at http://128.11.143.114/english/2004-11-26-voa13.cfm.

62. Ibraham Bani Odeh, a bomb maker for Hamas, was killed in November 2000, when the car he was driving exploded. Nobody else was reported hurt in the blast. Although

some Israeli officials denied responsibility for the death, Israel had issued a warning earlier in the week that it would hunt down terrorists. Jamie Tarabay, "Palestinians Blame Israel on Death,"Associated Press, November 25, 2000. Palestinians executed Bani Odeh's relative after finding him guilty of assisting Israel in the bombing. "Palestinians Executed for Israel Links," CNN, January 13, 2001; accessible at http://archives.cnn.com/2001/WORLD/meast/01/13/palestinian.executions/. In August 2001 undercover soldiers shot and killed Emad Abu Sneineh, a Fatah militant. No injuries were reported. Greg Myre, "Israeli Troops Kill Militia Leader," Associated Press, August 15, 2001. A member of Al Aqsa Martyrs Brigade was killed in June 2001 when the public telephone he was using exploded. Two bystanders "were lightly wounded by flying debris." Jamie Tarabay, "Palestinian Activist Killed in Explosion," Associated Press, June 24, 2001.

63. Margot Dudkevitch, "Shehadeh Was 'Ticking Bomb,'" *Jerusalem Post*, July 24, 2002, p. 3.

64. Ibid.

65. John Ward Anderson and Molly Moore, "Palestinians Vow Revenge after Gaza Missile Strike; Militants Said to Be Poised for Truce before Hamas Figure, 14 Others Died," *Washington Post*, July 24, 2002, p. A13.

66. Ibid.

67. Janine Zacharia and Gil Hoffman, "US Condemns 'Heavy-handed' Action," *Jerusalem Post*, July 24, 2002, p. 1.

68. Dudkevitch, op. cit.

69. Anderson and Moore, op. cit.

70. Ibid.

71. "Global Condemnation for Strike: U.S.: It was 'heavy-handed,'" *Ha'aretz*, July 23, 2002.

72. President Clinton authorized the targeted killing of Osama bin Laden in 1998, following "the bombing of two U.S. embassies in East Africa which Bin Laden was suspected of masterminding." "Clinton Ordered Bin Laden Killing," BBC News, September 23, 2001; accessible at http://news.bbc.co.uk/1/hi/world/americas/1558918.stm.

73. Alan M. Dershowitz, "Killing Terrorist Chieftains Is Legal," *Jerusalem Post*, April 22, 2004; accessible at http://www.jpost.com/servlet/Satellite?pagename=JPost/JPArticle/ShowFull+cid=1082606033932.

74. See HCJ 5100/94, *Public Committee against Torture in Israel v. Government of Israel*.

75. See Christopher Shea, "Countless," *Boston Globe*, November 7, 2004, p. D4.

76. Heymann and Kayyem, op. cit., pp. 63–64.

77. Ibid., p. 60 (internal quotation marks omitted).

78. For the details of the criteria, see ibid., p. 66.

79. The criteria proposed in the Heymann-Kayyem report are certainly an improvement over the current rules for covert actions, which, according to the report, include the following:

> If a targeted killing were to be carried out in the form of a covert action by an intelligence agency, the President would have to comply with specific procedures

under federal statutes. In order to authorize a covert action, the President must make a finding that (1) the action is necessary to support identifiable foreign policy objectives of the United States and (2) is important to the national security of the United States. . . . These findings must be sent to the congressional intelligence committees, but, in extraordinary circumstances, they may be sent only to the congressional leadership.

Ibid., pp. 60–61. This was precisely the sort of vague and open-ended criteria—"necessary to support identifiable foreign policy objectives of the United States" and "important to the *national security* of the United States"—that was used by some to justify our ignoble role in the death of the Western Hemisphere's first elected Marxist leader Salvadore Allende. See Diana Jean Schemo, "U.S. Victims of Chile's Coup: The Uncensored File," *New York Times*, February 13, 2000, p. 1. It would be difficult to imagine an assassination that could not be rationalized by reference to foreign policy objectives and national security interests. The only acceptable criteria for a preemptive targeted killing must relate to relatively certain terrorist threats involving mass casualties, multiple attacks, the acquisition of weapons of mass destruction, and the like.

80. Mark Lavie, "Israel Resumes Diplomatic Contacts with Palestinians, Halts Targeted Killings of Militants," Associated Press, January 26, 2005.

81. Ori Nir, "CIA-linked Study Warns of Bio-terrorist Attacks during the Next 15 Years," *Forward*, January 21, 2005, p. 1.

82. Ibid.

83. The health care apparatus in New Orleans did not fare well during the hurricane and its aftermath. One doctor wrote: "Hurricane Katrina struck a devastating blow to health care in New Orleans and the Gulf Coast, crippling most hospitals, destroying virtually all nursing homes, shutting down two medical schools and wiping out thousands of physicians' practices." Dr. Carmen A. Puliafito, "How to Hurricane-Proof Health Care," *Palm Beach Post* October 2, 2005; accessible at http://www.palmbeachpost .com/opinion/content/opinion/epaper/2005/10/02/ale_puliafito_1002.html.

84. There may, however, be psychological costs attached even to the construction of detox facilities. The large shower rooms remind some of the gas chambers at Auschwitz and other death camps, even though their purpose is to save life.

85. Ian Urbina, "Antiterror Test to Follow Winds and Determine Airborne Paths," *New York Times*, February 11, 2005, p. B1.

86. Ian Urbina, "City Weighs Plans to Deliver Medicine to Public after Attack," *New York Times*, February 7, 2005, p. B1.

87. "No one was reported killed by the seven Scud missiles that struck Israel, but Israel Radio reported that a 3-year-old Arab girl suffocated in a gas mask, that at least four elderly people died of heart attacks or suffocation while wearing gas masks, and that 12 people were injured." Michael Kranish, "Israel Weighing Response; US Hits Scud Sites after Iraqi Attack," *Boston Globe*, January 18, 1991, p. 1.

88. See, for example, David Shook, "Smallpox: 'We Eradicated It Before . . . ,'" *Business Week*

(October 25, 2001); accessible at http://www.businessweek.com/bwdaily/dnflash/oct2001/nf20011025_6673.htm.

89. Nicholas Wade, "A DNA Success Raises Bioterror Concerns," *New York Times*, January 12, 2005, p. A15.

90. According to the Web site for the Centers for Disease Control and Prevention, "In the past, about 1,000 people for every 1 million people vaccinated for the first time experienced reactions that, while not life-threatening, were serious," and "Rarely, people have had very bad reactions to the vaccine. In the past, between 14 and 52 people per 1 million people vaccinated for the first time experienced potentially life-threatening reactions." Centers for Disease Control and Prevention, "Smallpox Fact Sheet: Side Effects of Smallpox Vaccination"; accessible at http://www.bt.cdc.gov/agent/smallpox/vaccination/reactions-vacc-public.asp.

91. Alex R. Kemper et al., "Expected Adverse Events in a Mass Smallpox Vaccination Campaign," *Effective Clinical Practice* (March–April 2002); accessible at http://www.acponline.org/journals/ecp/marapr02/kemper.htm.

92. From the Web site for the Boston Public Health Commission:

> What is ring vaccination?
>
> This is a strategy that will be used for containing a smallpox outbreak. Vaccinating and monitoring a "ring" of persons around each smallpox case and his/her contacts will help protect those at greatest risk for developing disease and provide a buffer of immune persons to prevent the spread of disease within the community. Focused "ring" vaccination campaigns along with isolation of cases, intensive surveillance, and contact tracing will be the cornerstones for disease prevention and control.

Accessible at http://www.bphc.org/bphc/smallpoxvac_clin.asp.

93. This hypothetical may lack a basis for all its particulars. For example, the virus may not be contagious in the immediate aftermath of exposure. But there are several bio-events that would fit this hypothetical.

94. The original is "Martial law is to law as martial music is to music," but I like some martial music.

95. Wendy E. Parmet, "AIDS and Quarantine: The Revival of an Archaic Doctrine," *Hofstra Law Review* vol. 14 (1985), pp. 53–90.

96. See Dershowitz, *Shouting Fire*, loc. cit., pp. 163–75.

97. Ibid., pp. 163–75.

98. "Incitement to massacre the civilian Tutsi population over the radio air-waves of RTLM and Radio Rwanda can be directly imputed to Éliezer Niyitegeka for his failure to control the programming of the radio broadcasts or to curtail the anti-Tutsi programming, or to sanction or punish those that used radio broadcasts in a campaign of genocide." *The Prosecutor v. Éliezer Niyitegeka*, ICTR-96-14-T (May 16, 2003).

99. See these defendants' cases at http://www.ictr.org/ENGLISH/cases/completed.htm.

100. Jon Silverman, "Rwanda's 'Hate Media' on Trial," BBC News, June 29, 2002; accessible at http://news.bbc.co.uk/2/hi/africa/2075183.stm.

101. The First Amendment provides that Congress "shall make no law . . . abridging the freedom of speech. . . ."

102. *New York Times Co. v. United States*, 403 U.S. 713 (1971), p. 733.

103. See "Some Prior Restraints Squeaked By in Past Year, Says PLI Panel," *Media Law Reporter*, vol. 30, no. 46 (November 26, 2002); accessible at http://ipcenter.bna.com/pic2/ip.nsf/id/BNAP-5G5L3N?OpenDocument.

104. Adam Cohen, "The Latest Rumbling in the Blogosphere: Questions about Ethics," *New York Times*, May 8, 2005.

105. See Thomas L. Friedman, "If It's a Muslim Problem, It Needs a Muslim Solution," *New York Times*, July 8, 2005, p. A23.

106. See Dominic Casciani, "Q&A: Religious Hatred Law," BBC News, June 9, 2005; accessible at http://newsvote.bbc.co.uk/mpapps/pagetools/print/news.bbc.co.uk/1/hi/uk/3873323.stm.

107. See "France 'to Expel Radical Imams,'" BBC News, July 15, 2005; accessible at http://newsvote.bbc.co.uk/mpapps/pagetools/print/news.bbc.co.uk/2/hi/europe/4688111.stm; Samantha Maiden, "Costello Tells Firebrand Clerics to Get Out of Australia," *Australian,* August 23, 2005; and Philip Johnston, "Imams Who Praise Terrorism to Face Deportation," *London Telegraph*, July 21, 2005; accessible at http://www.opinion.telegraph.co.uk/news/main.jhtml?xml=/news/2005/07/21/nimam21.xml.

108. Law and morality must keep up with the ever-advancing technology and the constantly active human imagination. See Dershowitz, *Shouting Fire*, loc. cit., pp. 487–92.

CHAPTER 5.

Bush Doctrine on Preemption, the U.S. Attack against Iraq

1. The irony is that this sort of deterrent approach is almost certainly repugnant to international law, which forbids retaliatory attacks on civilian population centers. Because the United States had demonstrated its willingness to drop nuclear bombs on Japanese civilian population centers, our threat was credible, despite the prohibition on attacking civilian population centers that was made explicit by international law following Hiroshima and Nagasaki. The White House, "The National Security Strategy of the United States of America," September 2002; accessible at http://www.whitehouse.gov/nsc/nss.pdf.

2. By 1996 Libya had constructed "the world's largest underground chemical weapons plant" in the region of Tarhunah, and Clinton administration officials threatened to attack the installation unless weapons manufacturing ceased. Lenny Capello et al., "The Preemptive Use of Force: Analysis and Decision Making," National Security Pro-

gram Discussion Paper Series, Harvard University John F. Kennedy School of Government 1997, pp. 57–59. Clinton ordered missiles to be fired at targets in Sudan and Afghanistan in August 1998. James Bennet, "U.S. Cruise Missiles Strike Sudan and Afghan Targets Tied to Terrorist Network," *New York Times*, August 21, 1998, p. A1. Clinton also considered an attack in 1994 on North Korea's nuclear reactor. Toby Sterling, "Clinton Says He Had a Plan to Attack North Korean Reactor in 1994," Associated Press, December 15, 2002.

3. The difference between acting preemptively without having announced a preemptive policy and announcing such a policy will be considered later.

4. There is considerable debate in the scholarly literature over whether earlier anticipatory actions constitute preemptions, reactions, or something in between. See generally Laura Secor, "Grand Old Policy," *Boston Globe*, February 8, 2004, pp. H1, for a discussion of the work of Yale Professor John Lewis Gaddis, who argues that "Bush's doctrine of preemption has deep roots in American history."

5. Robert A. Pape, "Soft Balancing: How States Will Respond to America's Preventive War Strategy," TISS Conference paper, Duke University, January 17, 2003. Mark Dayton, writing in the *Washington Post*, characterized the proposed attack on Iraq as "something no president has done before." In support of that claim, he cited "researches at the Library of Congress" to the effect that "the United States has never in its 213 year history launched a preemptive attack against another country." Mark Dayton, "Go Slow on Iraq," *Washington Post*, September 28, 2002, p. A23.

6. United States Conference of Catholic Bishops, statement on Iraq, November 13, 2002.

7. See Mark Aarons and John Loftus, *Unholy Trinity: The Vatican, the Nazis, and the Swiss Banks* (New York: St. Martin's, 1998). The U.S. Conference of Catholic Bishops has generally been more "liberal" and more antiwar than some in the Vatican.

8. Richard Falk, "The New Bush Doctrine," *Nation* (July 15, 2002), p. 9.

9. Other scholars agreed with Professor Falk in distinguishing between unacceptable preventive wars and acceptable preemptive attacks.

> Preventive war is almost always a bad choice, strategically as well as morally. Preemption is another matter—legitimate in principle and sometimes advisable in practice. . . . Thus it is better to face the music sooner, when chances of military success are greater.
>
> Preemption is unobjectionable in principle, since it is only an act of anticipatory self-defense in a war effectively initiated by the enemy. If the term is used accurately, rather than in the sloppy or disingenuous manner in which the Bush administration has used it to justify preventive war against Iraq, preemption assumes detection of enemy mobilization of forces to attack, which represents the start of the war. Beating the enemy to the draw by striking before he launches his attack is reactive, even if it involves firing the first shot.

Richard K. Betts, "Striking First: A History of Thankfully Lost Opportunities,"

Carnegie Council on Ethics and International Affairs March 2, 2003; accessible at http://www.cceia.org/viewMedia.php/prmTemplateID/8/prmID/866.

So long as the word "always" is modified by "almost," it is difficult to quarrel with this formulation. But if the danger is great enough and its likelihood sufficiently probable, the case for preventive—as distinguished from preemptive—war becomes more compelling.

10. Joachim C. Fest, *The Face of the Third Reich: Portraits of the Nazi Leadership* (New York: Pantheon, 1970), p. 48.

11. Although the chemical plant at Tarhunah, with its potential for producing weapons of mass destruction, was the immediate precipitating factor in generating the debate over preemption, the threat of "nuclear leakage," especially to terrorist groups, "was also a concern. Preemption was a policy option to address our nuclear leakage and terrorist problems." Capello et al., op. cit., p. v.

12. Ibid.

13. Ibid., p. vi.

14. Ibid., pp. 75–76.

15. There were certainly many factors that contributed to the Libyan decision, including preventive measures, such as the interception by the United States of a freighter carrying "centrifuge parts made in Malaysia, along with other products of Dr. Khan's network, all bound for Libya. Confronted with the evidence, Libya finally agreed to surrender all of its nuclear program." William J. Broad and David E. Sanger, "As Nuclear Secrets Emerge, More Are Suspected," *New York Times*, December 26, 2004, p. 1.

16. In April 1986 U.S. planes bombed Tripoli and Benghazi, killing more than a hundred people. President Reagan justified the attack by blaming Libya for terrorist attacks. He cited a bombing ten days prior at a West Berlin nightclub that was frequented by U.S. service members. Ronald Reagan, "Address to the Nation on the United States Air Strike against Libya," April 14, 1986; accessible at http://www.reagan.utexas.edu/archives/speeches/1986/41486g.htm. A couple of days later, according to the BBC, "The extremist group Arab Revolutionary Cells said it murdered two British and one American hostage in Lebanon on 17 April 1986, in retaliation for the US attack." "On This Day: 15 April 1986," BBC News; accessible at http://news.bbc.co.uk/onthisday/hi/dates/stories/april/15/newsid_3975000/3975455.stm.

17. Clinton has said that he would have supported military action, but much more slowly. See *Larry King Weekend*, CNN, February 9, 2003.

18. Capello et al., op. cit., p. 75.

19. "Russia Warns of Strikes on Terror Camps, Posts Bounty for Chechen Leaders," Channel NewsAsia, September 8, 2004; accessible at http://www.channelnewsasia.com/stories/afp_world/view/105633/1/.html.

20. "Putin Tightens Grip on Russian Regions after Deadly Attacks," Agence France Presse, September 13, 2004. Previously Russia and its predecessor, the Soviet Union, had condemned preemptive and preventive attacks. Jing-dong Yuan, "A Promising Partnership Is Tested: Russia and China," *International Herald Tribune*, November 30, 2002, p. 4.

21. Charles Krauthammer, "Axis of Evil, Part Two," *Washington Post*, July 23, 2004, p. A29; and Douglas Davis, "A Syrian Bomb?," *Jerusalem Post*, September 10, 2004, p. 14.

22. Iran has already done this with regard to Israel, though it does not yet have the capacity to carry out its threat.

23. Jerome R. Corsi, *Atomic Iran: How the Terrorist Regime Bought the Bomb and American Politicians* (Nashville: WND Books, 2005), p. 39.

24. Some Israeli authorities believed that Egypt was preparing a first strike on its air force or its nuclear facility.

25. See p. 315, n. 61, *supra*. Recently, Prime Minister Howard advocated new antiterrorism laws. According to these measures, it would be made easier for the police to search, monitor, and detain terror suspects. The *New York Times* observed that "[t]he antiterrorism bill, which even some backers have described as draconian, contains the most sweeping changes to security apparatus since World War II." Raymond Bonner, "Australia to Present Strict Antiterrorism Statute," *New York Times*, November 3, 2005, p. 6A. The BBC reported that Australia is divided about these new terrorism laws. While some critics fear that Australia might to turn into a "police state," others support the new laws but think that the government must convince the country for its need. The BBC report quotes a terrorism analyst as follows: "One of the dilemmas the government is facing [is that] the police have proven that they can actually disrupt and foil alleged terrorist attacks with the existing legislation slightly amended, so the onus will be on them to prove why they need the wider laws." Phil Mercer, "Australia Split on New Terror Laws," *BBC News (Sydney)*, November 9, 2005; accessible at http://news.bbc.co.uk/2/hi/asia-pacific/4420558.stm.

26. Philip Stephens, "For All Bush's Bravado, the Preemption Doctrine Is Dead," *Financial Times*, July 16, 2004, p. 17.

27. James M. Lindsay and Ivo H. Daalder, "Shooting First: The Preemptive War Doctrine Has met an Early Death in Iraq," *Los Angeles Times*, May 30, 2004; accessible at http://www.cfr.org/pub7066/james_m_Lindsay_ivo_h_daalder/shooting_first_the_pre emptivewar_doctrine_has_met_an_early_death_in_iraq.php.

28. "Preventive War: A Failed Doctrine," *New York Times*, September 12, 2004, p. 12.

29. Michael Walzer has also distinguished between preventive war and preemptive attack. In an essay written in September 2002, he observed:

> The war that is being discussed is preventative, not preemptive—it is designed to respond to a more distant threat. The general argument for preventive war is very old; in its classic form it has to do with the balance of power . . . Whether or not war is properly the last resort, there seems no sufficient reason for making it the first.
>
> But the old argument for preventive war did not take into accounts weapons of mass destruction or delivery systems that allow no time for arguments about how to respond. Perhaps the gulf between preemption and prevention has now narrowed so that there is little strategic (and therefore moral) difference between them. The Israeli attack on the Iraqi nuclear reactor in 1981 is sometimes invoked as an example of a justified preventive attack that was also, in a sense,

preemptive: The Iraqi threat was not imminent, but an immediate attack was the only reasonable action against it.

Michael Walzer, *Arguing about War* (New Haven: Yale University Press, 2004), pp. 146–47.

30. The editorial concluded by criticizing Vice President Cheney's conception of preventive war: "Instead, he promises more preventive, offensive wars against hypothetical dangers like Iraq. Besides estranging America from its main European and Asian allies, and leaving Washington looking like an aggressor to much of the Arab and Muslim world, these policies kill American soldiers and civilians in the countries attacked, and they threaten to tie down the Army and Marine divisions America needs to have available for responding to real threats in the dangerous decades ahead."

31. Gary Schmitt, "Shooting First: Going after Perceived Threats Will Remain Part of the U.S. Arsenal," *Los Angeles Times*, May 30, 2004; accessible at http://www .newamericancentury.org/defense-20040601.htm.

32. Ruth Wedgwood, "The Fall of Saddam Hussein: Security Council Mandates and Preemptive Self-Defense," *American Journal of International Law*, vol. 97, no. 3 (July 2003), pp. 576–85. This raises the broad jurisprudential question of whether a single abstract standard can ever govern the justifications of preventive war or it will always depend, at least to some degree, on the nature and history of the actors. Two countries, each building identical nuclear weapons, will pose entirely different threats depending on the likely use to which the weapons will be put.

33. Miriam Sapiro, "Iraq: The Shifting Sands of Preemptive Self-Defense," *American Journal of International Law*, vol. 97, no. 3 (July 2003), pp. 599–607.

CHAPTER 6.

WOULD PREEMPTIVE ACTION AGAINST THE IRANIAN NUCLEAR PROGRAM BE JUSTIFIED?

1. To make matters even more complex, a former prime minister of Israel has said that Israel would not drop a nuclear bomb on an enemy population center, even in retaliation for a nuclear attack on Tel Aviv. See p. 96. It would rely on preemption against the military threats rather than deterrence by unlawful mutually assured destruction.

2. Suzanne Fields, "Confronting the New Anti-Semitism," *Washington Times*, July 25, 2004; accessible at http://washtimes.com/books/20040724-105243-9684r.htm.

3. Jerome R. Corsi, *Atomic Iran: How the Terrorist Regime Bought the Bomb and American Politicians* (Nashville: WND Books, 2005), p. 42.

4. Ibid., p. 19.

5. Craig S. Smith, "Iran Moves toward Enriching Uranium," *New York Times*, September 22, 2004, p. A12.

6. Ali Akbar Dareini, "Iranian Lawmakers, Shouting 'Death to America,' Vote Unanimously for Resuming Uranium Enrichment," Associated Press, October 31, 2004.

7. Ali Akbar Dareini, "Iran Confirms Converting 37 Tons of Raw Uranium into Gas," Associated Press, May 9, 2005.

8. Tom Hundley, "Pressure Builds on Iran; Blair Says UN Security Council Is Next Stop If Nuclear Work Resumes," *Chicago Tribune*, May 13, 2005.

9. "Iran angry at nuclear resolution," CNN, September 25, 2005; accessible at http://www.cnn.com/2005/WORLD/meast/09/25/iran.iaea/; and "UN adopts motion on nuclear Iran," BBC, September 24, 2005; accessible at http://news.bbc.co.uk/1/hi/world/middle_east/4277054.stm. In late November 2005, the Iranian parliament voted to block UN inspections of the nuclear facilities if Iran is referred to the Security Council.

10. "Crowd Attacks British Embassy," *Independent*, September 29, 2005, p. 29.

11. Nazila Fathi, "Iran's New President Says Israel 'Must Be Wiped Off the Map,'" *New York Times*, October 27, 2005, p. 8.

12. Ibid.

13. Steven R. Weisman, "Western Leaders Condemn the Iranian President's Threat to Israel," *New York Times*, October 28, 2005, p. 9.

14. Ibid.

15. Michael Slackman, "Many in Jordan See Old Enemy in Attack: Israel," *New York Times*, November 12, 2005, p. 1.

16. Ibid.

17. Joseph Nasr, "Egyptian Magazine: Israel-US Caused Tsunamis," Jerusalem Post, January 7, 2005, p. 4.

18. Seymour M. Hersh, "The Coming Wars," *New Yorker* (January 24 and 31, 2005); accessible at http://www.newyorker.com/fact/content/?050124fa_fact.

19. David E. Sanger, "Rice Says Iran Must Not Be Allowed to Develop Nuclear Arms," *New York Times*, August 9, 2004, p. A3.

20. Anton La Guardia, "Israel Challenges Iran's Nuclear Ambitions," *Daily Telegraph*, September 22, 2004; accessible at http://www.telegraph.co.uk/news/main.jhtml?xml=/news/2004/09/22/wnuke22.xml&sSheet=/portal/2004/09/22/ixportaltop.html.

21. Corsi, op. cit., p. 32.

22. Quoted in Hersh, op. cit., p. 44.

23. Quoted in H. D. S. Greenway, "Onward to Iran?," *Boston Globe*, February 4, 2005, p. A15.

24. "In order to ensure respect for and protection of the civilian population and civilian objects, the Parties to the conflict shall at all times distinguish between the civilian population and combatants and between civilian objects and military objectives and accordingly shall direct their operations only against military objectives." Geneva Conventions of 12 August 1949, and relating to the Protection of Victims of International Armed Conflicts, 8 June 1977, Part IV, Section I, Chapter I, Article 48.

25. Federal law states that "whoever . . . seizes or detains and threatens to kill, to injure, or to continue to detain another person in order to compel a third person or a governmental organization to do or abstain from doing any act as an explicit or implicit condition for the release of the person detained . . . shall be punished by imprisonment for

any term of years or for life and, *if the death of any person results*, shall be punished by death or life imprisonment." 18 U.S.C. 1203 (emphasis added). The law does not specify who must have caused the death; if someone dies, the hostage taker is responsible.

26. Menachem Begin said, in explaining the timing of the Osirak attack: "[I]f the reactor had become . . . hot, we couldn't do anything further. Because if . . . we would open it . . . a horrifying wave of radioactivity would come out from the reactor and cover the sky over Baghdad. . . . Hundreds of thousands of innocent citizens—residents, men, women and children—would have been hurt." Shlomo Nakdimon, *First Strike: The Exclusive Story of How Israel Foiled Iraq's Attempt to Get the Bomb* (New York: Summit, 1987), p. 239.

27. Corsi, op. cit., p. 32.

28. Ibid., p. 219.

29. Hersh, "The Coming Wars," loc. cit.

30. Ibid.

31. John Daniszewski, "Iran's Victor Urges Unity in Wake of Vote," *Los Angeles Times*, June 26, 2005, p. A10.

32. See Michael Slackman, "Victory Is Seen for Hard-Liner in Iranian Vote," *New York Times*, June 25, 2005, p. A1; and Charles A. Radin, "Hard-liner Wins Iran Presidency," *Boston Globe*, June 25, 2005, p. A4.

33. Hersh, "The Coming Wars," loc. cit.

34. Shirin Ebadi and Hadi Ghaemi, "The Human Rights Case against Attacking Iran," *New York Times*, February 8, 2005, p. A25.

35. The *New York Times* reported that the discovery of blueprints for an atomic bomb in the files of the Libyan weapons program "gave the experts a new appreciation of the audacity of the rogue nuclear network led by A. Q. Khan, a chief architect of Pakistan's bomb. Intelligence officials had watched Dr. Khan for years and suspected that he was trafficking in machinery for enriching uranium to make fuel for warheads. But the detailed design represented a new level of danger, particularly since the Libyans said he had thrown it in as a deal-sweetener when he sold them $100 million in nuclear gear." The report quotes "one American expert": "This was the first time we had ever seen a loose copy of a bomb design that clearly worked, and the question was: Who else had it? The Iranians? The Syrians? Al Qaeda?" William J. Broad and David E. Sanger, "As Nuclear Secrets Emerge, More Are Suspected," *New York Times*, December 26, 2004, p. 21.

36. Matthew Continetti, "International Men of Mystery," *Weekly Standard*, October 21, 2004.

37. Gareth Evans, President and Chief Executive of the International Crisis Group, and his committee might well favor military intervention as a last resort, but only following a vote by the Security Council, where a Chinese (and perhaps Russian and French) veto is likely. Professors Lee Feinstein and Ann-Marie Slaughter might favor military intervention by a regional organization such as NATO or—as an absolutely last resort—"unilateral action of coalitions of the willing." Others would never consider any military option in the absence of an imminent attack, regardless of how likely and catastrophic the threat.

CHAPTER 7.
TOWARD A JURISPRUDENCE OF PREVENTION AND PREEMPTION

1. Oliver Wendell Holmes, Jr., *The Common Law* (New York: Dover, 1991), p. 1.
2. Oliver Wendell Holmes, Jr., "The Path of the Law," *Harvard Law Review*, vol. 10, no. 8 (1897), p. 457.
3. George Santayana, *The Life of Reason: Reason in Common Sense* (New York: Dover, 1980), p. 284. As some wag once put it: "Anyone who has ever heard Santayana's bon mot is condemned to repeat it."
4. Alan Dershowitz, *Rights from Wrongs: A Secular Theory of the Origins of Rights* (New York: Basic Books, 2004), p. 8.
5. Alan M. Dershowitz, *The Genesis of Justice: Ten Stories of Biblical Injustice That Led to the Ten Commandments and Modern Law* (New York: Warner, 2000).
6. Roscoe Pound, quoted in *Christian Science Monitor*, April 24, 1963, quoted in Michael R. Stahlman et al., "New Developments in Search and Seizure: More than Just a Matter of Semantics," *Army Lawyer* (May 2002); accessible at http://www.jagcnet.army.mil/JAGCNETINTERNET/HOMEPAGES/AC/ARMYLAWYER.NSF/0/68866d468a3cf4fe85256e5b0054d0f4/$FILE/ATTHVHZB/Article%204.pdf.
7. There is a wonderful legend recounted in the Talmud: The great Rabbi Eliezer was engaged in an acrimonious dispute with the other sages about an arcane point of law. Eliezer was certain that his interpretation of the Torah was the correct one, and he "brought forward every imaginable argument, but they did not accept them." Finally, in desperation, he invoked the original intent of the author of the Torah, God himself. Eliezer implored, "If the halachah [the authoritative meaning of the law] agrees with me, let it be proved from Heaven!", whereupon a heavenly voice cried out to the others: "Why do ye dispute with R[abbi] Eliezer, seeing that . . . the halachah agrees with him!" But another of the rabbis rose up and rebuked God for interfering in this very human dispute. "Thou hast long since written the Torah," and "we pay no attention to a Heavenly Voice." The message was clear: God's children were telling their Father, "It is our job, as the rabbis, to give meaning to the Torah that you gave us. You gave us a document to interpret, and a methodology for interpreting it. Now leave us to do our job." God agreed, laughing with joy. "My . . . [children] have defeated Me in argument." Babylonian Talmud, Baba Mezi'a 59b, quoted in Alan M. Dershowitz, *Shouting Fire* (New York: Little, Brown, 2002), pp. 391–92.
8. Midrash Genesis Rabba.
9. Thomas Hobbes, *Leviathan* (1651), ch. 18.
10. Richard P. Feynman, *What Do You Care What Other People Think?* (New York: Norton, 1988), p. 245.
11. Louis Henkin, *How Nations Behave: Law and Foreign Policy* (New York: Columbia University Press, 1979), p. 47.
12. Talmud, Berakhot, quoted in Elizabeth Frost-Knappman and David S. Shrager, *The Quotable Lawyer* (New York: New England Publishing, 1998), p. 255.

13. *Brown v. United States*, 256 U.S. 335, 343 (1921).

14. Jacqui Goddard, "Florida Boosts Gun Rights, Igniting a Debate," *Christian Science Monitor*, May 10, 2005.

15. Steve Bousquet, "Bill Would Relax Rules on Self-defense," *St. Petersburg Times*, February 24, 2005; accessible at http://www.sptimes.com/2005/02/24/State/Bill_would _relax_rule.shtml.

16. Myres S. McDougal, "The Soviet-Cuban Quarantine and Self-Defense," *American Journal of International Law*, vol. 57 (1963), pp. 600–01, quoted in William C. Bradford, "'The Duty to Defend Them': A Natural Law Justification for the Bush Doctrine of Preventive War," *Notre Dame Law Review*, vol. 79 (2004), p. 1390, n. 87.

17. One reason why Israel may have become the laboratory for preemption is that it believes it cannot count on UN support or assistance to prevent any attack, as evidenced by the UN's hasty accession to Nasser's demand that its peacekeepers immediately leave the Sinai in 1967. See Michael B. Oren, *Six Days of War: June 1967 and the Making of the Modern Middle East* (Oxford: Oxford University Press, 2002), p. 67.

18. See Alan M. Dershowitz, *The Abuse Excuse: And Other Cop-outs, Sob Stories, and Evasions of Responsibility* (Boston: Little, Brown, 1994).

19. The UN did call for an immediate cease-fire, which was not implemented until several days later.

20. Letter from U.S. Secretary of State Daniel Webster to British Plenipotentiary Lord Ashburton, August 6, 1842, quoted in Bradford, op. cit., p. 1381.

21. United Nations High-level Panel on Threats, Challenges and Change, "A More Secure World: Our Shared Responsibility" (2004), p. 63; accessible at http://www.un .org./secureworld/.

22. Gareth Evans, "When Is It Right to Fight" *Survival* (Autumn 2004), pp. 59, 64–65; accessible at http://www.cfr.pdf./59-2.pdf. There were many nations at the UN that did "seriously suggest" that Israel acted unlawfully when it did not "wait to be fired upon" in 1967.

23. Ibid., p. 65.

24. "Excerpts: Annan interview," BBC News, September 16, 2004; accessible at http://news .bbc.co.uk/1/hi/world/middle_east/3661640.stm.

25. Jeffrey Goldberg, "The Great Terror," *New Yorker*, March 25, 2002; accessible at http://www.newyorker.com/fact/content/?020325fa_FACT1.

26. United Nations High-level Panel on Threats, Challenges and Change, op. cit., p. 63.

27. Ibid.

28. Ibid.

29. Evans, op. cit., p. 65.

30. Ibid., pp. 65–66.

31. Giordano Bruno, *De Monade, numero et figura* (1591), quoted in Frost-Knappman and Shrager, op. cit., p. 188.

32. Talmud Shabbath, 31a.

33. United Nations High-level Panel on Threats, Challenges and Change, op. cit., p. 67.

34. Michael J. Glennon, *Limits of Law, Prerogatives of Power* (New York: Palgrave, 2001), p. 2.

35. For example, *Bush v. Gore*, 531 U.S. (2000), p. 98. See Alan M. Dershowitz, *Supreme Injustice: How the High Court Hijacked Election 2000* (New York: Oxford University Press, 2001).

36. Until recently Israel was ineligible to sit on the Security Council, which requires membership in a regional group. While Israel geographically would be part of the Asian Group, several countries in that bloc, including Iran, Libya, and Syria, disqualified Israel for years. A consensus must exist among all the group's members in order to admit a new nation into a group. In 2000, Israel joined the Western European and Others Group (WEOG), which is the only group with membership that is not exclusively geographic. The United States, Australia, Canada, and Turkey are among its members. The admission of Israel was initially on a temporary basis, with a requirement that the country reapply every four years. Israel's membership in WEOG was extended in 2004.

   It is now theoretically possible for Israel to sit on the Security Council. (See Permanent Mission of Israel to the United Nations, "Israel's Membership in WEOG"; accessible at http://www.israel-un.org/israel_un/weog.htm.) But to date Israel has never been permitted to sit on this important body.

37. Russia's and China's veto power has often resulted in stalemates in votes relating to Israel.

38. Bob Burton, "Howard unmoved by 'preemption' furor," *Asia Times*, December 3, 2002; accessible at http://www.atimes.com/atimes/Southeast_Asia/DL03Ae02.html.

39. To be sure, there are some ideological anti-interventionists who oppose both anticipatory self-defense (at least when the threat is not immediate) and anticipatory protection of others. For an example of this isolationist viewpoint, see Patrick J. Buchanan, *A Republic, Not an Empire: Reclaiming America's Destiny* (Washington, D.C.: Regnery, 2002).

40. Samantha Power, *A Problem from Hell: America and the Age of Genocide* (New York: Basic Books, 2002), pp. 503, 504, 508.

41. For a brilliant discussion of these issues, see Ibid.

42. Anne Geran, "Powell: Tsunami Aid May Help Fight Terror," Associated Press, January 4, 2005.

43. Lee Feinstein and Ann-Marie Slaughter, "A Duty to Prevent," *Foreign Affairs* (January–February 2004), pp. 136–37.

44. Ibid., p. 137.

45. Ibid., pp. 141–42.

46. Ibid., p. 148.

47. Ibid., pp. 148–149.

48. Ibid., p. 149.

49. See also statement of Kenneth Adelman, quoted on p. 97.

50. See Alan Dershowitz, "Tortured Reasoning," in *Torture: A Collection*, ed. Sanford Levinson (New York: Oxford University Press, 2004); and Alan M. Dershowitz, *Why*

Terrorism Works: Understanding the Threat, Responding to the Challenge (New Haven: Yale University Press, 2002), pp. 131–63.

51. Alan Dershowitz, *The Case for Israel* (Hoboken: Wiley, 2003), p. 184.

52. Nathan Lewin, "Deterring Suicide Killers," *Sh'ma* (May 2002); accessible at http://www.shma.com/may02/nathan.htm.

53. Ami Eden, "Top Lawyer Urges Death for Families of Bombers," *Forward*, June 7, 2002; accessible at http://www.forward.com/issues/2002/02.06.07/news1.html.

54. Alan Dershowitz, "Death to the Bombers' Kin: Sacrilegious, or by the Book?," letter to the editor, *Forward*, June 21, 2002; accessible at http://www.forward.com/issues/2002/02.06.21/letters.html.

55. Fyodor Dostoevsky, *The Brothers Karamazov* (New York: Farrar, Straus & Giroux, 2002), p. 245.

56. Even before the most minimal and least intrusive military options are employed, there might be a range of nonmilitary options, including such coercive ones as sanctions and boycotts.

57. Israel did, however, *threaten* to destroy any new reactor capable of providing Iraq with nuclear weapons.

58. See Richard A. Posner, *Catastrophe: Risk and Response* (Oxford: Oxford University Press, 2004).

59. *Whitney v. California*, 274 U.S. 357 (1927). Just twelve years prior to the *Whitney* decision, Justice Oliver Wendell Holmes upheld the conviction of a newspaper editor who had published an article advocating nude swimming in isolated areas. This is what the great Holmes wrote:

> The printed matter in question . . . an article entitled, "The Nude and the Prudes," . . . predicts and encourages the boycott of those who thus interfere with the freedom of Home, concluding: "The boycott will be pushed until these invaders will come to see the brutal mistake of their action and so inform the people." Thus by indirection, but unmistakably, the article encourages and incites a persistence in what we must assume would be a breach of the state laws against indecent exposure. . . . [T]he argument that this act is both an unjustifiable restriction of liberty and too vague for a criminal law must fail. It does not appear and is not likely that the statute will be construed to prevent publications merely because they tend to produce unfavorable opinions of a particular statute or of law in general. In this present case the disrespect for law that was encouraged was disregard of it, an overt breach and technically criminal act.

Fox v. Washington, 236 U.S. 273 (1915), pp. 276–77.

60. Or even true positives, if the harm is remediable.

61. See Entebbe analysis, pp. 89–93.

62. See Dershowitz, *Genesis of Justice*, loc. cit., ch. 4, on God arguing with Abraham over sinners of Sodom.

63. See Patrick J. McDonnell and Jonathan Peterson, "Tightening Immigration Raises

Civil Liberties Flag," *Los Angeles Times*, September 23, 2001.

64. See Appendix A, p. 251.

65. See Michael J. Glennon, *Limits of Law, Prerogatives of Power* (New York: Palgrave, 2001), p. 208.

66. For an explanation of the justness of this type of arrangement, see John Rawls, *A Theory of Justice* (Cambridge: Belknap, 1999).

67. Eric A. Posner, "All Justice, Too, Is Local," *New York Times*, December 30, 2004, p. 23.

68. See, for example, Karen J. Alter, "The European Union's Legal System and Domestic Policy: Spillover or Backlash?" in *Legalization and World Politics*, ed. Judith Goldstein et al. (Cambridge: MIT Press, 2001).

69. Louis Rene Beres, "On Assassination as Anticipatory Self-Defense: The Case of Israel," *Hofstra Law Review*, vol. 20 (1991), p. 323, quoted in Bradford, op. cit., p. 1394, n. 99.

70. "Legality of the Threat or Use of Nuclear Weapons," 1996 I.C.J. 226, p. 263, quoted in ibid., p. 1390.

71. "Remarks by the Honorable Dean Acheson," *American Society of International Law Proceedings*, vol. 57 (1963), pp. 13, 14, ibid., p. 1470.

72. Concluding that a particular military option should be available as a matter of law or morality does not mean that it should always be employed as a matter of tactics or prudence.

73. See Alan M. Dershowitz, "Preventive Confinement: A Suggested Framework for Constitutional Analysis," *Texas Law Review*, vol. 51 (1973), p. 1295.

74. Some of that history is parallel to that outlined in Chapter 1 of this book, in which a distinction was drawn between the formal system of criminal justice and far less formal mechanisms of crime control.

75. Dershowitz, "Preventive Confinement, loc. cit., pp. 1295–96.

76. *United States v. Salerno*, 481 U.S. 739 (1987), pp. 747–48.

77. Taken to its logical conclusion, this "reasoning" could lead to an absurd ruling that therapeutic execution of the kind carried out in Nazi Germany was not "punishment" because the legislative purpose was eugenic and preventive.

78. "The Case of the Speluncean Explorers: A Fiftieth Anniversary Symposium," *Harvard Law Review*, vol. 112 (1999), pp. 1899–1913.

79. Samantha Power, *"A Problem from Hell": America and the Age of Genocide* (New York: Basic Books, 2002).

   Some of the world's most intractable problems grow out of the clash of absolute moral positions; many, but not all of them, religiously based. I have written elsewhere against the existence of moral absolutes. See Alan Dershowitz, *Rights from Wrongs: A Secular Theory of the Origin of Rights* (New York: Basic Books, 2005). I am now working on a project that asks whether many arguments that purport to be moral are not really based on hidden empirical assumptions. My soft claim—with which few will disagree—is that many complex arguments that purport to be moral contain significant empirical underpinnings. For example, the argument that capital punishment is morally wrong is often based on empirical assumptions about the deterrent effect of capital punishment, its racially and economically selective application, its deleterious impact on how life is valued, the possibility that innocent people may be executed, and other similar issues of fact (or at least mixed issues of fact and morality). Many current opponents of capital punishment would concede that if it could be proven beyond any doubt that the killing of a small number of indisputably guilty and culpable murderers—selected fairly and without racial, economic, or other invidious factors—would deter (and/or prevent) the killing of a much larger number (how much larger may be open to disagreement) of potential murder victims, while at the same time enhancing the value of life, that it would be morally permissible (some would say morally required) for the state to practice capital punishment. Some would argue that the deliberate taking of any life, as punishment, is immoral, but when their arguments are carefully deconstructed, it may well turn out that at least some of them are empirical, at least in part.

Even if I am correct about capital punishment, that does not prove my general assertion—even in its soft version—that many *other* moral arguments are, in reality, factual disputes dressed up as moral arguments. So long as I merely claim that "many" other moral arguments fit into this category, I can demonstrate that I am correct. Were I to assert the harder version of this claim—that *all* moral arguments are *always only* empirical claims in disguise—I would have a much more daunting burden to satisfy. First, I can never address *all* moral arguments, since there will always be some I have not considered. Second, it will be asserted that there are surely *some* moral claims that have *no* empirical underpinnings—that are purely normative. Kant comes to mind. His adamant rejection of all consequential considerations seems inconsistent with any empirical underpinnings, but I plan to show that a close reading even of Kant often reveals some hidden empirical assumptions.

In a more contemporary setting, let us consider the arguments for and against abortion. Advocates of a woman's right to choose abortion focus on several factors: equality, autonomy, health hazards to the woman, the status of the fetus as a non-human being; the risks of bringing unwanted children into this world, the effect on population control, and other considerations. Opponents of abortion argue that the fetus is an innocent human life; that allowing a fetus to be killed diminishes the value of all life; that abortion encourages promiscuous sex; that the Bible prohibits abortion. This later argument raises the broader issue of faith-based "empirical" assumptions not subject to null hypothesis. For example, if God gave the Ten Commandments to Moses, it might follow that its rules are morally compelled, but if the Ten Commandments (and the Bible in general) were written by mere mortals, then they are simply part of the marketplace of morality. Why should we expect absolutes based on this human invention, when no other inventions are perfect?

This sort of deconstruction of moral arguments, particularly those that lead to moral absolutes, is the subject of one of my current projects that I hope to publish in the near future.

APPENDIX A.
PREVENTIVE DISBARMENT:
THE NUMBERS ARE AGAINST IT

1. Michael A. Bishop and J. D. Trout, "50 Years of Successful Predictive Modeling Should Be Enough: Lessons for Philosophy of Science," *Philosophy of Science,* vol. 69, p. S198, accessible at http://www.niu.edu/phil~bishop/50%20years%20of%20successful%20predictive%20modeling%20should%20be%20enough%20Lessons%20for%20philosophy%20of%20science.pdf.

APPENDIX B.
KARYOTYPE, PREDICTABILITY AND CULPABILITY

1. Lewis Carroll, *Through the Looking-Glass and What Alice Found There* (New York: William Morrow, 1993), p. 97.
2. A. Sandberg, G. F. Koepf, T. Ishihara, et al., "XYY Human Male," *Lancet* (1961), p. 488.
3. P. A. Jacobs, M. Brunton, M. M. Melville, et al., "Aggressive Behavior, Mental Subnormality and the XYY Male," *Nature* 208 (1965), p. 1351.
4. D. R. Owen, "The 47 XYY Male: A Review," *Psychology Bulletin* 78 (1972), p. 209.
5. Walzer eventually ended the screening, after facing intense public criticism. See Philip Weiss, "Ending the Test for Extra Chromosomes," *Harvard Crimson,* September 15, 1975.
6. A. M. Dershowitz, "Preventive Disbarment: The Numbers Are Against It," *American Bar Association Journal* 58 (1972), p. 815.
7. W. Blackstone, *Blackstone Commentaries on the Laws of England,* vol. 4 (London: J. Murray, 1857), p. 25.

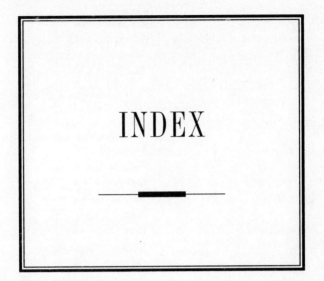

INDEX

References beginning with page 277 are endnotes.